The Acoustic City

The Acoustic City

MATTHEW GANDY, BJ NILSEN [EDS.]

jovis

PREFACE

1   URBAN SOUNDSCAPES

2   ACOUSTIC FLÂNERIE

3   SOUND CULTURES

4 ACOUSTIC ECOLOGIES

5 THE POLITICS OF NOISE

PREFACE

Matthew Gandy
BJ Nilsen

This essay collection and its accompanying CD have emerged from a sense that the field of sound, and our understanding of it, are undergoing a set of changes. The starting point for the idea arose from a Leverhulme Artist-in-Residence Fellowship held by BJ Nilsen in the UCL Urban Laboratory during 2012. Other points of connection include the regular Stadtklang events organized by the Urban Laboratory, and emerging intersections at UCL between architecture, acoustic ecology, and the study of urban soundscapes.

Our critical engagement with sound has been facilitated through the development of inter-disciplinary fields such as "acoustic ecology" and "sound studies," yet the topic is nonetheless extremely difficult to accommodate within existing approaches to the organization of knowledge. The study of sound is marked by a series of intersecting domains derived from history, physics, law, musicology, and many other areas—each bringing its own set of intellectual concerns and institutional entanglements.

The Acoustic City comprises five thematic sections: *urban soundscapes* with an emphasis on the distinctiveness of the urban acoustic realm; *acoustic flânerie* and the recording of sonic environments; *sound cultures* arising from specific associations between music, place, and sound; *acoustic ecologies* including relationships between architecture, sound, and urban design; and *the politics of noise* extending to different instances of anxiety or conflict over sound. In putting together this collection, we have also sought to de-centre some of the implicit assumptions underlying earlier approaches to the study of sound by including feminist insights, post-colonial threads, and other approaches that necessitate a more nuanced reflection on the sensory realms of modernity.

Financial support for the production of this book was provided by the Leverhulme Trust, the UCL Urban Laboratory, and the UCL Grand Challenges programme. At UCL, we would like to thank Ben Campkin, Andrew Harris, Kate E. Jones, Louis Moreno, James Paskins, and Ian Scott. Thanks also to Stephen Barber, Yasminah Beebeejaun, and Michael Flitner for their thoughtful comments and advice at different stages of the project. We are grateful to Inez Templeton for her careful copy-editing of the text and to Knut Enderlein and René Lehmann at Loki-Found for assistence with the production of the CD. We owe special thanks to Sandra Jasper who provided extensive editorial support for the project, including original research for many of the images used in the collection. We would also like to thank Philipp Sperrle, Susanne Rösler, Franziska Fritzsche, and Jutta Bornholdt-Cassetti at jovis for their superb input to the project at every stage.

ACOUSTIC TERRAINS: AN INTRODUCTION

Matthew Gandy

The lower level of the Spichernstrasse U-Bahn station, located in the former West Berlin, has an unusual feature. Set in the wall of the southbound platform is an illuminated case containing details of an installation completed by the sound artist Gabriele Stirl as part of the refurbishment of the station in 1987.[1] The pattern of coloured tiles chosen by Stirl for the tunnel walls corresponds to a musical score comprising twelve colour-sound (*Farbklang*) instruments. Her synesthetic response to the redesign of a utilitarian space connects with wider interest in the aesthetic complexity of urban soundscapes, encompassing fields such as acoustics, musicology, and multiple cultural discourses surrounding the meaning, significance, and perception of different sources of sound.

Urban soundscapes are marked by a dense layering of sound that ranges from the humming spaces of the domestic interior to vast infrastructures of noise extending across the city. The acoustic city has a porous and disruptive spatiality through which we may encounter "the Other" or simply others. In one of Siegfried Kracauer's vignettes from Weimar-era Berlin, he describes being startled by sudden screams or shouts in the night as if the streets themselves could no longer bear the emotional burden of their human inhabitants.[2] Similarly, Jonathan Raban's encounter with early 1970s London in *Soft City* is suffused by a series of dense soundscapes that mirror the social heterogeneity of the inner urban neighbourhoods at the time.[3] Sound is a concrete phenomenon that is spatially distributed: it can be experienced across great distances; it exhibits immense variability through its diverse material and environmental interactions; and it may also impact vast areas if the source itself is mobile. Yet sound is not only a measurable focus of regulatory control or scientific research but also a highly subjective realm of perception encompassing different degrees of sensitivity to acoustic stimuli. There is a spatial intricacy to sound so that different sources of potential disruption may mask each other to produce different fields of sonic anxiety. As sound enters the cultural and political domain, we find that it increasingly eludes the grasp of techno-scientific understanding.[4]

The incessant and sometimes dramatic incursions of sound into domestic environments betoken a fragility in the socio-spatial order of modernity. The multilayered phenomenon of "background noise" is constituted through a mix of corporeal, imaginary, and material sources that can be punctuated by moments of what the musicologist and philosopher Jean-François Augoyard refers to as "agonizing silence," when mechanical systems such as air-conditioning units, refrigeration appliances, and other elements of techno-modernity temporarily cease operation.[5] The auditory realm of modernity is marked by a contrast between spaces of intense collective listening, exemplified by the purpose-built concert hall, and micro-spheres of individualized indifference that transform the sensory realm into a meaningful or endurable form.

For the literary critic Steven Connor, sound has the "capacity to disintegrate and reconfigure space." Connor's rendition of the "auditory self" dispels bounded conceptions of the human subject and challenges "the flat rationality of Cartesian cartography."[6] The changing cultural significance of sound can be placed in the context of an implicit yet unstable "hierarchy of the senses"—in some historical periods, vision was placed below hearing or touch in order of significance—so that the acoustic realm has effectively been rediscovered as part of a recurring critique of ocularcentrism in modern thought. Yet, it would be misleading to draw too schematic a distinction between the role of the senses before and after the Enlightenment, since a distrust in vision alone forms a recurring element in aesthetic discourse from at least the late eighteenth century onwards and emerging interest in darkness, the sublime, and different forms of heightened sensory awareness under European romanticism.[7] In parallel with the cartographic impulse of urban modernity, and its new technological instruments of control and representation, an emerging counter discourse can be discerned, elaborated especially through phenomenological concerns with the capacity of vision to adequately capture the experience of time or the full richness of human sensory perception.[8]

The intersections between sound and vision are perhaps most strikingly represented through the concept of the "soundscape," which plays on the established notion of an optical field of sensory perception. Yet, the Canadian composer R. Murray Schafer's influential use of the term soundscape, which he elaborated from the late 1960s onwards, belies a tension between the idea of the soundscape as a form of direct sensory experience and a proliferation of artificial, modified, or pre-recorded soundscapes.[9] More nuanced approaches to the categorization of acoustic spaces have emerged since the 1970s, ranging from site-specific dimensions to auditory experience to more complex conceptions of sound dynamics and their effective reproduction.[10] Yet even here, in the burgeoning fields of "acoustic ecology" and "sound studies," we find tensions between an emphasis on the spatio-temporal complexities of sound as an acoustic phenomenon and the wider social or historical context within which sound is experienced.[11] We are perhaps better served by the historian Alain Corbin's conception of the "auditory landscape" as a sensory realm that forms part of a geographically defined historical process rather than an inchoate amalgam of sonic traces.[12]

The shift in emphasis from the visual experience of landscape towards other modes of sensory perception does not necessarily involve a critical reworking of the concept of landscape itself, since many of the implicit assumptions concerning the bounded human subject and the "naturalization" of space and time persist. In this respect, Schafer's approach to the understanding of auditory culture holds parallels with the architect Kevin Lynch's concerns with spatial legibility and earlier topographic explorations of the sensory realm that form part of the cartographic impulse of modernity.[13] The idea of the "natural" soundscape is in any case a cultural construction that downplays the human presence in nature and the extent to which any soundscape is refracted through specific forms of human experience, aesthetic longing, or even technological means of mobility to reach ostensibly purer sonic realms.

Under conditions of sensory deprivation the experience of hearing becomes radically modified. Studies of the effects of blindness, for example, reveal very different experiences of the acoustic environment: we find that a seemingly innocuous space such as a university building can be perceived as a disorientating labyrinth of strange echoes.[14] In a similar vein, radically different sonic environments such as underwater spaces reveal the enhanced significance of reverberations and the limited ability of the human ear to accurately perceive the directionality of sound. The anthropologist Stefan Helmreich's study of the "deep-sea soundscape" reveals an array of sound sources that can be technologically transduced into a perceptible form. His study of the use of a submersible to explore deep-sea environments emphasizes a cyborgian dimension to the acoustic realm whereby ostensibly silent worlds can be brought within the scope of human hearing.[15] The cyborgian acoustic realm can be extended to include the use of specific devices such as ultrasound recorders to render the inaudible accessible. Beyond the limitations of human hearing, there are a myriad of acoustic worlds ranging from the echolocation calls of bats to the unheard micro-cosmos in soil, water, and other ecological niches.[16] At any one time, we are only tuned into a small fraction of the acoustic realm, even if we can feel the physiological effects of indiscernible frequencies or notice the material traces left by the "acoustic emissions" of weathering processes on the exposed surfaces of the city.

The attempt to reveal hidden or neglected sonic worlds can also be extended to the historical imagination and the use of available sources to reconstruct what the cultural geographer

David Lowenthal refers to as "the audible past."[17] Early modern European soundscapes were very different to those of the industrial metropolis—dominated by sounds such as blacksmiths, bells, windmills, and human voices. Much of this sound would have been concentrated in higher frequency ranges than contemporary soundscapes, it would have been affected to a greater extent by seasonal rhythms, and it would show strong diurnal variations with a much more restricted acoustic realm during hours of darkness.[18] By the eighteenth century, however, noise was increasingly regarded as a problem, especially in larger towns and cities. In William Hogarth's engraving entitled *The Enraged Musician* (1741), we see the agony of a violinist trying to practise by an open window, forced to listen to the maddening tumult of the crowded London street below.

With the spread of industrialization, the impact of noise further intensified. The theatre critic Mel Gordon describes how the working-class districts of industrializing towns and cities in Europe during the 1840s and 1850s were characterized by "a constant din of construction and pounding, of the shrieking of metal sheets being cut and the endless thump of press machinery, of ear-splitting blasts from huge steam whistles, sirens, and electric bells that beckoned and dismissed shifts of first-generation urbanized laborers from their unending and repetitive days."[19] This acoustically defined disciplinary landscape reinforced both class distinctions and emerging geographies of excessive noise. The surge of sonic disturbance experienced in the expanding nineteenth-century city forms part of the emerging rationale for "zoning" and the rationalization of urban space; a process that gathered further momentum in the twentieth century with the development of technological means to measure noise and impose new forms of standardization.[20]

During the twentieth century, we find growing ambivalence towards urban noise, which is variously characterized as a symbol of progress and prosperity, a disorientating and potentially health threatening source of social disorder, or a fascinating realm of cultural experimentation.[21] Writing in 1946, for example, Aldous Huxley named the twentieth century as "the Age of Noise." Huxley's concern with the "pre-fabricated din" enabled by radios, mass advertising, and "a babel of distractions" connects with Theodor Adorno's criticism of "emotional listening" and the use of music for social control.[22] Changing sensitivities to noise also reflect wider anxieties over the "effects of modernity," especially in the early decades of the twentieth century with emerging psychoanalytic interest in forms of sensory "over stimulation" as a source of nervous shock.[23]

The fraying of distinctions between music and sound during the twentieth century forms part of a wider pattern of acoustic experimentation that would extend to architecture, synesthetic dimensions to the visual arts, and new technological advances in the recording, manipulation, and broadcast of the auditory realm.[24] The auditory dimensions to space, and the struggle to interpret or represent these worlds, became part of a wider set of contentions and developments within the phenomenology of the modern sensory realm.[25] A flurry of technological innovations for the recording of sound during the 1930s displaced the rudimentary magnetic wire recorders of the past. These new advances in acoustic mimicry, including the introduction of stereo recording and the rise of magnetic audio tape, provided new possibilities for editing and mixing. The commercial availability of tape recorders from the early 1940s onwards also allowed music to be created more easily without conventional notation systems. John Cage, for example, describes how the tape recorder gave composers access to "the entire field of sound," so that the distinction between musical and non-musical sound became increasingly irrelevant.[26] The introduction of non-pitched sounds into music by Edgard Varèse and Cage, for example, or the direct use of mechanical noise such as airplane propellers in George Antheil's *Ballet Mécanique* (1926), illustrate how the redefinition of music formed part of a wider field of modernist sound experimentation.[27] The spatial aspects of musical experimentation from the 1960s onwards, and the intensified challenge to regularized post-Renaissance musical forms, also institute a new kind of sonic geography. Works such as György Ligeti's *Atmosphères* (1961), used to dramatic effect in Stanley Kubrick's *2001: A Space Odyssey* (1968), indicate a new fluidity between experimental sound textures and popular culture.

Sound itself can form part of the political dynamics of urban space: in nineteenth-century Brazil, for example, the violent suppression of slave festivities such as *capoeira* explicitly linked sonic disruption with the fear of crowds and political insurrection.[28] More recently, the *cacerolazos* phenomenon of public protests through the banging of metal pots in Latin American cities illustrates how fleeting control over sonic space can serve as a symbolic challenge to state authority. The cacerolazos is a spreading phenomenon; a clattering that surges forth, like a strange tide, to produce an acoustic ripple across the surface of the city.[29] Various types of "acoustic torment" have been used as a form of cultural redress. In the case of Kolkata (Calcutta), for example, the political scientist Sudipta Kaviraj describes how the poor make use of possibilities offered by religious festivals to produce "blaring music throughout the night directed precisely at the middle-class houses." Noise in this context constitutes a type of "currency for repayment" in the face of pervasive poverty and powerlessness. These types of sonic disruption also expose the limits to a particular kind of European understanding of modernity and the socio-spatial constitution of the public sphere.[30] Noise can be used as a weapon, or as a means to assert control over space. Social conflict over noise appears to be growing, in part driven by the "acoustic gentrification" underway in many inner urban areas and the increasing density of bars and nightclubs.[31] A further facet of this acoustic gentrification, ironically revolving around cultures of sonic authenticity, involves various forms of "acoustic boosterism" through the design of prestige concert halls, international music festivals, and other types of cultural events. The experience of sound, and music in particular, is being shaped by new configurations in public culture.

A further critique of contemporary soundscapes concerns the ubiquity of MP3-dominated acoustic environments. The development of an increasingly sophisticated acoustic carapace for individual urbanites, observable since the early development of the Walkman in the

1980s, marks part of a choreography of socio-spatial disengagement.[32] The "auditory self" is now immersed in new forms of digital governmentality that extend to other aspects of the sensory environment. The contemporary city increasingly resonates to a strange chorus of disembodied digital voices that seek to direct human behaviour.[33] The generalized low-grade digital reproduction of music generates distinctive kinds of cultural relationships to sound that are further removed from the "acoustic authenticity" of original sources. The pervasive use of music for the marketing of commodities and the ubiquitous crafting of "lifestyle soundtracks" marks just one element in this unfolding dynamic between the acoustic realm and late capital.

In parallel with the growing political salience of noise, there has been an increasing emphasis on the social and cultural significance of silence. In 1969, for example, the International Music Council of UNESCO passed a motion calling for "the right of everyone to silence." This officially sanctioned emphasis on silence marks a somewhat ironic regulatory echo to the minimalist acoustic experimentation of Cage and other avant-garde artists. In fact, the experience of anything approaching silence is rather rare: following the Icelandic volcanic ash cloud of 2010, for example, the temporary absence of aircraft produced an eerie stillness across the skies of north-west Europe, as the subsonic aerial soundscapes of the early twenty-first century temporarily receded.

Cultural and political concerns with noise, and especially the synthetic acoustic realm, have frequently been aligned with a broader critique of modernity. On Earth Day 2005, for instance, an area within the temperate rain forest of the Olympic National Park in Washington State called "One Square Inch of Silence" was created in order to "protect and preserve the natural soundscape." Considered to be "the quietest place in the United States," the logic behind this project is that by defending one inch of the park from noise, a vast zone of tranquillity can be realized.[34] In this instance, the right to silence and the protection of a "natural soundscape" connects with an ecological critique of modernity and the attempt to create an imaginary acoustic landscape. The rejection of noise also resonates with long-standing anti-urban sentiments and a distrust in technologically mediated environments.

The cultural politics of sound has tended to downplay the historical specificities of acoustic authenticity and the "embodied universalism" that pervades phenomenological studies of sound. Anxieties or desires in relation to the sonic realm are ineffably entangled with the co-evolutionary dynamics of the body, space, and technology; there is an oscillatory dynamic between the material and measurable, the symbolic and phantasmatic. Whereas visual culture rests on a degree of distanciation between the observer and the direct object of the gaze, auditory experience is marked by a greater degree of spatial intimacy and material permeability. Yet the separation of the listener from the original sound source can engender its own forms of acoustic alienation. Recent writing on sound has sought to delineate a more nuanced auditory realm. The acoustic city transcends the limitations of the human ear; its full resonance eludes even the most ardent of listeners.

Endnotes

1 The full title of Gabriele Stirl's installation is *Visualisierung einer seriel-len Klangpartitur für 12 Instrumente.*

2 Siegfried Kracauer, "Schreie auf der Straße," in *Straßen in Berlin und anderswo* (Berlin: Arsenal, 1987 [1964]) pp. 26–28.

3 Jonathan Raban, *Soft City* (London: Hamish Hamilton, 1974).

4 See Michael Flitner, *Lärm an der Grenze. Fluglärm und Umwelt-gerechtigkeit am Beispiel des binationalen Flughafens Basel-Mulhouse* (Stuttgart: Franz Steiner, 2007).

5 Jean-François Augoyard, *Step by Step: Everyday Walks in a French Urban Housing Project*, trans. David Ames Curtis (Minneapolis: University of Minnesota Press, 2007) p. 148.

6 Steven Connor, "The modern auditory I," in *Rewriting the Self: Histories of the Renaissance to the Present*, ed. Roy Porter (London: Routledge, 1997) pp. 206, 221, and "Rustications: Animals in the Urban Mix" in this volume.

7 See Martin Jay, *Downcast Eyes: The Denigration of Vision in Twenti-eth-century French Thought* (Berkeley: University of California Press, 1993).

8 Ibid. See in particular chapter 3, "The crisis of the ancien scopic regime: from the impressionists to Bergson" pp. 149–209.

9 See R. Murray Schafer, *The Soundscape: Listening to the Twentieth Century* (New York: Alfred Knopf, 1977).

10 See, for example, Jean-François Augoyard and Henry Torgue, ed., *Sonic Experience: A Guide to Everyday Sounds*, trans. Andrea McCartney and David Paquette (Montréal: McGill-Queen's University Press, 2005); Michel Chion, *Audio-vision: Sound on Screen*, trans. Claudia Gorbman (New York: Columbia University Press, 1994 [1990]); Don Ihde, *Listening and Voice: A Phenomenology of Sound* (Athens: OH: University of Ohio Press, 1976); Brandon LaBelle, *Background Noise: Perspectives on Sound Art* (New York: Continuum, 2006); George Revill, "*El tren fantasma*: Arcs of Sound and the Acoustic Spaces of Landscape," *Transactions of the Institute of British Geographers* (in press); Trevor Wishart, "Sound Symbols and Landscape," in Simon Emmerson, ed., *The Language of Electroacoustic Music* (London: Macmillan, 1986) pp. 41–60.

11 See Georgina Born, "Introduction," to *Music, Sound and Space: Transformations of Public and Private Experience*, ed. Georgina Born (Cambridge: Cambridge University Press, 2013) pp. 1–69.

12 Alain Corbin, *Village Bells: Sound and Meaning in the Nineteenth-century French Countryside*, trans. Martin Thom (New York: Columbia University Press, 1998 [1994]).

13 See Kevin Lynch, *The Image of the City* (Cambridge, MA: The MIT Press, 1960).

14 See Ann Heylighen and Jasmien Herssens, "Designerly Ways of Not Knowing. What Designers Can Learn about Space from People Who Are Blind," *Journal of Urban Design* (in press).

15 Stefan Helmreich, "An Anthropologist Underwater: Immersive Soundscapes, Submarine Cyborgs, and Transductive Ethnography," *American Ethnologist* 34 (4) (2007): 621–641.

16 Listen, for example, to Lee Patterson's recordings of micro-spaces of urban life on the CD that accompanies this volume.

17 See David Lowenthal, "The Audible Past," in International Music Council, *The Canada Music Book 11/12* (Montréal: Canada Music Council, 1975–76) pp. 209–217.

18 See, for example, Schafer, *The Soundscape.*

19 Mel Gordon, "Songs from the Museum of the Future: Russian Sound Creation (1910–1930)," in *Wireless Imagination: Sound, Radio, and the Avant-garde*, ed. Douglas Kahn and Gregory Whitehead (Cambridge, MA: The MIT Press, 1992) p. 197.

20 See, for example, Karin Bijsterveld, "'The City of Din': Decibels, Noise, and Neighbors in the Netherlands, 1910–1980," *Osiris* 18 (2003): 173–193; Karin Bijsterveld, "Listening to Machines: Industrial Noise, Hearing Loss, and the Cultural Meaning of Sound," *Interdisciplinary Science Reviews* 31 (4) (2006): 323–337; Emily Thompson, *The Soundscape of Modernity: Architectural Acoustics and the Culture of Listening in America, 1900–1933* (Cambridge, MA: The MIT Press, 2002).

21 See, for example, Douglas Kahn, *Noise, Water, Meat: A History of Sound in the Arts* (Cambridge, MA: The MIT Press, 1999); Andrey Smirnov and Liubov Pchelkina, "Generation Z: Renoise—Experiments in Sound and Electronic Music in Early Twentieth-century Russia," in *Dis Continuity. Select Trajectories in Experimental and Electronic Music* (Berlin: CTM—Festival for Adventurous Music and Art, Berlin, 2014) pp. 4–9.

22 See Aldous Huxley, "Silence, Liberty, and Peace—A Thoughtful Analysis of the Individual Today and his Future in the World," in *The Perennial Philosophy* (New York: Harper & Brothers Publishers, 1946) pp. 218–219 and Theodor Adorno, *Quasi una fantasia*, trans. Rodney Livingstone (London: Verso: 1992 [1963]). On the ideological dimensions to music, listening, and modern soundscapes, see also Jacques Attali, *Noise: The Political Economy of Music*, trans. Brian Massumi (Minneapolis: University of Minnesota Press, 1985 [1977]); Carolyn Birdsall, *Nazi Soundscapes: Sound, Technology and Urban Space in Germany, 1933–1945* (Amsterdam: University of Amsterdam Press, 2012); George Revill, "Music and the Politics of Sound: Nationalism, Citizenship, and the Auditory Space," *Environment and Planning D: Society and Space* 18 (2000): 597–613; Susan J. Smith, "Soundscape," *Area* 26 (3) (1994): 232–240.

23 See, for example, Andreas Killen, *Berlin Electropolis: Shock, Nerves, and German Modernity* (Berkeley: University of California Press, 2006) and Anthony Vidler, *Warped Space: Art, Architecture, and Anxiety in Modern Culture* (Cambridge, MA: The MIT Press, 2000).

24 See Born, "Introduction."

25 Ibid. See also Merijn Royaards "The Space Between: A Cartographic Experiment" in this volume.

26 John Cage cited in Christoph Cox and Daniel Warner, ed., *Audio Culture: Readings in Modern Music* (London: Continuum, 2009) p. 5. See also Dieter Daniels and Inke Arns, ed., *Sounds Like Silence* (Leipzig: Spector Books, 2012).

27 See Alex Ross, *The Rest is Noise* (New York: Farrar, Straus and Giroux, 2007).

28 See, for example, Simone Pondé Vassalo, "Capoeiras e intelectuais: a construção coletiva de capoeira 'autêntica,'" *Estudos Históricos* 32 (2003): 106–124.

29 See Leandro Minuchin, "Noise, Language, and Public Protest: The *Cacerolazos* in Buenos Aires" in this volume.

30 Sudipta Kaviraj, "Filth and the Public Sphere: Concepts and Practices about Waste in Calcutta," *Public Culture* 10 (1) (1997): 111–112.

31 See Joanna Kusiak, "Acoustic Warfare: The Silence of Warsaw's Acoustic Gentrification" in this volume.

32 See Michael Bull, *Sounding out the City: Personal Stereos and the Management of Everyday Life* (Oxford: Berg, 2000), Jonathan Sterne, *MP3: The Meaning of a Format* (Durham, NC: Duke University Press, 2012), and Heike Weber, "Stereo City: Mobile Listening in the 1980s" in this volume.

33 See Nina Power, "Soft Coercion, the City, and the Recorded Female Voice" in this volume.

34 http://onesquareinch.org/ (accessed 23 January 2014).

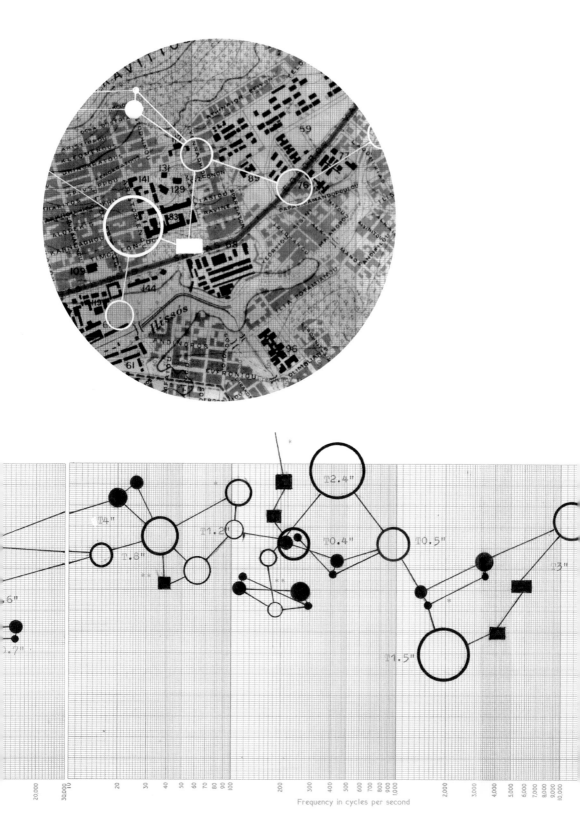

1

URBAN
SOUNDSCAPES

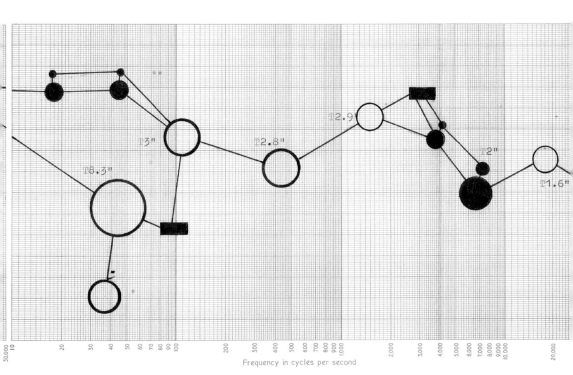

Frequency in cycles per second

RUSTICATIONS: ANIMALS IN THE URBAN MIX

Steven Connor

What is a soundscape? It is a word that we seem to have been able to do without until it was coined by R. Murray Schafer in 1969. At the beginning of *The Tuning of the World* (1977), Schafer defines a soundscape as "any acoustic field of study," whether that be "a musical composition," "a radio program," or "an acoustic environment." Schafer makes the point that a soundscape cannot be captured in the same way that a landscape can be captured in a photograph. Unlike a camera, a microphone samples details: "It gives the close-up but nothing corresponding to aerial photography."[1] Where a map provides a representation of a landscape that one may easily learn to read, making sense of the many different kinds of sound notation required to document a given soundscape requires both much more information, and much more training. And, where maps are iconically congruous with what they represent (they are a visible representation of a visual scene), the notations of soundscapes are translations of sound into visible or legible form.

The success of the idea of the soundscape is suggested by the promotion of the term into the title of Schafer's *Tuning of the World* when it was reissued in 1993, the year that marked the foundation of the World Forum for Acoustic Ecology, followed in 2000 by the first issue of *Soundscape: The Journal of Acoustic Ecology*. It was not just that the concept of the soundscape has been elevated to star billing in Schafer's 1993 book: it is that giving the book this title means that the book itself was now itself conceivable as a kind of soundscape—that is, as a certain gathering-together or taking-to-be of the whole field of modern sound that may itself count as a kind of soundscape. Indeed, we might note that, though there is a great deal in Schafer's book about individual elements of the soundscape, whether natural or human—waves, winds, birds, bells, cars, electric fans—relatively little is said about their fields of interrelationship, perhaps because it is the book itself which constitutes that field. For a soundscape, like a landscape, is the outcome of a particular act of associative attention, an effort or aptness to hear certain sounds as consonant, though we will see that there are markedly different forms of synopsis, or synaudience, for the "sounding together" of sounds.

It should not be a surprise that the two definitions of the word soundscape offered by the *Oxford English Dictionary*—"(a) a musical composition consisting of a texture of sounds; (b) the sounds which form an auditory environment"—should associate the ideas of a composition and a disposition, a sound arrangement made, and a sound arrangement to be made out. The making out of a soundscape, whether in the mode of construction or construal, involves, first of all, a disaggregation of an ensemble of sounds from the contexts of action and significance in which they are embedded (in which, odd though it may seem, they may be heard, but not heard as "sound" at all), and second a new aggregation of these disjoined sounds with each other, in such a way that they may seem to be brought on to a single plane of expression and intelligibility.

There is a curious effect of advancing and recession involved in the composition of a soundscape. A soundscape must be pulled out, or "foregrounded" from a previously formless condition, or rather something that is not in any kind of "condition," formed or formless, at all. But, insofar as it is in fact a soundscape, what it is foregrounded as is a kind of background, making it the making manifest of an implicitness. It is for this reason that the kinds of musical compositions that tend to be called soundscapes are ones that suggest reservoirs or repertoires of possibility, environments of sound, against which other kinds of sound might stand out, rather than specific actualizations of sound. There is something loose and latent in the idea of a soundscape, which is always somehow in advance of its collection as sound. A soundscape is therefore a kind of precomposition, a score rather than a performance.

There is an added complexity that comes when the sounds involved are those of animals. For most, the sounds that constitute a soundscape are sonically autonomous, existing as pure and distinct sounds, with a purely contingent relation to other sounds in the environment. The sound made by an aeroplane coming in to land may have a relation to the sound of the highway I can hear in the distance, in that the highway will get me to the airport to meet a passenger on the incoming plane, but this is a relation between the things making the sounds, not between the making of the sounds. If there is a dialogue between highway and skyway, it is one that takes place because of my act of attention. But if I hear a blackbird at its sweet rippling ruckus on the gable of the house opposite, and then a second or two later a call from another blackbird that seems to answer it, a response that may then prompt a further bawling sally from the principal, then I am hearing a diaphony that has a specifically sonorous relatedness. Here I am not just knitting together a soundscape out of the coincidence of my attention, I am apprehending a pattern of sonorous interaction that is already in itself, to borrow the Ignation formula, a kind of "composition of place."[2] Once one starts to hear the call and response, one begins to hear the periods of suspended song as hollowed out by listening. The interlacing of action and latency forms a sonorous field that is, in Sartrean locution, "for-itself" as well as being "in-itself," or "in-itself-for-me." Listening to animal sounds is therefore, in a replete sense, an "overhearing," or hearing to the second degree, in that in it I lend an ear to other listenings; I listen in on the knitting of a soundscape by and for other ears than my own. A soundscape is a disposition of points and sounds that is referable to a particular point of audition: a soundscape populated by animals is polycentric, a disposition of dispositions that listens and replies to itself. The sound of animals gives to a soundscape interiority, even saturation—for it includes other centricities or points of audition. This is one of the many features of a soundscape that renders it something that is not simply available either to be captured, or let be, or both, as in the dreams of acoustic ecology. In a soundscape in part populated by auditory actants, my very listening is an active and productive part of the soundscape.

There is another sense in which animal sounds signify a circuit of produced and heard sound. Just as the interrelations of animal sounds make silence sonorously positive, so the hearing of animal sounds signifies the retreat or diminution of human sound. The rhythm of our own remission is often accordingly what we hear in animal sound, especially in the roaring urban circumstance.

So soundscapes are more than sounds—they are sounds joined by relations, whether these are external, as when one assembles sounds into a soundscape by an act of listening, or internal, as when sounds reveal themselves to be produced in interchange. If a tree falls in the forest with nobody to hear it, it may well make a sound, but it cannot be part of any kind of soundscape. A soundscape is a sound plus a certain kind of relation. The sounds in a soundscape must always be for me, in something of the way that a landscape must always be for me; but, buried within that relation, they must also always be for-each-other-for-me, made consonant with each other by being included within the scope of my auditory attention. This has an important and often overlooked consequence. It means that sound is not enough to constitute a soundscape: for a soundscape is sound plus relation, and that relation need not be fully and in itself sonorous. The being-for-me of an urban soundscape is not of the order of the sonorous, precisely because it is a relation, even though it may be a relation between sounds. In fact, I think we have to take a further step, and say that it is necessary that there be this ontological adulteration. For sound to be heard *as sound*, it must paradoxically be denatured, or taken out of its being. A soundscape must be composed of sound, and only sound; but it can only be so composed through something that is not itself sonorous.

A soundscape is formed autonomously of unaccommodated sound; but that autonomy is heteronomous, for what is essential in the making of a soundscape is this anacoustic element of relation—not inaudible, but rather not of the order of the audible.

First of all, human beings enclosed wild animals, drawing them into shared habitation through domestication; then, without any manumission, the growth of cities has led to a banishment of animals—out of sight, hearing, and mind of the urban dweller. To speak of the urban is to seem to evoke a place emptied of animals. This is a much more recent phenomenon than we may tend to assume. The gradient of the approach roads to London bridges was defined both by the need for horses to be able to draw the conveyances they were pulling up to the level of the bridge, and their capacity to resist the forward impulsion of their loads on the way down. London is full of water troughs provided by the Metropolitan Drinking Fountain and Cattle Trough Association, set up in 1859 to provide free drinking fountains, and then extended in 1867 to the provision of troughs for horses and cattle. Their ubiquity in London, with particular concentrations in the City of London as one gets closer to Smithfield Market, is a reminder of what prodigious numbers of animals one might have encountered in the heart of the largest and most powerful city in the world in the second half of the nineteenth century. Many of these were horses, which provided almost all of the transportation, but huge numbers of animals were driven through the city to the market for slaughter and sale. Charles Dickens, Jr. estimated that "a single trough has supplied the wants of 1,800 horses in one period of 24 hours."[3]

With the replacement of horse-drawn transport with cars, and the progressive eviction of slaughterhouses from the centre of cities, the city has become increasingly emptied of animals, apart from domestic pets, which is to say, almost exclusively cats and dogs. Unowned animals live surreptitious or parasitic lives. There are very few sounds of animals to be heard in the city, but the animals that do dwell in the city will tend to make themselves known predominantly through sound, precisely because that is what is left to them. Perhaps it is the sound of animals that most impresses us with the sense of a specifically sonic field of action and awareness, precisely because the sound of unowned animals is usually separated from visual confirmation. Whether it be the whirr of cicadas, the twittering of birds, or the hum of bees, the animal sounds that we hear are normally separated from their sources. It is as though the sounding species had not so much occupied a niche within an ecology of sound, but had been drawn into the niche of sound itself. Non-domestic animals do not dwell in the city, so much as haunt it, and their disembodied cries and whispers are a sign of this haunting. Charles Dickens anticipates this haunting from the midst of the horse-drawn city, in the passage evoking the neighbourhood near Todgers's in chapter 9 of *Martin Chuzzlewit,* which alerts its reader to the fact that "deep among the foundations of these buildings, the ground was undermined and burrowed out into stables, where cart-horses, troubled by rats, might be heard on a quiet Sunday rattling their halters, as disturbed spirits in tales of haunted houses are said to clank their chains."[4]

There are significant variations across cities in different parts of the world however. Indeed, the sounds of animals may be one of the only identifying soundmarks in the increasingly homogenous sound of traffic. The chatter of monkeys may be one of the only sonorous features that would identify the city of Kolkata, while the growl of prowling bears has become a common urban noise in some North American and Canadian towns.

Since Rachel Carson, the survival or silencing of birdsong has become a sonorous measure of environmental degradation. In fact, however, there is some reason to believe that we may be forcing birds to become louder rather than quieter. Hans Slabbekoorn of Leiden University studied the songs of Great Tits, *Parus major,* in a number of Northern European cities, and found that they routinely sang faster and higher, incorporating fewer low-frequency notes than birds in the wild. It seems very likely that this is in order to compensate for the low-frequency hum of traffic that would otherwise mask their song. This is no mere behavioural adaptation—in that such birds would be unlikely to be able to mate with members of their own species from rural areas who would sing in a different register, the birds may be undergoing a kind of acoustic respeciation. In many species of bird, females seem to prefer males with lower-pitched songs, which may well put such birds at a double disadvantage, in having to expend more energy on overcoming noise while also not attracting as many mates. The sheer quantity of competing noise is not the only feature of the urban environment with which birds have to contend. Other studies have suggested that birds are responsive, not just to raw noise levels, but also to the acoustic features of their physical environment. Hard, impervious surfaces like brick and concrete reflect and scatter more of the sound energy of birdsong, this effect being more marked in high-frequency signals than low frequency. As this can make the signal unintelligible, it exerts pressure on birds in urban environments to lower rather than to lift the frequency of their song. Since highly reverberant surfaces and high levels of low-frequency noise often coexist in urban environments, this may create paradoxical pressures—if a bird sings at higher frequencies and with shorter stabs of song in order to overcome the masking effects of low-frequency noise, this may in turn make the song more vulnerable to acoustic scattering from highly reflective surfaces.[5]

Another of the ways in which birds have adapted to city life is through time-shifts. The European Robin, *Erithacus rubecula,* has taken to singing at night in order perhaps to compensate for its restricted opportunities to establish territory during the day. If you hear a nightingale singing in Berkeley Square, the chances are that it will be singing much louder now than in 1939. In fact, the toning and tempering of the time of the city is one of the most important ways in which animal sounds interact with, rather than simply struggle through or stand out against urban noise.

Despite the many features in play in urban birdsong—frequency, amplitude, phrasing, syntax, patterning, redundancy—the model governing ecological studies of urban birdsong is predominantly that of a zero-sum game involving only two parameters, that of the bird's song, and the urban noise that either obstructs or is overcome by it. This is because the question driving such research is, principally, how are birds doing in noisy towns?

This model is surely too simple. It would be a mistake, for example, to counterpose "urban" and "rural" environments in such a way as to suggest that the former are always noisy and the latter always soothingly serene. In fact, the very capacity of birds to adapt their songs—whether through singing differently, selective pressure on the transmission from adult to chick of different kinds of song, or selective pressure on breeding—derives from the fact that there are many sources of noise in the natural world. The theoretical prediction that a bird singing against masking noise might increase the serial redundancy of its song (repeating its song more often, just like somebody shouting through a gale or over a poor phone-connection) has been borne out in studies of Chaffinches, *Fringilla coelebs*, living near waterfalls.[6] There may be a great deal of noise to contend with in urban environments, but this should not imply that there is no noise in "natural" environments.

For there is noise everywhere; what is more, there is no information without noise. The birds that adapt their songs in cities may be there because their songs have been formed in circumstances in which very similar kinds of noise—wind, water, or the sounds of other species—have to be overcome.[7] The dawn chorus, often taken as an image of the orchestral plenitude of nature, is in fact an extremely stressful acoustic environment, an order that is formed in and through competing noise. Signal is the opposite of noise, but information is found in the emergence of signal from noise, and therefore in a certain signal-noise coupling. So there is no signal without noise, and there is noise in and around every signal. In fact, this is the very reason for the importance of birds and birdsong in human history—since birdsong represents the very principle of meaning amidst noisiness, and the intensification of meaning that comes from the intensification of noise.

There is one kind of creature with whom cities have a positive affinity, namely insects. R. Murray Schafer suggests that insects provide a rare example in the nonhuman world of what he calls "flat-line" sounds—that is, sounds involving repeated automatic processes, in humming, buzzing, or stridulation.[8] Where the sight and sound of other animals may strike the city-dweller as an anomaly or annunciation, insects in a certain sense are the city. The beehive has long been taken as a metaphor for the structure and operations of the city, and it is indeed the case that, at a time when bee colonies are under intense pressure worldwide, bees are often healthier in the city than in the surrounding countryside, partly perhaps because of the diversity of plant species available to them to feed on, compared to the condition of grimly depleted monoculture that characterizes many rural locations. Even where insects are not physically present or audible, they are evoked in the metaphors of humming and buzzing that are so often applied to the background sounds of city life. My suggestion is that this metaphorical texture is in fact part of the animal soundscape of the city.

It has become clear that the work of conservation can less than ever be conceived simply as a work of holding back, piping down, and letting be, important though all of these are. Soundscapes are always constructed, and the construction of soundscape should be regarded as part of the larger work of what Peter Sloterdijk has usefully called the work of "explicitation" in modernity.[9] Insofar as explication means the bringing into the foreground for the purposes of management and design of what had previously been merely given or implicit, and since the soundscape must be defined as a foregrounding of a background phenomenon, the making of a field into a figure, the construction of soundscape is part of the huge effort of rethinking the relations between the human and the natural that must characterize our future. In a world in which, as Michel Serres has repeatedly said, "we depend on things that depend on us,"[10] there seems no possibility of returning to a condition of immanence or innocence.

I began by suggesting that the concept of the soundscape both draws our attention to the particularity of sound and also draws us away from sound, or places sound beside itself. I then proposed that the audible presence of animals in urban sound is both a kind of haunting and a hollowing out of the tinnitant self-enclosure of human sound. Even as it points to the eviction of animals from the characteristically urban spaces of the modern world, the anomalous sounds of animals in the city point to a new, delocalized, even evaporated kind of urbanism, one in which the urban and the rural interpenetrate each other. This haunting serves to point us away from the cramping idea of location, of the factitious and reactionary notion of the here-and-now that hovers around every notion of the soundscape, and to adumbrate a newer, more conjugated, and convivial auditorium of the world.

Endnotes

1   R. Murray Schafer, *The Tuning of the World* (New York: Alfred A. Knopf, 1977) p. 7.
2   St. Ignatius of Loyola, *Spiritual Exercises*, trans. Micheal Ivens (Leominster: Gracewing, 2004) p. 19.
3   Charles Dickens, Jr., *Dickens's Dictionary of London*. 4th ed. (London: Macmillan and Co, 1882) p. 96.
4   Charles Dickens, *Martin Chuzzlewit*, ed. Margaret Cardwell (Oxford: Oxford University Press, 1984) pp. 113–14.
5   J. L. Dowling, D. A. Luther, and P. P. Marra, "Comparative Effects of Urban Development and Anthropogenic Noise on Bird Songs," *Behavioral Ecology* (23) (2012): 201–9.
6   H. Brumm and P. J. B. Slater, "Ambient Noise, Motor Fatigue and Serial redundancy in Chaffinch Song," *Behavioral Ecology and Sociobiology* (60) (2006): pp. 475–81.
7   Alejandro Ariel Ríos-Chelén, "Bird Song: The Interplay Between Urban Noise and Sexual Selection," *Oecologia Australis* (13) (2009): 153–64, here p. 155.
8   Schafer, *The Tuning of the World* p. 78.
9   Peter Sloterdijk, *Schäume: Sphären, Vol. 3: Plurale Sphärologie* (Frankfurt: Suhrkamp, 2004) p. 87.
10 Michel Serres, *Temps des crises* (Paris: Le Pommier, 2009) p. 36 [my translation].

SOFT COERCION, THE CITY, AND THE RECORDED FEMALE VOICE

Nina Power

Four questions to begin with: What is the pitch of the neo-liberal city? How does the pitch of the city construct images of and for the humanity that travels through it? How does gender relate to control of this space—corporate, commercial, privatized space, and the few remaining places we might (often erroneously, or perhaps nostalgically) refer to as "public space"? How does the soundscape of the city relate to forms of control—what I will call here "soft coercion"—that often goes unnoticed, or at least blends into the background and becomes simply part of the tapestry of the urban sonic environment, alongside the whirr of traffic, the babble of the crowd, birdsong, sirens? We may think of the sound of the city as somehow being "neutral" on its own terms, or at least cacophonous enough to escape linear description, but by paying careful attention to the patterns of urban sounds, we do more than simply listen: the overfamiliarity of certain sonic tropes starts to tell us something signifcant about the way in which both gender and control are constructed and reinforced. This essay considers the now-ubiquitous use of female-sounding voices in a variety of urban settings: information announcements on public transport, especially buses, trains, and train stations; instructions on supermarket machines; security announcements[1]. The references here will apply mainly to the UK context, but it is apparent that many European and North American cities will exhibit similar features. Much of what I am looking at also applies to more domestic and intimate technologies, such as mobile phones (consider, for example, the "Siri" application—a voice-activated knowledge locater that responds with a female voice on the default setting in most countries), GPS, or commercial automated telephone answering systems. But my focus here will be on the female-sounding voice as encountered in the context of the city, as a traveller, shopper, or commuter, in particular, where the choice of the gender of the voice is far less available to the listener, and where the voice operates at a generic or collective level, rather than relating to specific individual instructions. Here, the listener is perhaps passing through a transport hub, or buying food at a supermarket terminal on his or her way home hearing multiple recorded voices intermingle. This is the sound of the banal, everyday urban experience, rather than that of an ecstatic night out or serious state of emergency (although a low-level fear enters into the picture when we think about the way in which the message "in these times of heightened security…" becomes the norm and "if you see anything suspicious please contact a member of staff" is the sonic fabric of the everyday). It operates as a kind of aural clutter, but one whose pitch is supposed to remind us of a certain kind of female-sounding voice: in the British context, this voice is clipped, upper-middle class, brusque, sensible. It asks "have you swiped your Nectar card?" in the same way we might imagine a nurse in a field hospital in World War Two would ask if you'd been drinking enough fluids or getting enough rest.[2] It tells us which tube station is coming up next in a firm, bureaucratic way,[3] such that we feel reassured we know where we're going, but also faintly controlled and guided by some sort of invisible Mary Poppins. It is the regionless accent of BBC Radio 4, of a slight nostalgia for the War and post-war period, of hard work and no nonsense, of pragmatism and benevolent strictness. It conjures up images of governesses and schoolmistresses and films from the 1940s. It is the sound of Received Pronunciation and the Queen's English, of the voice that Margaret Thatcher never quite managed to get to sound anything other than forced.

This voice of soft coercion ("Go here if you want to do that," "Have you done x? It's for your own good, you know") announces something of a paradox: although women have yet to achieve quantitative representation in positions of power (as of 2013, in the UK women are 51 per cent of the population but only 22 per cent of MPs, 23 per cent of judges, and 31 per cent of local councillors[4]), their voices—albeit ghostly, disembodied, usually pre-recorded and extremely narrow in terms of origin, class, and pitch—are everywhere. This flooding of the commercial and transportational economy with female-sounding voices is inversely correlated to the number of women in parliament, with recorded female voices outnumbering male voices five to one.[5]

There are some observations to make, some technical, some political. The female voice in the places focused on here is typically pre-recorded, either as complete phrases (such as the name of the places on the tube map[6]), or as fragments of phrases that are later reconstituted by a second technology ("concatenation"). Think about those announcements you get that are ubiquitous but contingent, such as an announcement regarding the "late running" of a particular train. Here you are likely to hear a female-sounding voice that seems more fragmentary than usual: "Due to signal failure the … 9:52 … to … Penzance … will be approximately … 17 … minutes late. We apologize for any inconvenience this may cause." The pre-recorded blocks are played like notes in a particularly avant-garde piece, where the conductor is a machine and commuters the unwitting audience, rushing from one machine to the other at the behest of incorporeal commandments. But why make these voices female-sounding? Why not embrace a gender-neutral machinic-sounding pitch? Or to put it another way, what is it about male-sounding voices that train companies, supermarkets, and so on dislike? The clue perhaps lies in the separation between the everyday and the emergency, between the supposed smooth running of things and the potential for things to go wrong. If the role of the female-sounding voice is to reassure but also to direct, is the implication that a male-sounding voice would sound too dictatorial, too bossy, too "serious"? With personal technologies such as Siri, the implication that her (default) female voice fits into a continuum of secretaries and personal assistants is clear (if you ask Siri who "she" is, she will respond "I am your humble personal assistant"). In places that see a large number of passing human traffic, the situation is somewhat different—you do not command the machine, the machine "commands" you by informing, instructing, softly controlling. As female-sounding recorded messages take over more and more sonic space, we notice them bleed over into even those scenarios where emergency can be calculated and prepared for, albeit only sonically: not just the late running of trains, but coded messages for fire alerts in train stations ("Would Inspector Sands please report to Platform 2") are often "female-sounding." The soft coercion of the everyday thus includes and incorporates its own contingency.

But we could go further and ask what if the smooth running of things *was* the emergency? This would make the female-sounding voice the sound of quiet catastrophe, of social control as such, rather than just the ordinary running of things. This particular construction of gender—albeit of a disembodied, ghostly kind—would make the recorded female voice a kind of cover story for a normalcy that is in fact a state of emergency, of crisis, of barbarism, and capitalism. It would be more honest for this voice to be shouting, chastising, authoritarian, and perhaps therefore male-sounding to reflect the balance of power, but perhaps it is more alarming to reflect on why it doesn't need to be to have the same effect: the co-optation of the female-sounding voice as the voice of everyday control is no longer the voice of authority conceived as male (as in the pioneering voice work of Laurie Anderson for example), but of control regendered and recoded as female.[7] What effects might this have on the way in which we conceive of gender above and beyond our repeated fragmentary experience of the disembodied voice in urban spaces? Do the often unnoticed voices really have any effect on how we conceive of political representation, of the "public," of where "real" power lies? In so far as female-sounding voices represent order and soft coercion in a sensible mode, they arguably do present a misleading impression of gender and the real control of property and space. The voices float monotonously over commercial and privatized zones, fusing an image of feminized "Englishness" with that of corporate culture. In other words, they are *symbolic* of the destruction of the welfare state and the ambiguity of the "public," as we witness it being finally hacked to death, but they are not *representative* of those doing the destroying (need it be pointed out that it is women and children who suffer most in times of economic crisis and benefit cuts). They are ideological sonic veneer for what lies beneath, the sonic equivalent of the "Keep Calm and Carry On" poster and its myriad spin-offs, a fusion of war and crisis made cute for the middle classes.

But what shall we do with the voices, the recordings that have replaced the real bodies of announcers and cashiers? We could do worse than to begin to pay attention to what they are saying, and not saying; of what they tell us about gender and the contemporary city, of where the power lies and where it doesn't, of the ideological function of "certain" voices and the exclusion of others. The protester in the street chanting spontaneous slogans hears her opponent in every beat of the neo-liberal city: to reclaim the machines—from supermarket tills to parliamentary processes—we must first identify who speaks in the voice of the enemy, and who speaks from elsewhere.

Endnotes

1 I use the term "female-sounding" to indicate that I am not interested in the normative question—what should "men" and "women" sound like if they are to perform "maleness" and "femaleness," as if this was anyway decidable—but rather for examining the intention of the companies that use voices that they have explicitly picked to "sound female." It is clear that when hearing voices we tend to "gender" them quickly, and often without reflecting on any assumptions that follow from this apparent recognition. I want to ask instead why the "female-sounding" voice has become a key sonic element in the urban landscape, and ask what it means for the maintenance of the running and order of the city.

2 A Nectar card is a reward card that contains points gathered through purchasing.

3 Though it should be noted that the story of Emma Clarke and her tube announcements is rather more complicated than we might initially think. See my earlier short piece on "The Dystopian Technology of the Female Voice" for the Her Noise Archive (2012): http://hernoise.org/nina-power/

4 http://www.parliament.uk/briefing-papers/SN02936/women-international-womens-day-2013-background-statistics.

5 http://britishlibrary.typepad.co.uk/archival_sounds/2010/08/womens-voices-calling-the-shots-in-recorded-announcements.html.

6 "Old Street," for example always comes to mind, as the way Emma Clarke pronounces it captures exactly the pitch and tone I mention above.

7 See her track "From The Air" from her LP *Big Science* (1982), and her widespread use of audio drag filters.

A BEAUTIFUL NOISE EMERGING FROM THE APPARATUS OF AN OBSTACLE: TRAINS AND THE SOUNDS OF THE JAPANESE CITY

David Novak

Japan's modernity has long been characterized by the proposal of its unique sensory culture, and the question of its survival in the face of urbanization. As early as 1898, Lafcadio Hearn described Japanese attention to environmental sounds as part of a special perceptual mode, which, he argued, was a cultural resource endangered by industrial Westernization:

> *Surely we have something to learn from the people in whose mind the simple chant of a cricket can awaken whole fairy-swarms of tender and delicate fancies. We may boast of being their masters in the mechanical, their teachers of the artificial in all its varieties of ugliness; but in the knowledge of the natural—in the feeling of the joy and beauty of earth—they exceed us like the Greeks of old. Yet perhaps it will be only when our blind aggressive industrialism has wasted and sterilized their paradise—substituting everywhere for beauty the utilitarian, the conventional, the vulgar, the utterly hideous—that we shall begin with remorseful amazement to comprehend the charm of that which we destroyed.*[1]

Hearn's identification of this local senseworld, then, was (like so many other fascinated narratives of intercultural discovery) already marked by its inevitable extinction. The future of the Japanese soundscape was bound up, part and parcel, with the colonial construction of the Japanese nation-state; the inexorable loss of native culture was projected forward into the destructive technoculture of the global industrial city.

Then, as now, the major sonic feature of cities was noise. Public attention to street noise helped establish new divisions between public and private space, and became a crucial point of dispute for class-biased social reforms. The characterization of a particular neighbourhood as "noisy" often turned on the threat of a destabilizing (and often foreign) urban population, which needed to be reduced or eliminated in order to maintain or recover the "original" local soundscape. In Victorian London, for example, anti-noise campaigns targeted Italian organ grinders, whose street music triggered bourgeois anxiety about migrant labour.[2] Both in the changing labour market, and in the advancement of machines into public life, noise was so closely tied to modern progress that "noise pollution" appeared to be a kind of waste created by urbanization.[3] Noise was considered powerful and technologically progressive, but fundamentally uncivilized and dangerous; thus it quickly became a key sonic metaphor for rapid and unfettered social change, as well as the magical transformations of urban modern space. Identifications of noise were increasingly mitigated by the demands of cultural progress. In the fatalistic words of an 1878 noise ruling regarding the new elevated train in New York City, the noise of industrial society simply "has to be."[4]

But specific city soundscapes can yet be heard to possess unique mixes of noise, which help organize the sonic and affective sensibilities of their populations. In a "typical" Tokyo district (the pseudonymically-named Miyamoto-cho) circa 1983, Theodore Bestor catalogued the distinctively "raucous and annoying" sounds of everyday "daytime noise" that mixed "the honking of horns and the screeching of brakes; the blare of stereos and televisions on display in local shops; the many loudspeaker trucks making political commercials, or public service announcements; the recorded music from the shopping street; the junior high school's outdoor public address system; the rumble of passing trains."[5] The local sound "mix" helps to mark the experience of place, as the ringing of bells, for example, sonically marked the boundaries of eighteenth-century French villages,[6] or as the commercial "village" of a shopping mall uses pre-recorded music to organize the social and spatial experiences of wandering customers.[7]

The special character of Tokyo's soundscape is often symbolized through its technological noises. Canadian experimental composer Sarah Peebles' soundscape recording *108–Walking through Tokyo at the Turn of the Century* mixes sounds ranging from pre-taped advertisements and video games, to the short electronic tunes played as trains arrive in Shinjuku station, the clanking of wheels on the Sobu line, and the resonant almost-chanted voices of the announcements played in subway cars. These sounds, Yoshimura Hiroshi argues in the liner notes, represent "something extra" beyond the "uniform information of the globalized digital world" in Tokyo's soundscape; "almost like body odor, so that the noise of the city that might have been perceived as bothersome becomes soothing."[8]

One of the most commonly identified features of the modern Japanese soundscape is the special sensory and social environment of its trains. In 1966, the Capitol LP *Japan: Its Sounds and People* used recordings of trains to represent aspects of the local Tokyo soundscape, claiming to represent an array of essentially Japanese sounds, "infinite in variety," which include several recordings of musical performance, food vendors, and festivals. Although the liner notes claim "noise is not truly typical of Japan," most of the public sounds on the album were dominated by mechanical noise, including a recording of an electric train, described by narrator Rose Okugawa as a "distinctive Japanese sound."[9] How does the noise of the train—that ubiquitous machine and core metaphor of modern technological civilization—come to symbolize any kind of specificity, sonic or otherwise, about Japanese urban culture?

As Walter Benjamin put it, the sounds of mechanized transport are "the signature tunes of modern cities"—"the diesel stammer of London taxis, the wheeze of its buses. The clatter of the Melbourne tram. The two-stroke sputter of Rome ... the many sirens of different cities"—these different machine sounds "remind us the city is a sort of machine" replicated in industrial societies around the world.[10]

Wolfgang Schivelbusch described the introduction of the train as a formative project of modern subjectivity.[11] The train made social life calculable: it ran by a timetable and separated travellers into compartments, "annihilating" space and time in a decontextualized and blurred "panorama." Peripheral local places were detached from their isolation, and brought into the range of the cities. The train forced the reordering of urban space to accommodate changes in human traffic, and demanded new contexts of circulation in the exchange of goods, people, and modes of communication. Populations sped toward the cities, and the physical jolt of the train on the tracks communicated a new and shocking experience of travel beyond human and animal capacity. In short, the sensory environment of the train mediated the public experience of urban modernity on a global scale.

For Japan, the introduction of the train system was iconic of the nation's entry into global modernity: the *shinkansen* (bullet train), in particular, became a marker of Japan's post-war economic ascendance. The cultural symbolism of the train system also reflects dark anxieties about the precariousness of millennial Japanese society. The 1996 sarin gas attacks resonated as much for the misanthropic assault on the inviolable social space of the train, as for the spectacle of religious fanaticism presented by the Aum Shinrikyo cult. In April 2005, more than one hundred commuters were killed when a Japan Railways train jumped the tracks and crashed into an apartment building in Amagasaki, just north of Osaka. And, famously, the train tracks are a place for suicides, reported as "body accidents" that clot the circulatory flow of Tokyo's vast railway network.[12]

But for many Japanese, the local train also epitomizes the communal aspects of public space, and the shared sensory experience provides a sense of cultural intimacy. In stark contrast to the aura of progress, loneliness, and distance of the train in the American soundscape, the train is marked as a domestic-but-urban-space in Japanese city life. While the interiors of trains are inherently noisy places, Japanese riders tend to fall asleep, somehow rising and disembarking just as they arrive at their desired station. In the noisy enclosure of the homebound train, there is a kind of public contemplation of a balanced human and mechanical environment that feels natural.

Sound artist Suzuki Akio captured the homey and nostalgic qualities of the Japanese railway through his mix of field recordings made on station platforms in the outskirts of Tokyo:

> *I made records of the sound of the ticket punchers on the Yamanote Line—they've changed over to automatic wickets now, so you can't hear that sound anymore. I started noticing these masterly performances and took the outer track of the line from Tokyo Station all the way around, got off, and made recordings of that "chaki, chaki" sound at each station. The recordings were divided between the A and B side according to the order of the stations, and the endless locking ring at the end of each side had the shrill sound of the train's departure bell. In the midst of the ticket punching sounds, you can hear the cute voices of elementary school students on their way home saying things like, "Bye-bye! See you!"*[3]

Suzuki's recordings capture a personal memory of a specific local cultural space, but also recall the recurrence of railway sounds in the historical register of post-war experimental music. It is no coincidence that the sound chosen by Pierre Schaeffer for the first *musique concrète* piece *Étude aux Chemins de Fer* (*Railway Study*) (1948), was, as the title suggests, a recording of a train, its whistle, and the conductor's announcement. And yet, despite their global ubiquity, trains and other technological sounds can be heard as markers of local place and associated with sensory qualities of cultural intimacy.

In his early writings about Japanese aural sensibilities, the post-war composer Takemitsu Tōru described his discovery of noise as a context of listening to silence. He used the word *chinmoku* to refer to silence in his famous 1971 essay "Oto, Chinmoku to hakariaeru hodo ni," included with others written over the course of several decades in his influential book *Confronting Silence*. There is an interesting slippage between the Japanese title of the book—which means something like "considering sound and silence"—and the English-language translation. "Silence" here is *chinmoku*, a word that implies an internal state of contemplation that is reticent to action. This "hesitation in silence" reflects considered listening, in which silence naturally occurs in the world through human perception. Distinct from confrontation, this state "considers" (or alternately, "measures," or "observes" [*hakaru*]) silence in relation to sound; here Takemitsu chooses *oto*, a word that does not distinguish between musical sounds and noise. In other words, "noise" and "silence" are not mutually exclusive, but related experiences within a broad spectrum of environmental "soundings" realized in listening.

Takemitsu's interest in environmental silence was entwined with an equally radical attention to technological noise. His compositions, he argued, do not describe natural spaces devoid of "seamy" human life, but aspire to harmonize humanity with nature by using noise, to "confront silence." For example, in the noisy *sawari* sound made when the string buzzes against the grooved plate of a *biwa*, Takemitsu heard a "deliberate obstruction" that was yet a central part of the instrument's expression—a "beautiful noise" emerging from the "apparatus of an obstacle."[14] Beginning in his early experiments in the NHK electronic music studio, the composer was attracted to "beautiful noises" that were created by the new synthesizer technology.

But for Takemitsu, noise was isolated neither to electronically generated sounds, nor to the rich noise sonorities of traditional Japanese instruments. Rather, noise was a fundamentally "peopled" vibration foundational in the human sensorium, which must be included in music that seeks to reflect the nature of the world. In his later compositions, noise became a musical value that reconciled composition with the "diverse, sometimes contradictory sounds around us."

As early as 1955, Takemitsu mixed recordings of the Tokyo countryside with noises of the city soundscape in *Hi* (Fire), a collaboration with poet Yasushi Inoue created for the NHK programme *Shin Nihon Hôsô* (New Japanese Radio); he later remixed the same soundscapes for a later piece called *Static Relief*.[15] It was after intense listening to the "continuous, unbroken movement" of Tokyo's subway in the 1940s that he began to consider mixing "random noise" into his work:

> In the dim lights of the subway, I was conscious only of the rhythm of the train and its physical effect on me. The regular rhythm of the train coursed through our bodies, pounded our perspiring skins; and I and the others in the subway leaned on this rhythm, receiving some kind of rest from it … The train stopped at a station. Passengers entered and left. Then again in the fast-moving train people settled down, regaining that repose from the regular vibrations … That rich world of sound around me … those are the sounds that I should have the courage to let live within my music.[16]

In his sudden, social awareness of the affective qualities of ambient mechanical noise, Takemitsu "became aware that composing is giving meaning to that stream of sounds that penetrates the world we live in."[17] Takemitsu's story of sensory immersion in the interior of the train—which tells of a profoundly social soundscape—anchors his long-term fascination with the musical value of noise in the feelings of humans contained in a technological environment. The train emits a shared, unbroken stream of sound as a felt vibration, in which noise is a natural part of the inhabited, "peopled" experience of the Japanese urban soundscape. Noise can be homey, warm, and profound: not just the "interruptive" character of sound, but the noisy but natural vibrations of human life in the city.

Endnotes

1   Lafcadio Hearn, "Insect Musicians," in *Exotics and Retrospectives* (Boston: Little & Brown, 1898) p. 63.
2   John Picker, *Victorian Soundscapes* (Oxford/New York: Oxford University Press, 2003).
3   Karin Bijsterveld, *Mechanical Sound: Technology, Culture, and Public Problems of Noise in the Twentieth Century* (Cambridge: MIT Press, 2008).
4   Emily Thompson, *The Soundscape of Modernity: Architectural Acoustics and the Culture of Listening in America, 1900–1933* (Cambridge, MA: MIT Press, 2002) p. 120.
5   Theodore C. Bestor, *Neighborhood Tokyo* (Stanford: Stanford University Press, 1989) p. 38.
6   Alain Corbin, *Village Bells: Sound and Meaning in the Nineteenth-century French Countryside* (New York: Columbia University Press, 1998).
7   Jonathan Sterne, "Sounds Like the Mall of America: Programmed Music and the Architectonics of Commercial Space," *Ethnomusicology* (41) (Winter 1997): 22–50.
8   Yoshimura Hiroshi. Liner notes for Sarah Peebles' *108- Walking through Tokyo at the Turn of the Century* (Post-Concrete 004, 2002).
9   Rose Okugawa, Liner notes for *Japan: Its Sounds and People* (Capitol Records, 1966).
10 Walter Benjamin, *One-Way Street and Other Writings* (London: Verso, 1985 [1925–26]) p. 82.
11 Wolfgang Schivelbusch, *The Railway Journey: Trains and Travel in the 19th Century*, trans. Anselm Hollo (New York: Urizen, 1980 [1977]).
12 Michael Fisch, "Tokyo's Commuter Train Suicides and the Society of Emergence," *Cultural Anthropology* 28 (12) (2013).
13 Interview with Akio Suzuki by Nobushisa Shimoda, *Sound Arts* (6) (1993), XEBEC. http://www.sukothai.com/X6.suzuki.html
14 Tōru Takemitsu, *Confronting Silence: Selected Writings* (Berkeley: Fallen Leaf Press, 1995) p. 64. Japanese publication as *Oto, Chinmoku to Hakariaeru hodo ni* (Tokyo: Shinchōsha, 1971).
15 Luciana Galliano, *Yōgaku: Japanese Music in the 20th Century*, trans. M. Mayes (Lanham: Scarecrow Press, 2002).
16 Takemitsu, *Confronting Silence* p. 79.
17 Ibid. p. 81.

STRANGE ACCUMULATIONS: SOUNDSCAPES OF LATE MODERNITY IN J. G. BALLARD'S "THE SOUND-SWEEP"

Matthew Gandy

In the fiction of J. G. Ballard, urban space is conceived as a technological totality comprising an intersecting field of corporeal geographies. It is through the failure or disruption of technological systems that the vulnerability of the human body is exposed and existing social relations are placed under strain: consider the violent ruptures of *Crash* (1973), the absurd enclave of marooned commuters in *Concrete Island* (1974), or the intricate technological matrices of *High Rise* (1975). The body-technology couplings explored by Ballard move beyond the aeronautical preoccupations of Cold War cybernetics or more simplistic forms of bodily augmentation to encompass an unusual synthesis of cultural and technological elements. In this respect, his vivid explorations of the body-machine complex are redolent of modernist pioneers in graphic art such as Fritz Kahn whose work heralded an increasing interest in the liberatory potential of science and technology.[1] Ballard's familiarity with human anatomy, a result of his training as a medical student, forms a distinctive element in his corporeal style of writing. Yet his scientifically inspired literary imagination is also tempered by an ironic neo-Hobbesian fascination with modernity's denouement through eco-catastrophe or violent disorder. Ballard's world is suffused with an ideological ambivalence between the naturalization of capitalist urbanization and existing social relations, and emerging landscapes of technological possibility.

Ballard's short story entitled "The Sound-Sweep," first published in 1960 as a "novelette" in the British science fiction journal *Science Fantasy*, provides an intriguing encounter with the cultural and political complexities of late-modern soundscapes.[2] The story is set in a future city that appears to be a kind of hybrid between mid-twentieth-century London and Los Angeles: we encounter a divided, transmogrified, and car-dominated cityscape that combines more familiar topographic zones with new types of acoustically differentiated spaces. The increasing focus on sound has led to a series of changes in the sensory environment, including the replacement of audible sounds—such as music—with new forms of ultrasound. The direct experience of music has been increasingly replaced by an inaudible yet tightly controlled form of synthetic silence. We learn that although the classical repertoire is being "re-scored for the much wider range of the ultrasonic orchestra," the human voice, as the one instrument that cannot be satisfactorily replaced by ultrasound, is fast becoming a musical anachronism:

> *Since the introduction a few years earlier of ultrasonic music, the human voice—indeed, audible music of any type—had gone completely out of fashion. Ultrasonic music, employing a vastly greater range of octaves, chords and chromatic scales than are audible by the human ear, provided a direct neural link between the sound stream and the auditory lobes, generating an apparently sourceless sensation of harmony, rhythm, cadence and melody uncontaminated by the noise and vibration of audible music.*[3]

The emergence of an increasingly synthetic acoustic realm also marks a sophisticated form of social control through the neurological effects of ultrasound. The city is increasingly marked by the prevalence of what Pierre Schaeffer and Jérome Peignot term the *acousmatique*, whereby sounds are experienced separately from their causes to produce a "new paradigm of dislocation."[4] Since the time in which Ballard was writing, the use of sound as a means of behavioural manipulation and also as a commodified realm in its own right has significantly expanded. Indeed, recent developments in acoustic ecology, evolutionary biology, and neurophysiology have even suggested the presence of genetically coded forms of originary soundscapes that are amenable to ultrasonic forms of sound stimulation.[5] We find that techno-modernity has radically expanded into human subjectivity itself through intensified efforts to control the sensory realm.[6]

"The Sound-Sweep" opens with a description of an abandoned sound stage, now lying beneath the "endless din" of an eight-lane flyover, where an embittered former opera singer lives—her career having been ruined by the switch to ultrasonic music. In Ballard's city, sonic distinctions increasingly intersect with late-modern topographies of anxiety and dislocation. We are immersed in an acoustic realm where sound does not fade away but accumulates in the fabric of the city. The entire city has become a kind of acoustic sponge or giant recording device where walls and other surfaces retain a permanent trace of their sonic environment. As sound acquires a material presence in the city, the distinction between spatial and temporal dimensions to urban space has become increasingly blurred. Architecture acquires an incriminating presence through its storage of sounds and conversations. Rather than a discretely reproducible phenomenon, sound has become a generalized source of potential disorder. It is feared that the failure to clear away "unswept sonic resonances" will not only undermine social order but also endanger the physical foundations of the city itself.[7] The central protagonist in Ballard's story is Mangon, a municipal "sound sweep" since the age of fourteen with the Metropolitan Sonic Disposal Service, who removes the accumulation of sound from buildings, walls and other sound retaining surfaces using a device called a "sonovac." We learn that Mangon, like many other sound sweeps, has been a mute from an early age, and has consequently developed extremely sensitive hearing, which allows him to detect any trace of "embedded sounds."[8] Despite these essential skills, however, the sound sweeps are held in contempt by wider society:

> *Regarded as little better than garbage collectors, the sound-sweeps were an outcast group of illiterates, mutes (the city authorities preferred these—their discretion could be relied upon) and social cripples who lived in a chain of isolated shacks on the edge of an old explosives plant in the sand dunes to the north of the city which served as the sonic dump.*[9]

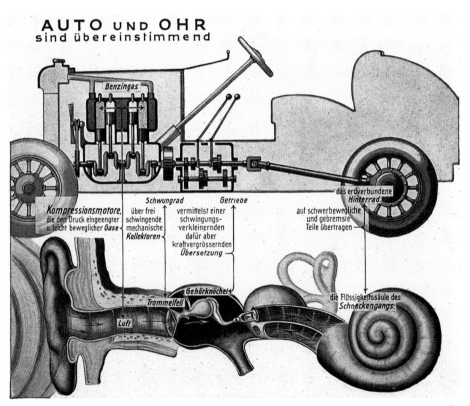

1

1 Fritz Kahn, *Car and ear* (1929).
Source: Fritz Kahn, *Das Leben des Menschen IV* (Stuttgart: Franckh'sche Verlagshandlung, 1929).

2 Haus-Rucker-Co, *Environmental Transformer Project* (1968). Courtesy of the Architekturbüro O&O Baukunst.

This acoustically defined form of social stratification represents a late-modern variant of the association between dirt—in this case sonic detritus—and extreme forms of social and spatial marginalization: there are certain parallels here with the role of scheduled castes in India or the *burakumin* of Japan, who are largely restricted to dirty, menial, or dangerous forms of labour. The presence of sound sweeps in the future city underlines the continuing necessity of human labour in order to allow urban space to function: this is no automated science fiction utopia, but a noisy future metropolis riven by stark forms of social difference. The relegation of the sound sweeps to residential zones near the city's "sonic dump" is reminiscent of those communities that eke out a living from waste, living in or around the vast garbage dumps that have developed in parallel with modern cities.

Through his work as a sound sweep, Mangon traverses the acoustic terrain of the city meeting different clients who require his specialist sound removal services. He enters the foyer of a "huge forty-storey apartment block" where "the marble walls and columns buzzed softly with the echoing chatter of guests leaving parties four or five hours earlier."[10] On entering the penthouse apartment, he meets the appropriately named Ray Alto, who is described as a "doyen of ultrasonic composers," and clearly part of the new sonic elite. "Noise, noise, noise—the greatest single disease-vector of civilization," declares Alto, whose apartment's "wide studio windows" take in an "elegant panorama" of the city below.[11] For Alto and his wealthy neighbours, sound has become yet another focus of anxiety stalking their architectural citadels; a source of contamination that serves to blur distinctions between inside and outside, yet simultaneously enables the emergence of specialist kinds of acoustic consumption.

In a later passage, Mangon drives out towards "the stockade" used for the storage of unwanted sound:

> *Here and there among the dunes they could see the low ruined outbuildings of the old explosives plant, the white galvanized iron roof of one of the sound-sweep's cabins. Desolate and unfrequented, the dunes ran on for miles. They passed the remains of a gateway that had collapsed to one side of the road; originally a continuous fence ringed the stockade, but no one had any reason for wanting to penetrate it. A place of strange echoes and festering silences, overhung by a gloomy miasma of a million compacted sounds, it remained remote and haunted, the graveyard of countless private babels.*[12]

Ballard's evocation of an acoustic miasma connects his imaginary late-modern metropolis with nineteenth-century fears of contamination. The city's sonic edgelands mark the apotheosis of a new acoustic order in which the poor are relegated to an increasingly noisy existence. These sonic dumps have a complex topography of residual sounds contained in their "sound-absorbent baffles" that only Mangon and the other sound-sweeps can safely navigate. The sonic detritus of the city has acquired a distinctive stratigraphy derived from different sources over time to produce a multilayered cacophonic landscape that is in "a continuous state of uproar."[13] Like all waste dumps, however, there is the looming threat of accidents or saturation:

> *Occasionally, when super-saturation was reached after one of the summer holiday periods, the sonic pressure fields would split and discharge, venting back into the stockades a nightmarish cataract of noise, raining on to the sound-sweeps not only the howling of cats and dogs, but the multi-lunged tumult of cars, express trains, fairgrounds and aircraft, the cacophonic musique concrète of civilization.*[14]

Here, Ballard makes an oblique reference to experimental developments in electroacoustic music, which indicates an ambivalence towards twentieth-century modernism. Ballard's somewhat sly use of the term musique concrète, most closely associated with the compositional experiments of Pierre Schaeffer, also alludes to an association between the material properties of concrete and aspects of twentieth-century modernism.[15] Different materials, along with their characteristic topographies and architectural forms, are integral to the physical texture of urban space in Ballard's writings, and it is his fascination with the sound-material interface that is perhaps the most striking element of the story. Ballard's description of the conversion of music into ultrasound resonates with the emerging tension in the 1950s between different modes of musical composition and the shifting boundaries between music and "noise."[16]

Ballard's interest in sound as a source of anxiety links to historical concerns with bells, machinery, traffic, and other forms of sonic disturbance.[17] In his story, however, the nature of sound has changed, along with its lingering presence, so that sound increasingly resembles matter through the accretion of acoustic debris on the edge of the city. Ballard's story can be read as a portent of the contemporary accumulation of information exemplified by vast repositories of digital data. Like the sonic dumping grounds described by Ballard, the "soft landscapes" of the digital realm have produced their own edgelands in banks of humming servers and stockpiles of toxic waste.[18]

The politics of sound is more than just a question of "noise abatement," but forms part of a symbolic critique of the sensory realm of modernity and its disconnection from "authentic" forms of aesthetic experience. The emphasis on enhancing the experience of listening by R. Murray Schafer, Barry Truax, and others is rooted in the development of more critically aware forms of acoustic ecology. Their concerns with a diminished or degraded auditory realm feed into a broader critique of the alienating effects of techno-modernity on everyday life.[19] Yet, at the same time, the search for distinctive forms of "acoustic fidelity" are not located outside of their precise cultural or historical context: the elision between aspects of acoustic ecology and the ecological critique of modernity, for example, belies the limits to Eurocentric conceptions of the universal human subject, which have been pervasive in musicology, neurophysiology, and many other disciplines. Recent interest in the "right to silence" finds parallels with reactions towards intrusive synthetic realms such as light pollution or artificial smells. Yet silence itself remains an elusive goal since even spaces without any external sound serve merely to accentuate the sounds of the body itself.[20]

For Ballard, the sonic realm has both a temporal and spatial porosity. There is a sense that sound, like memory, cannot be completely eradicated. Yet the chaotic accumulation of sonic waste cannot be organized into a form of collective memory that is amenable to archives, monuments, or narrative accounts of historical change. The sonic dumps on the edge of Ballard's city, with their sound-adsorbent baffles, provide a kind of negative sonic imprint, a medley of archaeological traces of human lives like the eerie plaster casts produced from the excavations of Pompeii. These strange accumulations are also to be found in Félix Nadar's essay on the jumbled bones of the Paris catacombs, which were once people who "had loved, had been loved."[21] The sonic catacombs located on the edge of Ballard's future city, with their acoustic residues of unsorted human lives, betoken a sense of dislocation between life and death, between signal and pure noise.

Endnotes

1 Cornelius Borck, "Communicating the Modern Body: Fritz Kahn's Popular Images of Human Physiology as an Industrialized World," *Canadian Journal of Communication* 32 (2007): 495–520.

2 J. G. Ballard, "The Sound-Sweep," *Science Fantasy* 39 (13) (1960): 2–39. The "novelette" is also reprinted in J. G. Ballard, *The Four-Dimensional Nightmare* (London: Penguin, 1977 [1960]) pp. 42–82.

3 Ballard, "The Sound-Sweep" p. 49.

4 Michael Fowler, "On Listening in a Future City," *Grey Room* 42 (2011): 26. See also Brian Kane, "*L'objet sonore maintenant*: Pierre Schaeffer, Sound Objects and the Phenomenological Reduction," *Organized Sound* 12 (1) (2007): 15–24; and Pierre Schaeffer, *Traité des objets musicaux* (Paris: Editions Le Seuil, 1966).

5 Fowler, "On Listening in a Future City" p. 30.

6 GegenSichKollektiv, "Anti-Self: Experience-less Noise," in ed. Michael Goddard, Benjamin Halligan and Paul Hegarty, *Reverberations: The Philosophy, Aesthetics and Politics of Noise* (London: Continuum) p. 194.

7 Ballard, "The Sound-Sweep" p. 49.

8 Ibid. p. 45.

9 Ibid. p. 47.

10 Ibid. p. 53.

11 Ibid. p. 54.

12 Ibid. p. 63.

13 Ibid. p. 66.

14 Ibid. p. 64.

15 Adrian Forty, *Concrete and Culture* (London: Reaktion, 2013).

16 See, for example, Alex Ross, *The Rest Is Noise: Listening to the Twentieth Century* (New York: Farrar Straus and Giroux, 2007).

17 Emily Thompson, "Noise and Noise Abatement in the Modern City," in *Sense of the City: An Alternative Approach to Urbanism*, ed. Mirko Zardini (Montréal: Canadian Centre for Architecture/Lars Müller Publishers, 2005) pp. 190–199.

18 The term "soft landscapes" is taken from Akira Suzuki, *Do Android Crows Fly over the Skies of an Electronic Tokyo?* (London: Architectural Association, 2001).

19 Fowler, "On Listening in a Future City."

20 On the absence of silence, see Stefan Helmreich, "An Anthropologist Underwater: Immersive Soundscapes, Submarine Cyborgs and Transductive Ethnography," *American Ethnologist* 34 (4) (2007): 621–627.

21 Félix Nadar's essay, "Le Dessus et le dessous de Paris," was first published in 1867 and is cited in Shelley Rice, *Parisian Views* (Cambridge, MA: MIT Press, 1997) p. 159.

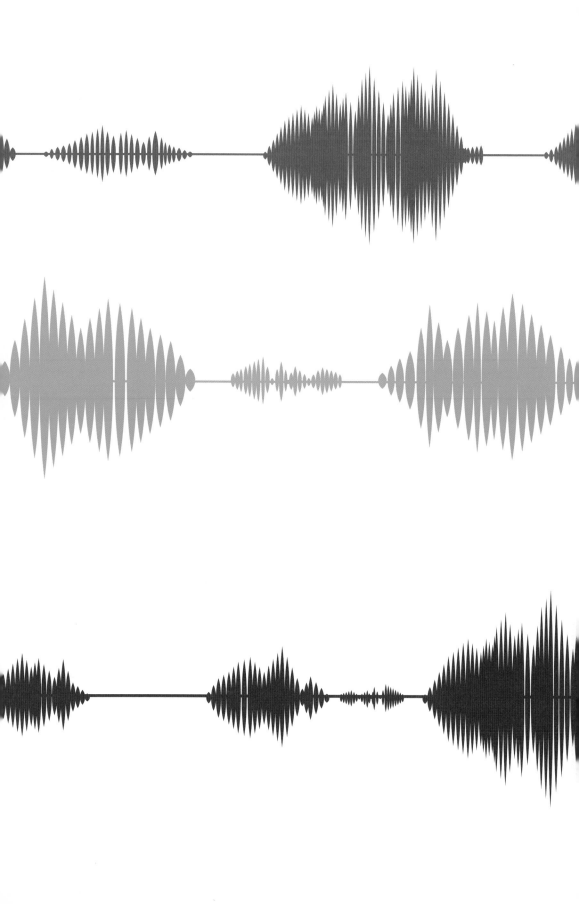

ACOUSTIC FLÂNERIE

SILENT CITY: LISTENING TO BIRDS IN URBAN NATURE

Joeri Bruyninckx

At half past four on a crisp July morning in 1952, a man could be seen leaning over the balcony of his room at the luxury London Savoy Hotel. Below his feet, the city was only beginning to wake up, but radio personality, broadcaster, and naturalist Ludwig Koch had kept himself awake all night. He had spent hours concentrating on the sounds coming through his headphones, and the long wait near his improvised recording studio had been interrupted only by quick glimpses across the balcony. Behind the legs of a cherub statue, the hotel management had found a nest of kestrel eggs—the high façade being an ideal habitat for the breeding pair. Realizing the opportunity, Koch now tried to record the sounds of the parents feeding their fledglings.

But through his earphones that morning, he heard no sound of a chick. "The noises of all kinds, including those of Waterloo Station, were deafening." By the time he stopped recording at ten o'clock, he had finally succeeded in recording its typical notes, luckily "clearly audible above the din of London." Nonetheless, the city had kept sounding through—with anything from the traffic noises below, to Big Ben chiming in the background—imposing itself on the ornithologist and future listeners to his recording.[1]

Although ornithologists have predominantly situated their inquiries in the rural landscape, the urban context serves as a preferred habitat for a plethora of avian species. As a result of

1

birds adopting urban and industrial infrastructure such as canals, landfills, factories, and old buildings as their habitats, ornithologists have also been progressively inspired to redefine the boundaries between the rural field and the city.[2] These new spatial contexts, however, also presented the ornithologist with a social and material ordering that was substantially different from the traditional ornithological field-site. This ordering, as geographers, historians, and sociologists of science have repeatedly highlighted, has also had a bearing on the production of knowledge taking place in the city.[3] Recent scholarship has pointed out, for instance, that "how scientists chose their research topics and framed them conceptually; how they organized their research practices; and how they articulated and stabilized certain beliefs as valid scientific claims," has been affected by the city's socio-spatial setting.[4] But just as research practices have been affected by the spatial and temporal rhythms with which urban life unfolds, I propose, they have also been intricately textured by the sensory distractions and city acoustics that resulted from them.

For Ludwig Koch, the urban context had long provided a familiar background for his observations and recordings. As director of the cultural branch of Electrical and Musical Industries Ltd[5] from the early 1930s, he had been well positioned to explore the new possibilities of electrical means of amplification and recording outdoors, while applying these in the production of a series of gramophone sound books on educational topics. Although Koch initially began recording commissioned soundscapes of German cities such as Cologne and Leipzig, he soon specialized in publishing natural history recordings. Intended both for a general public and scientific study on animal vocalizations, Koch produced these recordings in close collaboration with a host of prominent ornithologists and conservationists at

1 Ludwig Koch (left) with an improvised studio in the field. Photo by L. Lascelles Whitfield.

Source: Ludwig Koch, *Memoirs of a bird man* (London: Phoenix House, 1955).

the time, collecting his material in the zoological gardens of major European cities such as Antwerp, Berlin, and London. Often situated in the centre of these cities, these zoos provided a space advantageously sheltered from the bustle on the streets, but with convenient access to power supply. As such, they allowed an improvised recording studio to be set up in close proximity to the animals. By the mid-1930s, however, Koch and his fellow pioneers in wildlife recording had also become increasingly concerned with the possible distortions that animal cages presented to their recordings, both with regard to their acoustical aesthetics and the naturalness of the animals' behaviour.[6] This had led them to progressively prefer the open air of city parks and gardens. Indeed, as field recordists at Cornell University pointed out, to enhance the fidelity of their recordings, bird vocalizations should not only be recorded outdoors but, during demonstrations, ideally also be played back outdoors, as the acoustics of a room might render a sound unnatural, or even unintelligible.[7]

But although such city parks seemed to provide a more "natural" setting for bird vocalizations to be studied and recorded in, they also required more flexibility of the recording engineer. Power supply was often short, with recordists depending on unreliable dry cell batteries or a noisy dynamotor to make their mobile studio run. Sometimes, these urban spaces provided new opportunities to exploit: Danish radio engineer Carl Weismann, for instance, set up his first recording outfits next to a railway ten kilometres from Copenhagen and used the telegraph wires to send the recording signal of a singing bird to a wax disc recorder in the Danish radio headquarters.[8] More often, though, urban nature presented the listener with small disturbances. On one occasion, for instance, Ludwig Koch had detected Crested Larks, *Galerida cristata*, which often resided around slag heaps and factories, at a Philips factory terrain. The noisy industrial activity at the location, however, only allowed him a very short window of night-time, between three and five a.m., during which the species could be recorded without much disturbance. In a similar vein, while observing local species in the parks of the Belgian Royal Palace in Laeken, Koch and his recording crew found themselves perturbed by the heavy background sound coming from Brussels, even though the town was located over three miles away: "The spots I had in mind proved impossible, and I had to seek others more sheltered from the waves of sound from the city."[9]

But even at a comfortable distance from the city, the rural field was never the acoustically pristine wilderness that it might appear. As another pioneering wildlife recordist in New York warned his readers, "… it is not as simple as it would seem to get a location where there is absolute quiet … Too great proximity to a traffic road, for instance, makes recording impossible."[10] Students of urban nature generally complained that their recordings were repeatedly interrupted by a passing airplane or turned out to be unfeasible because of the hum of a distant highway. Invariably, the fields, parks, and nature reserves where these ornithologists worked were bordered by urban infrastructure. Although often located several miles out of sight, its sounds often embraced listeners in the field. British conservationist Max Nicholson observed, for instance, that "just as smoke pollution helps to swamp a town

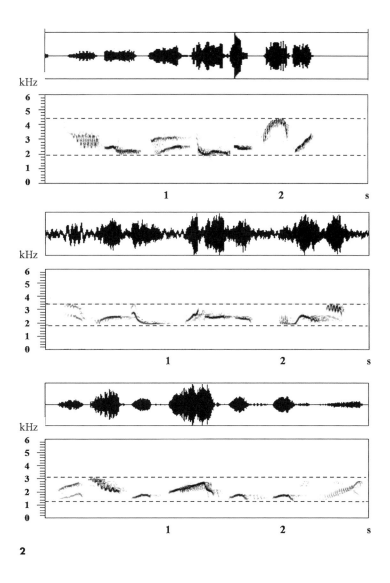

2 An Example of a Sonogram. A Blackbird in Urban, Periurban and Rural Settings.

under fog, so the natural peace of the country was drowned under the indefinable hum of distant engines and wheels." Noise abatement campaigns had taken off since the late nineteenth century, and between 1910 and 1940 became increasingly organized in cities such as London and New York. Clearly though, concerns with such "sonic exhaust" were never exclusive only to inhabitants of the metropolitan agglomeration.[11]

Along with its infrastructure then, urban sounds became fully, yet often initially imperceivably, entrenched within the landscape. This was not only due to obvious acoustic changes in the soundscapes of the mechanical age. It was also due to the increased sensitivity of mechanical equipment and recording instruments that recordists deployed in their service.[12]

2 An Example of a Sonogram. A Blackbird in Urban, Periurban and Rural Settings.

Source: Solange Mendes et al., "Bird Song Variations along an Urban Gradient: The Case of the European blackbird (Turdus merula)," Landscape and Urban Planning (99) (2011).

Granted, ever since the nineteenth century, ornithologists have had to negotiate their aural attention with other people and activities present. One naturalist listener in 1916, for instance, registered his frustration with "an energetic brass band with a particularly enthusiastic bass drummer, and a merry-go-round with the usual depressing music, traction-engine whistle and other noise producers."[13] But it was the electrical microphone, these recordists concluded, that amplified those sounds beyond their control. Even sounds that were hardly noticeable or simply too familiar to the human ear to stand out were picked up within a several mile radius and exaggerated. For example, American ornithologists at Cornell University quickly learned not to station their improvised field studio too close to power lines, as this would expose their recordings to an unpleasant electrical static that would render them useless. Other nature recordists learned to judge the urban landscape not only by what they heard for themselves, but also by the potential disturbances that it afforded. Far from a simple prosthesis for the ear, then, the microphone had begun to remediate and thereby restructure the urban soundscape, determining where and when one was able to listen and record.

The microphone drew attention to an acoustically complex habitat, in which the distinctions between urban and rural became progressively diffuse. But although wildlife recordists like Koch wanted to convey a sense of the singing birds' "natural" background, they were significantly less tolerant of interfering urban sounds. Whether their recordings were played back on low-tech consumer gramophones, broadcast over the radio, or reproduced on a visual film for scientific study, noise was found to diminish the recordings' intelligibility and pleasant consumption. As a result of such technical restrictions, these field recordists sought to balance their desire for the fidelity of an acoustically evocative setting with the demand for an attractively intelligible sound. Although their sound records were to capture the atmosphere of a natural scene as truthfully as possible, such records were still produced to be enjoyed by—and thus to privilege—the human listener.[14]

Reproducing the sounds of urban nature required considerable intervention. As media historian Jonathan Sterne has highlighted, the very act of recording always implies mediation and selection.[15] Koch and his recording team tackled the problem of interference by arranging up to six different microphones to enclose the bird's song perch. With each of these microphones linked to a control panel, recordists would hope to get as close as possible to the bird, to reduce interference by any background noise. Other wildlife recordists deployed highly directional types of microphones that amplified the sounds they were aimed at, "zooming in" on the birds. Permitting a far more selective recording, such microphones enabled recordists to capture the singing bird, and nothing but the bird, with minimal interference from its acoustic context. To the extent that regular microphones permitted at least the suggestion of immersion in a landscape, this was mostly offset by the close-up. These recording techniques provided a way to distil from the urban context a sonic landscape that was clear and tranquil, but also as free of urban disturbances as possible.[16]

Since the 1930s, this very concern with urban sounds as an aesthetic and analytic disturbance, and the preference for a close-up and sterilized aesthetic, has been crystallized in a variety of tools, techniques, and routines that ornithologists developed to record and analyze bird song. But by staging the experience of listening to birds as one that is devoid of urban interference, these field recordists not only acted upon an idea of what nature ideally should be, but in doing so also performed one. These recordings not only represented the city as an acoustic space, but also actively transformed it: moulding it into a private acoustic space fit for consumption and analysis. Building on anthropologist Steven Feld's notion of "acoustemology," Paul Greene and Thomas Porcello proposed the term "techoustemology" to foreground the implication of technological mediations of sound on individuals' knowledge and interpretations of, sensations in, and consequent actions upon their acoustic environments.[17] It alerts us to the ways in which these recordings enacted, suggested, and perpetuated a specific listening experience. They did so not just for these field recordists themselves. Through their circulation on commercial gramophone records, they also did so for a large group of other listeners—scientists, amateur birdwatchers, a general audience.

Grasping the extent to which such recordings came to filter urban nature provides one compelling way of understanding how biologists' investigations of the aural ecologies of the field privileged the natural over the technological and deeply human. Even despite, and often in spite of, ornithologists' and recordists' continuous immersion in, and annoyance with, interference by anthropogenic sound.

Such techoustemologies are not, however, inexhaustible and may be combined with other ways of listening, other ways of knowing. In 2003, the Dutch ecologist Hans Slabbekoorn and his colleagues at Leiden University published a paper in *Nature* that seemed to signal a remarkable behavioural adaptation of birds to their environments.[18] The authors observed that the ongoing spread of urban areas, highways, and airports throughout the world made anthropogenic noise virtually omnipresent. And such sounds, they found, created new selection pressures for birds. Slabbekoorn and his co-author Margriet Peet had studied groups of urban Great Tits, *Parus major,* in much the same way as their colleagues had done before them; they sampled their songs using a highly selective microphone, but they had combined this conventional technique with an omnidirectional microphone that allowed them to record, on a different channel, the city noise levels they previously had sought to eliminate. Slabbekoorn's study found that passerines that live in noisy urban environments generally sing with a higher minimum frequency than the same species living in a forest environment where there is significantly less anthropogenic noise. This, the authors proposed, suggested that the species adapted its vocal repertoires to a higher-frequency range in order to prevent its song from being effectively masked by low-frequency noises. Such interfering noises, bio-acousticians had begun to suggest elsewhere, made signals more difficult to detect or recognize by birds.[19] This has been recognized to constitute a competition for "signal space" between species. If its song would be structurally disguised by other sounds, this would give the birds a serious evolutionary disadvantage; after all, the bird would be less successful in using its song to defend its territory or attract a mate.[20] In the wake of this paper several other studies began to consider the urban, not just as an acoustic backdrop, but as a factor shaping birds' singing behaviour.[21]

Far from artificially segmenting and separating this behaviour from its original habitat and acoustic context, then, this research has begun to acoustically inscribe the bird in the city and vice versa, the city in the bird. Although Slabbekoorn's multichannel listening and recording technique still aimed to provide the urban listener a detached, privileged control over the soundscape rather than the turbulence of immersion, this approach also opens up a first step, a cautious reflection on the city as a shared space, physically as well as acoustically, where anthropogenic and biological sounds may begin to resonate with and into each other. Listening in such a way is to open up to and bring in contact the heterogeneous realities surrounding us, and to attend to the complex ecologies within which signals are broadcast, received, manipulated, impeded and, sometimes, exchanged.

Endnotes

1   Ludwig Koch, *Memoirs of a Birdman* (London: Phoenix House, 1955) p. 166.
2   For more on urban ecological science, see Jens Lachmund, "Exploring the City of Rubble. Botanical Fieldwork in Bombed Cities in Germany after World War II," *Osiris* 18 (2003): 234–254. For more on ornithology in relation to the urban environment, see Raf de Bont, "Poetry and Precision: Johannes Thienemann, the Bird Observatory in Rossitten and Civic Ornithology, 1900–1930," *Journal of the History of Biology* 44, no. 2 (2009): 171–203.
3   See David Livingstone, *Putting Science in Its Place: Geographies of Scientific Knowledge* (Chicago/London: The University of Chicago Press, 2003); and A. Ophir, Steven Shapin & Simon Schaffer, "The Place of Knowledge: The Spatial Setting and Its Relation to the Production of Knowledge," *Science in Context* 4 (1) (1991).
4   Sven Dierig, Jens Lachmund, and J. Andrew Mendelsohn, "Introduction: Toward an Urban History of Science," *Osiris* 18 (January 1, 2003): 1–19.
5   The company was formed by a merger of two of the largest record companies: Gramophone Company, which had been established by Emile Berliner, the inventor of the gramophone; and the American Columbia Phonograph Company.
6   Edward Max Nicholson and Ludwig Koch, *More Songs of Wild Birds* (London: H. F. & G. Witherby, Limited, 1937).
7   Albert R. Brand, *More Songs of Wild Birds* (New York: Thomas Nelson & Sons, 1936) p. 30.
8   Interview with Carl Weismann, by Patrick J. Sellar (March 28, 1983). British Library C90/02/01.
9   Koch, *Memoirs of a Birdman* pp. 55–6.
10 Albert R. Brand, "Recording Sounds of Wild Birds," *The Auk* 49 (4) (October 1, 1932): 436–439.

11 See for instance David Matless, "Sonic Geography in a Nature Region," *Social & Cultural Geography* 6 (5) (2005): 745–766.
12 Karin Bijsterveld, *Mechanical Sound. Technology, Culture, and Public Problems of Noise in the Twentieth Century* (Cambridge: MIT Press, 2008).
13 Henry Oldys, "Rhythmical Singing of Veeries" 33 (1) (1916): 19.
14 Rick Altman, *Sound Theory/Sound Practice* (New York & London: Routledge, 1992).
15 Jonathan Sterne, *The Audible Past: Cultural Origins of Sound Reproduction* (Durham: Duke University Press, 2003).
16 Altman, *Sound Theory/Sound Practice.*
17 Paul D. Greene and Thomas Porcello, *Wired for Sound: Engineering and Technologies in Sonic Cultures* (Middletown, CO: Wesleyan University Press, 2005).
18 Hans Slabbekoorn and Margriet Peet, "Ecology: Birds Sing at a Higher Pitch in Urban Noise," *Nature* 424 (6946) (2003): 267.
19 Ulrike Langemann, B. Gauger, and G. M. Klump, "Auditory Sensitivity in the Great Tit: Perception of Signals in the Presence and Absence of Noise," *Animal Behaviour* 56 (3) (1998): 763–9; R. H. Wiley and D. G. Richards, "Adaptations for Acoustic Communication in Birds, Sound Transmission and Signal Detection," in *Acoustic Communication in Birds, Vol. 1. Production, Perception, and Design Features of Sounds*, ed. D. E. Kroodsma and E. H. Miller (New York: Academic Press, 1982) pp. 132–81.
20 Slabbekoorn and Peet, "Birds Sing at a Higher Pitch in Urban Noise."
21 H. Brumm and D. Todt, "Noise-dependent Song Amplitude Regulation in a Territorial Songbird," *Animal Behaviour* 63 (5) (2002): 891–897; Jeffrey Cynx et al., "Amplitude Regulation of Vocalizations in Noise by a Songbird, Taeniopygia Guttata," *Animal Behaviour* 56 (1) (1998): 107–113; Paige S. Warren et al., "Urban Bio-acoustics: It's Not Just Noise," *Animal Behaviour* 71 (3) (2006): 491–502.

SONIC ECOLOGY: THE UNDETECTABLE SOUNDS OF THE CITY

Kate E. Jones

It is one of those balmy late summer evenings and the last rays of city sunlight reflect off the surface of the boating lake in London's Regent's Park. It is an absolutely perfect spot to investigate the sounds that the city can't hear. The group of people gathered around me on the lake's edge have come to listen to bats. However, as bat calls are too high for most people to hear, the group are relying on me to somehow reveal this sonic secret world.

Bats are surprisingly good city dwellers and have been reported in some of the most urban of city parks—New York's Central Park, and this evening's Regent's Park being just some examples. Although many people have negative perceptions of bats, bats are mammals just like us, and act as important pest controllers for many insects, including mosquitoes.[1] Bats have evolved flight by modifying their hands and spreading their fingers to form wings, enabling them to expertly navigate a variety of landscapes from lake surfaces to dense vegetation. Many species have also evolved sophisticated sonar systems to help them navigate and find food, which is especially useful when hunting aerial insects in the pitch dark. This "echolocation" system works by bats interpreting echoes as their calls bounce off objects, and then calculating exactly what and where things are.[2]

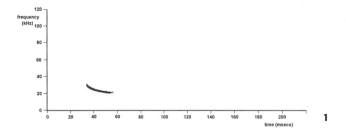

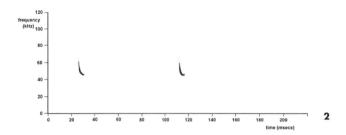

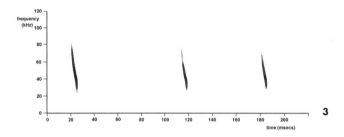

Bat calls can range from 9–212 kHz. To put that into perspective, humans can only hear up to 20 kHz, and even this drops off rapidly with age, meaning that most bat calls are beyond human hearing. Listening in on bats requires specialist acoustic equipment and the huge plastic box in front of me full of "bat detectors" will transform bat calls into hearing range.[3] Different species of bats use sound in slightly different ways, meaning that it is possible to tell some species apart from their calls. By the end of the evening, I hope that my group will all be experts in identifying the park's bats.

Some species of bats have louder calls and use higher frequencies than others, and these and other characteristics reflect how a species has adapted to navigate and find food. For example, a loud call can travel long distances and these types of calls are used by species that forage in the open. Quieter calls are used by species that forage in more dense vegetation or closer to water surfaces, where calls don't need to travel far. Lower frequency calls can also travel longer distances than higher frequency calls, but the returning echoes only

1 Spectrograms of echolocation calls of noctule bats (*Nyctalus noctula*). Source: Kate E. Jones.

2 Spectrograms of echolocation calls of pipistrelle bats (*Pipistrellus* sp.). Source: Kate E. Jones.

3 Spectrograms of echolocation calls of Daubenton's bats (*Myotis daubentonii*). Source: Kate E. Jones.

contain coarse information about the object. Higher frequency calls can only travel shorter distances, but contain finer details about the object of interest. Species that hunt in dense vegetation are better off using higher frequency calls, or a wider range of frequencies, because they need more information about their surroundings to navigate successfully.[4]

As the light starts to fade, I lead my group—each armed with a bat detector—around the lake. They soon have a chance to try out the detectors, as one of the devices springs to life with an extremely loud *chip chop* sound.[5] Looking up, bats are foraging very high over the lake, swooping down occasionally to catch insects. The detectors tell us that these are low-frequency calls around 20 kHz. In fact, they belong to noctule bats (*Nyctalus noctula*), one of the largest bat species found in London and long residents of Regent's Park. These bats are usually first to appear after sunset and they are highly efficient aerial insectivores, seemingly replacing swallows and swifts in the sky as the day passes into night. The evening air now fills with the noctule bats' loud calls, occasionally interrupted by buzzes (like someone is rudely blowing raspberries). These buzzes are "feeding calls," which are made when a bat hones in on an insect and increases its call rate to make a capture. These types of calls provide the bat with the maximum amount of information about the insect's speed and direction as it narrows down on its location.

Some species of insects have evolved a number of ingenious adaptations to avoid bats. For example, noctuid moths (Family Noctuidae) have evolved tiny organs in their ears to hear bat calls, and will employ drastic aversion tactics when they hear a call by folding up their wings and falling out of the sky. Some tiger moth species (Family Arctiidae) can even emit high frequency pulses that effectively jam the call, confusing the bat long enough for the moth to escape. Not all interactions with other species are as antagonistic: bats are important pollinators and seed dispersers of many tropical plant species and some plants have evolved acoustic beacons that reflect a bat's echolocation call acting to attract the bats to the plant's nectar.[6]

Despite my group's excitement at hearing their first bats, we move over to a more covered area of the lake with lots of overhanging trees and shrubs. The detectors crackle again but this time the calls are different, much higher frequency at 40–60 kHz, and sounding like *wet slaps*. Although not visible at first, we can now make out a cloud of much smaller bats flitting erratically in and out of the trees just above head height. The noise from the detectors is tremendous, as the bats swoop close by feeding on the insects accumulating over our heads. It seems incredible now, but I doubt any of us would have even noticed the bats if it weren't for the detectors first tuning our senses into them.

The bats flying above us are pipistrelle bats, one of the smallest and most common bats in the UK, and generally found in urban areas. Although one of the longest studied bat species in the world, it was only in 1997 that geneticists discovered that what had been previously considered as one species (*Pipistrellus pipistrellus*) was in fact two (*P. pipistrellus* and *pygmaeus*).[7] As well as the genetic differences, these species also can be separated by their echolocation calls: the common pipistrelle (*P. pipistrellus*) echolocating around a peak of 45 kHz, and the soprano pipistrelle (*P. pygmaeus*) peaking around 55 kHz. Using different frequencies means that the two species interpret the world slightly differently: the soprano pipistrelle can echolocate smaller insects invisible to the common pipistrelle using its lower frequency call. It seems a mixture of both species are here this evening.

Our group moves off and we stop on a bridge crossing the lake where it narrows. As well as the pipistrelles calling overhead, we can hear another occasional sound on the detectors like *rapid machine gun fire* at around 40–60 kHz.[8] Shining a torch beam on the lake's surface reveals a bat with long narrow wings doing leisurely turns around the lake foraging for insects inches above the surface. This is a Daubenton's bat (*Myotis daubentonii*) and is commonly associated with rivers, canals, and lakes—even in heavily urbanized areas (figure 4). It has a call that uses a range of frequencies, emitting calls in rapid succession to gain as much information about its environment as possible as it forages so close to the lake's surface.

The "heterodyne" bat detector, which the group are using, is converting the frequency of ultrasonic calls into sounds we can hear. Heterodyne means "different sound" and describes the way that these types of detectors work. For example, the detector receives a bat call, and mixes that frequency with its internal frequency, and emits the difference between the two signals. For example, if a bat was echolocating at 45 kHz, and if the internal frequency of the detector was set at 44 kHz, then we hear 1 kHz (within our hearing range). The internal frequency setting of the detector is changed with the dial and this alters the species that the detector can pick up. For example, to hear noctule bats, the dial would have to be lowered to around 20 kHz, or else their lower frequency calls might be missed.

One or two of the group are lucky enough to have more sophisticated bat detectors, which convert the sounds rather differently by slowing down the calls and thereby lowering the frequency into our hearing range. You can hear how the bat call really sounds using these "time expansion" detectors (albeit slowed down ten times). Bat calls sound more like short bird *chirps* rather than wet slaps or machine guns. It is also possible to see visible representations of the calls on some detectors in the form of spectrograms, so the call can be heard and seen as the bat flies past. Spectrograms are graphs that plot the frequency of sound over time (figures 1–3). Noctule bat echolocation calls can be seen as low frequency, long curved shapes; Pipistrelle bat echolocation calls look a little like noctule calls but are thinner and narrower, and of higher frequency. Daubenton's bat echolocation calls are extremely short calls that are nearly straight lines and cover a wide range of frequencies. Feeding buzzes are seen in spectrograms as a sequence of calls that get closer and closer together as the bat hones in on its target.

We listen on the bridge for a while, marvelling at the cacophony of sounds around us. However, feeding buzzes and echolocation calls are not the only sounds that bats make: during the breeding season in the late autumn, social calls are often also heard. The precise meaning of these calls is not well known but it is thought that bats use these calls to sing to

4

each other and to attract mates. Social calls sound like chirpy trills and are often of lower frequency, and some people can even hear them without a detector. I thought we might be lucky and hear a social call tonight, but it is not to be this time; perhaps it's a little bit too early in the year.

Although there are around eighteen species of bats in the UK, only some have been found to occur in London. There may be more species present in the city, but bats are extremely cryptic. Using bat echolocation calls to identify species is a great way to survey bats. However, bat call identification is a tricky business, many species can sound similar, and the same species can sound unalike in different habitats. For example, many species in the genus *Myotis* (including the Daubenton's bat) are almost indistinguishable from each other, and a pipistrelle bat call may sound more like the noctule in open habitats, and more like the Daubenton's bat in dense woodland canopies. Recent developments in voice recognition technology have led to the development of automatic call identification tools for bats.[9] These technologies have the potential to transform our understanding of the distribution of bats in our city and beyond.

The detector I am using tonight is pretty experimental—I attached one of the time expansion detectors to my smartphone and an app displays the calls on my phone's screen. I hope that in a few years this system will be commonplace and bat detectors will be just a small, cheap add-on that you attach to a smartphone, opening up this acoustic world to

4 Daubenton's bat (*Myotis daubentonii*). Source: Hugh Clark, Bat Conservation Trust.

many more people. Bat numbers have seen severe historical declines and it is important to monitor their populations, in order to understand how to help them recover and flourish. Anyone can get involved in bat monitoring as part of the National Bat Monitoring Programme at The Bat Conservation Trust or by joining their local bat group.[10] I hand out some information to the group about getting involved in bat conservation, before showing them out of the park and shutting the black iron gates behind us. That's it for tonight but I hope at least some of them have had their preconceptions changed about bats and are as amazed and inspired as I am about the undetectable sounds of our city.

Endnotes

1 See G. Jones et al., "Carpe Noctem: The importance of Bats as Bio-indicators," *Endangered Species Research* 8 (2009): 93–115.

2 See A. Maltby, Kate E. Jones, and G. Jones, "Understanding the Evolutionary Origin and Diversification of Bat Echolocation Calls," in *Handbook of Mammalian Vocalization: An Integrative Neuroscience Approach*, ed. Stefan M. Brudzynski (London: Elsevier, 2010) pp. 37–47.

3 For a recent review of bat detectors, see D. Waters and K. Barlow, "Bat Detectors: Past, Present and Future," *British Wildlife* 25 (2) (2013): 86–92; and for more details, see http://www.bats.org.uk/pages/bat_detectors.html

4 For bat identification guides, see Kate E. Jones, *A Guide to British Bats*, (Shropshire: Field Studies Council, 2001); and J. Russ, *British Bat Calls: A Guide to Species Identification* (Exeter: Pelagic Publishing, 2012).

5 Hear the CD accompanying this volume for heterodyne detector recordings of echolocation calls of the Noctule Bat.

6 For other species' adaptations to bat acoustics, see A. J. Corcoran, J. R. Barber, and W. E. Conner, "Tiger Moth Jams Bat Sonar," *Science* 325 (2009): 325–327; and R. Simon et al., "Floral Acoustics: Conspicuous Echoes of a Dish-shaped Leaf Attract Bat Pollinators," *Science* 333 (2011): 631–633.

7 See E. M. Barratt, et al., "DNA Answers the Call of the Pipistrelle Bat Species," *Nature* 387 (1997): 138–139.

8 Hear the CD accompanying this volume for heterodyne detector recordings of echolocation calls of the Pipistrelle and Daubenton's Bats.

9 See www.bbc.co.uk/news/science-environment-19147545 for information about an automatic bat call identification system.

10 See Bat Conservation Trust website for more details about getting involved in bat conservation and monitoring www.bats.org.uk.

RECORDING THE CITY: BERLIN, LONDON, NAPLES

BJ Nilsen

1 Willy Römer, *Der Gänsehirt ist da! Ein Artist mit hölzernen Gänsen und ein Drehorgelspieler in einem Hinterhof.* (The goose herder is here! An artist with wooden geese and an organ grinder in an inner courtyard), 1926. Courtesy of the bpk / Kunstbibliothek, SMB.

A city without sound does not exist. Every location, passageway, alley, road, park, contains its own world of isolated sound events and patterns.[1]

In my work as composer, sound, and recording artist, I explore the sound of nature and its perception by humans. I primarily use field recordings and electronic composition as a working method. The overall interest of my current work with sound is inspired by the following questions: What is the sound of a city? How do cities sound differently? What does sound mean to us? Can we trace urban change and transformation through sound?

The exploration of the acoustic realm of a city can be done in as many ways as there are sounds. Whenever travelling, I get familiar with my sound surroundings—such as the street life below my window, the sounds in my room, or the sounds in the courtyard. I have my recording gear set up, so I can easily capture spontaneous sound events, which might occur at any given time. The practice of recording the city has many parallels to the ways writers and urban flâneurs walk and explore the city. These acoustic observations are later composed into a personal reflection.

In the opening essay "Loggias," from his book *Berlin Childhood Around 1900*, Walter Benjamin reflects upon hearing various sound events occurring in the courtyard, such as carpet beating, the rhythm of overground trains, the sound of running water, and the brushing of leaves.[2] The *Hinterhöfe* (inner courtyards of Berlin's typical tenement buildings) contain interesting acoustic variations even today. Courtyards act as a kind of amplifier, letting the sounds bounce and blend between the buildings to finally settle down in the loggias. If we compare contemporary urban soundscapes to Benjamin's descriptions, they have changed quite a lot—maybe even radically. From the standpoint of an acoustic ecologist, we can explore how the sonic environment can be read as a reflection of our contemporary social structures and living standards. Do Hinterhöfe in different neighbourhoods contain different sound worlds? How do these sound worlds change with depth and height, walking from one courtyard into the next, further and further away from the street?

Today, typical sounds in a Hinterhof might include the hissing sound of streetcars, banging and shrieking of the trash collection, the rattle of bicycles, voices of neighbours, phones ringing, children on their way to school, musical practice, clattering of kitchenware, sounds of shops and cafes filtering through their rear walls, sirens, birds, dogs, rain patterns, thunder, and the low glissando of airplanes. However, the closed-in world of the courtyard might create a more intimate sound world controlled by its inhabitants than the loggias facing the busy high streets. Some larger courtyards with an open, park-like structure have the luxury of trees and bushes allowing wildlife as an audible presence. Although we can register all these diverse sounds, have the courtyards become more silent over time?

The writer and flâneur Franz Hessel noted during his walks through the city in the 1920s: "Sometimes I would like to enter the courtyards. In the older parts of Berlin, life in the back of the tenements becomes denser and more intimate … the frames for beating carpets, the rubbish bins and the wells that survive from the time before water pipes. In the mornings, I succeed only when the singers and fiddlers perform or the barrel organ man … or the amazing fellow who plays snare in front and a bass drum in back."[3]

In the early 1900s, a common practice was to extend the scene of the street into the courtyards with theatrical and musical play. Photographer Willy Römer successfully depicted these scenes of everyday working life in Berlin (figure 1).[4] Such performative events are recollected in Werner Herzog's film *Stroszek* (1977), where Bruno S. can be seen playing a glockenspiel and accordion, while the camera pans up and around the building, spotting a few spectators looking out of their windows.

In the summer of 2013, I visited Berlin's Tempelhof airfield, now open for the public to walk around or bike freely. Standing on the old runway, I listened to the construction work in the former terminals and hangars, possibly preparations for the Berlin Music Festival that takes place there each summer. The clanging of metal, roaring of vehicles, and sporadic shouts from the workers were thrown out and spread across the field decaying behind me in a wide natural reverb, a unique experience for being in the middle of the city. In some of the green areas covering the sides of the runways, the grass has been allowed to grow high. These spaces are now a habitat for rare and endangered birds such as the Red-backed Shrike (*Lanius collurio*), Skylark (*Alauda arvensis*), Tawny Pipit (*Anthus campestris*), and Wheatear (*Oenanthe oenanthe*). The busy backdrop of the city is far away enough to let us rest our ears for a moment.

Standing on Francis Street behind Victoria Station in London, it is a sunny spring afternoon and the air is crisp. For a location so central, it is a quiet street, for about ten seconds …. As the bells of a nearby church in the Diocese of Westminster start to chime, I press record. They merge into a vehicle and then into a woman on a bike, and as she brakes to make a turn, in the distance a cell phone rings. All the time, a train engine has been idling.

London pulls you towards water. You are bound to reach the river at some point. On a grey and foggy afternoon, I walk along the bank of the Thames during low tide. There, the sand, algae, mud, and brick buildings isolated the acoustics, revealing great detail. An almost interior space, surrounded by old shoes, pieces of porcelain, half a chair, bones, bricks, wood structures, and washed-up electronics; it felt like looking into the future as well as the past. To the left, there were the obscured towers of Canary Wharf, and to the right, Tower Bridge completely shrouded in fog. The drones of the clippers on the river suddenly sounded electronic, the occasional vague beep of metal detectors belonging to coin hunters tracing our past. A chainsaw starts up from one of the workshops nearby.

It is midday, outside a *pescheria* (fish market) somewhere in the old town of Naples, I have chosen not to look at my map and now I am lost. Taken in by the sounds and activity of the fish market I decide to stick around for a while. The only recollection of me ever being there will be my recordings.

Listening back I can almost visualize exactly what I encountered, even faces, and although my memory reads in a hazy dreamlike quality, it is filled with information. It is the month of May and sunny, very comfortable weather. (Usually, I create a voice index of the recording location with time and date. Even weather is noted, although I often recollect it later as a personal memory.)

Like a river, an endless stream of people is flowing through the street, chatting while carrying their newly purchased groceries in noisy plastic bags. Their conversations merge with the twittering of caged canary birds that people hang outside their windows or keep on their balconies. I adjust the volume of my recorder as the hacking of the tuna fish is peaking in my headphone, a hard fish to get through it seems. In the background, the constant sound of fresh water being poured into containers full of live seafood.

It is a good location and I decide to stay a little longer. The close-up recordings of people's discussions and the original quality of their voices is fascinating. My small omnidirectional microphones are clipped onto each side of my bag. The microphones are not very visible and I can remain incognito while recording, only the big headphones make me stand out in the crowd. I decide to change to small in-ear headphones, because they provide better cover.

Now almost dizzy from the auditory and visual activity, I decide to walk away, heading for a small side street in the old city grid. Naples is quite hilly. I start on the top of one of the narrowest and longest streets and walk through. It is very quiet, apart from the sound of cutlery by people setting tables above me for lunchtime. Radios and TVs bleed through with what sounds like talk shows, or are they political debates? People live so close to each other they can probably borrow salt from the neighbouring window.

Through a door that looks more like a prototype than an actual door, I step into a Neapolitan courtyard with not much activity except for a distant coughing from an elderly person. I think again of Franz Hessel who wrote: "In order to gain an impression of the lives of the inhabitants, one must penetrate the courtyards."[5] In order not to be intrusive, I step back out in the road.

Being in the middle of this small narrow street you cannot escape the scooters. Without any shops or people on this section of the street, the drivers allow themselves to rush through full speed like arrows. Wearing headphones, one has to be on guard. The scooter is the "signature" sound of Naples and can be heard and encountered at any time. Here is one racing down the street, and as I listen it pans quickly from my left to my right ear with a disappearing trail of dense reverberation.

Back in Berlin, at home in my studio, which happens to face the first Hinterhof of our building, I am listening to the recordings, and a surreal city begins to unfold. Without the multisensory impressions and visual synchronizations at the moment of recording, certain memories and perceptions seem to grow stronger. I decide to layer and merge the locations from these cities and play around with them. We can suddenly be in London and Berlin at the same time.[6] We can even place the fish market from Naples in the Berlin courtyard, or let scooters run parallel to the Thames clippers.

Endnotes

1   Liner notes taken from BJ Nilsen, *The Eye Of The Microphone* CD TO:95.

2   Walter Benjamin, *Berlin Childhood around 1900*, trans. Howard Eiland (Cambridge, MA: Harvard University Press, 2006 [1932–1938]) p. 38.

3   Franz Hessel, *Ein Flaneur in Berlin* (Berlin: Das Arsenal, 1984) p. 8. Hessel quotes translated into English by Wolfgang Kaschuba, Berlin Streetlife: Scenes and scenarios, Humboldt Universität Berlin, Transatlantisches Graduiertenkolleg.

4   Diethard Kerbs, *Der Fotograf Willy Römer 1887–1979. Auf den Strassen von Berlin* (Bönen: DruckVerlag Kettler, 2004) p. 229.

5   Franz Hessel, *Ein Flaneur in Berlin* p. 220.

6   For an example of mixing locations listen to the CD accompanying this volume.

EAVESDROPPING

Anders Albrechtslund

Eavesdropping is a type of surveillance that involves listening to private conversations in secret. Today, this auditory-focused practice seems to stand in the shadow of CCTV in particular, but also advanced hi-tech surveillance methods involving drones, data mining, and location technologies. A dominant understanding of surveillance today is that it is something extremely precise, effective, and constant, developed from a stereotypical interpretation of George Orwell's *Nineteen Eighty-Four* and the Panopticon.[1] This representation of surveillance is dominant in popular culture as well, where films like the *Bourne* series (2002–2012), *Minority Report* (2002), and *Eagle Eye* (2008) all focus on CCTV surveillance, only a few films such as *The Lives of Others* (2006) and *The Conversation* (1974) centre their narratives on auditory surveillance activities.

In this essay, my ambition is to nuance this one-sided understanding and use eavesdropping as a lens to explore aural surveillance as something that can also be limited, fragile, and partial. As a phenomenon, eavesdropping stands out from visual forms of surveillance and this might make it easier to escape the inadequate Big Brother image, and here Bruno Latour's concept "oligopticon"—introduced in his book *Paris: Invisible City*—is useful.[2] Oligoptica are specific, grounded views, and according to Latour, we should think of these as the opposite of the all-seeing Panopticon. This means that instead of thinking about surveillance

1, 2 *The Conversation*, 1974,
dir. Francis Ford Coppola
Courtesy of the British Film
Institute.

in terms of an absolute, omnipotent view that potentially embraces everything, it is much more accurate and productive to think of it as a form of observation that might be very clear and specific, but also lacks any kind of overview. In other words, surveillance is always situated and partial.

Latour uses oligoptica to illustrate the complex infrastructure of different Parisian organizations, which are all characterized by narrow gazes. For example, when we take in Paris from the top floor of the Eiffel Tower, this panoramic view of the city is not a complete picture. Rather, we only see a very limited part of Paris, because we cannot see behind buildings, the underground, and so on. In fact, there is no physical location from where the whole of Paris is visible. Instead of an all-encompassing view of the city as a whole, the gaze itself must produce invisibilities. The surveillance practices depicted in Francis Ford Coppola's 1974 Palme d'Or winner, *The Conversation*, illustrate how this more limited gaze is produced and how fragile it can be.

The film takes up the theme of eavesdropping, as the wiretapping expert, Harry Caul (played by Gene Hackman), is trying to understand and eventually intervene in an apparent murder scheme (figures 1 and 2). During work on a particularly demanding job, which is to bug a conversation between two individuals moving through Union Square, San Francisco, Harry becomes suspicious and hesitates to turn over the finished recording to his employers. He fears that the material will be used to harm innocent people; and due to his personal torment, he gradually loses his professional distance from the whole situation in which he reluctantly takes part. Instead, he decides to take action by launching a private wiretapping operation in an effort to prevent the imminent killings.

Harry Caul's job is to listen and observe, and he is therefore unable to intervene. He simply listens as a passive witness from the hotel room next door as the murder seems to be carried out, and his feeling of guilt relates to this lack of intervention. The guilt also relates to a previous assignment, where his surveillance work resulted in the death of an entire family. Harry claims to be indifferent to his clients and the people he records: "I don't care what they're talking about; all I want is a nice, fat recording,"[3] but in the course of the film, his guilt transforms him from cynical surveillance machine to a human being with feelings that he does not know how to act on. This increasingly alienated man guards his own privacy with an obsessive zeal and the irony is, of course, that his lonely life does not seem to have anything worth protecting: "I don't have anything personal. Nothing of value, except my keys" which makes Coppola's film a dystopian study of a paranoid voyeur.

The conversation in the opening scene, which is the pivotal point of Coppola's film, takes place in a crowded situation. For several minutes we zoom from a wide shot of Union Square in San Francisco to focus on a mime artist who, as it happens, begins to imitate Harry Caul. Here, we are introduced to some of the main themes of the film. There is a somewhat confusing asymmetry between what we see and what we hear which suggests Harry's inability to fully understand the elusive conversation he is trying to eavesdrop on. Throughout the film, Harry takes on the role of professional voyeur, yet as in the scene with the mime artist, he is involuntarily exposed. This theme of Harry's invisibility and visibility is revisited in the scene where his landlord puts a birthday present in his apartment and thereby bypasses the security system. More extreme, is the final scene where Harry is convinced that someone is watching him, which is emphasized by the cinematic perspective panning just like a surveillance camera. In a sense, the difficulty Harry experiences in trying to capture a clean and clear recording is a depiction of the modern urban experience of searching for coherence in a constantly changeable environment filled with sensory impressions.

Despite the chaos of the noisy outdoor space, Harry's surveillance team is able to record a considerable part of the words spoken. But still, the words are disconnected and lack an overall meaning. Harry's transformation is linked to his attempt to make sense of the conversation, and throughout the film he puts the words together and adds new bits of cleaned recordings as if doing a jigsaw puzzle. The twist is that the meaning of the conversation is dependent on human interpretation, and after his careful piecing together, Harry simply misinterprets. Several times during the film we see a young couple talk and then hear the sentence "he'd kill us if he got the chance," which Harry (and the audience) interprets as if someone wants to kill them, possibly people from the corporation where they both work, and which assigned Harry the bugging job. When Harry realizes that this is not the case—on the contrary—we hear the sentence with the crucial inflection: "he'd kill *us* if he got the chance." Thus, the presumed victims are in fact the killers, and this reveals Harry's inability to act.

The scene in the hotel further demonstrates Harry's passivity as he, weak and confused, sits on the bathroom floor while using his homemade surveillance equipment to spy on the people in the room next door. It has been suggested that this scene also compares the act of eavesdropping and spying with the behaviour of a child.[4] Similarly, when Harry realizes his inability to act on his suspicion that a murder will take place in the room next door, he turns on the television very loud, as if these childish defence techniques will make everything go away.

The concluding scene of *The Conversation* is a study of a man tormented by paranoid suspicions. Harry interprets his excessive self-consciousness as an invasion of privacy from an unknown enemy. He tears his room apart, obsessively searching for some hidden microphone or clue as to what ingenious surveillance method his "enemy" is using. Finally, the last stronghold of Harry's personality, his Catholic faith, is torn down as he smashes his figurine of the Virgin Mary, suspecting it to hide the unknown bugging device. We, the audience, cannot know to what extent Harry is right about his suspicions, since all we know is his perception of things, including dreams and hallucinations, such as the hotel scene where the toilet overflows with blood. Yet it can be concluded that Harry's looming madness relates to the tension between his strong voyeuristic interests, at first professionally directed and then gradually privately orientated, and, on the other hand, his extreme fear of being seen by others.

The Conversation offers the opportunity to broaden our perspective on eavesdropping and surveillance. Popular culture is a rich source for the cultural sediments of our more or less tacit understandings of surveillance. Although Harry Caul is a fictitious character, his trouble with the ethical dimensions to the gaze touches us in several ways. Popular culture obviously influences our understanding of the world in the sense that ideas and conceptions originate in, and are formed through, cultural artefacts such as books and films, and this is certainly also true when it comes to the discourse surrounding surveillance, where the fictitious character of Big Brother has dominated both public and academic debate. Harry's struggles demonstrate the burden of responsibility connected to secretly obtained information. The film illustrates the ambiguities inherent to eavesdropping as Harry embodies the ethical dilemma of surveillance at the film's conclusion.

Coppola's film shows how sturdy the gaze might seem and, at the same time, how fragile it really is. Latour writes that "the tiniest bug can blind oligoptica,"[5] and for Harry this little bug is the infliction "he'd kill *us* if he got the chance," which completely collapses and redefines his understanding of the situation. It seems ironic that Harry's whole apparatus of employees, self-built bugging equipment, and eavesdropping tactics is vulnerable to a simple misunderstanding of one word in a conversation. We see this fragility not only in the world of fiction, as recent mass surveillance scandals remind us. Here, for example, Edward Snowden was the "bug in the eye" of an advanced and widespread US-based global mass surveillance program, as he disclosed information about how the system works. Of course, this has not destroyed the National Security Agency, but it spurred global discussion and caused much embarrassment, as well as presumably damage, to the covert surveillance apparatus of the USA and its partners.

In comparison to oligoptica, the absolute gaze of the Panopticon seems invulnerable. My main argument is that this ostensibly superior vantage point and perhaps many of its derived concepts are not always very useful to describe the surveillance technologies and practices we meet in everyday life. Rather, it is part of a fantasy or "double disease of total paranoia and total megalomania" as Latour has described it.[6] This can easily be related to familiar positions in the general debate about surveillance. They stem from the same notion of surveillance as something stabile, all-encompassing, and extraordinarily effective. However, an understanding of surveillance as network-produced oligoptica offers a "cure" in the sense that it incites a focus on specific surveillance situations, without giving in to fears and fantasies.

Such an understanding of surveillance is mirrored in *The Conversation*. Here, the practice of surveillance—in this case eavesdropping—does not entail absolute control of the situation. Harry carries out the surveillance, but he is certainly not in command, as his bugging only leads to confusion and passivity on his side. However, the people under surveillance are not in control either. Their actions are unrelated to the surveillance and though the plot—involving murderers and victims—is probably affected by the material produced by the bugging, it is not Harry who is directing the action. Here, a conventional understanding of surveillance as hierarchies of power is challenged. In the Orwellian sense, surveillance is part of the destruction of the subjectivity under surveillance and the effort to render the lifeworld meaningless. We see the opposite in Coppola's film, as Harry's bugging displays the surveillant's own shame and inability to take control of the situation. Harry's world does not become more meaningful through surveillance, instead it eventually destroys him. Unlike the main character in *Enemy of the State*, Dean (played by Will Smith), who turns the tide by taking control of the surveillance technologies, Harry's situation doesn't offer any redemption. Surveillance isn't utopian, rather, it has frictions, malfunctions, and complications like most other dimensions to everyday life.

In my view, the insights gained from these thoughts on eavesdropping lead to an argument for a pluralistic understanding of surveillance. We should give the Orwellian-inspired concept a rest along with the idea of the surveillance state and the surveillance society. It seems more prudent to think of our world as permeated with surveillance cultures, which allow for a range of different perspectives.[7] This will shift the focus of discussion from surveillance technologies and practices (are they good or bad?), to the contexts and relations in which they are aligned, translated, and negotiated.

Endnotes

1 G. Orwell, *Nineteen Eighty-Four* (London: Secker & Warburg, 1949). See also J. Bentham and M. Bozovic, *The Panopticon Writings* (London/New York: Verso, 1995); M. Foucault, *Discipline and Punish: The Birth of the Prison* (New York: Pantheon, 1977).

2 B. Latour and E. Hermant, *Paris, ville invisible* (Paris: Institut Synthélabo, 1999).

3 *The Conversation*, directed by F. F. Coppola (Paramount Pictures, 1974).

4 M. Ratner, "Notes on The Conversation" (10 February 2008). http://www.sensesofcinema.com/2001/13/conversation (accessed 15 March 2014).

5 B. Latour, *Reassembling the Social: An Introduction to Actor-Network-Theory* (New York: Oxford University Press, 2005) p. 181.

6 Ibid.

7 D. Lyon, "The Culture of Surveillance: Who's watching whom, now?," lecture given at the University of Sydney (1 March, 2012).

3

SOUND CULTURES

OF LONGITUDE, LATITUDE, AND ZENITH: LOS ANGELES, *VAN HALEN*, AND THE AESTHETICS OF "BACKYARDISM"

John Scanlan

1

Writing in 1971, Reyner Banham suggested that one of the many reasons that the culture of Los Angeles was remarkable, and worthy of celebration, was that its aesthetic sensibility was driven by unconventional approaches to creativity that were not so evident elsewhere. Citing the city's custom car phenomenon as one example of a vernacular culture that emerged from "delinquent origins," Banham marvelled at the "wonders wrought in backyards by high-school dropouts" offering up for the public gaze vehicles that were transformed into "wild extravaganzas of richly coloured and exotically shaped métal."[1] But as interesting as the car in all its customized varieties was was to understanding the human ecology of Los Angeles, it is the fact that a kind of unschooled or haphazard aesthetics emerged from such unlikely origins that is interesting. Here was an environment in which backyard tinkering was elevated to new creative heights through the reconfiguration and modification of some of the most familiar products of mass culture, which would take on a look and style that made a virtue of the backyard origins of the creative process. And so, out by the Pacific Ocean at Venice Beach in the 1970s, a gang of young surfers with no waves to catch after the sea had gone out for the day decided they would reinvent surfing as skateboarding. Skateboards had already existed, of course, but what the new innovators did was to throw out its dull show-pony origins, with its rules and performance set pieces, and open the way to the idea that the skateboard was a means for some kind of self-invention. They sought out the curved concrete swimming pools of empty residential properties—drained of water and left to dry out in the long summers—which soon provided something akin to a concrete wave that could be "surfed" all day.

At the other end of the creative scale, we might point to a similar aesthetic at work in some of the Los Angeles buildings of Frank Gehry, which seemed to do no less than celebrate "Metropolitan Los Angeles as an unfinished city."[2] The casual observer driving past Gehry's famous Santa Monica residence would see a construction seemingly thrown together from materials that looked as if they were recovered from the leftovers of a storm that had blown through his property—corrugated metal siding, plywood, chain link fence, and so on—and reconfigured to present the back as the front.

And just as the Gehry residence became an icon of the city, so Edward Van Halen's famous self-built "Frankenstein" guitar and the experiments he conducted with sound and amplification would express the sonic aesthetics of a Los Angeles "backyardism."[3] But in dabbling with technology and acoustics, and arriving at a unique sonic identity that would come to be associated with the city, Van Halen sought to satisfy a more general synaesthetic crav-

1 The first publicly seen version of the "Frankenstein" guitar, 1978. It may look like a Fender Stratocaster with a custom paint job, but all elements of the instrument were specially built by, or for, the teenage Van Halen—the wood of the body is about twice as thick as a normal Fender (to aid tonal quality), the neck is broader and slimmer (more like a classical guitar than an electric guitar) and has been left unfinished/unlacquered and inlaid with "thick, fat" frets; the pickup was made by the guitarist and dipped in surfboard wax to cut out feedback, and instead of having three control knobs, the guitar has one—which reads "TONE." Source: Getty Images.

ing for what he would refer to as the "brown sound." The colour brown here stood for the tonal qualities he was driven to discover; it was variously "warm," "sweet," "fat," or "thick," "wood"-like, as well as "buttery" and "meaty." As the historian Olivia Mattis has written, the correspondence of sound to colour is an important element of how musicians in particular make sense of music:

> Tone color, or timbre, is one of sound's five parameters; the others are pitch, volume, duration, and envelope (the attack and decay of a sound). Tone color is the aspect of sound that allows the listener to differentiate, say, a violin from a clarinet.[4]

And it was precisely his pursuit of tone through sonic modifications that enhanced the remaining parameters of sound, thereby enabling the guitarist's backyardism to find expression on the 1978 *Van Halen* album.

As a musician in a rock'n'roll band, one of the motivations for Van Halen's experiments with sound was to find a way to play at high volumes without losing tonal warmth. But attaining this "brown sound" rested on the matter of how to make an electric guitar "hum" and "blow" at high volume without generating screeching feedback or the discordant sounds that were characteristic of a fuzz pedal. Van Halen's sonic ideals were saxophone, clarinet, and other wind instruments—whose tonal quality he revered and sought to emulate—which were able to maintain their specific character while, for example, increasing volume or modifying the attack and decay of musical notes. This was made possible by the use of breath, which could be a very subtle means of articulating musical ideas. Blowing through the notes, a wind player's two hands were free to manipulate the sound that air—breathing—first begins to articulate. But this sense of pushing air did not seem to be a quality of musical articulation that was available to a guitarist; rather, a guitar player's ability to achieve sustain came more obviously via the use of hands to attain vibrato, and effects such as fuzz, wah-wah, echo, and amplification. Working in his parents' Pasadena garage in the mid-1970s, Van Halen began work on the instrument and electronics that would produce the sound he heard in his head, and the end result went some way to imitating the kind of "breathing" quality that he sought.

To deal with the effect of volume on tone, amplifiers were dangerously modified to allow the voltage feed to be a source for controlling loudness, with a domestic light dimmer switch employed as a means of reducing or increasing the power input to the amplifier. By turning all the amplifier controls up, and "dimming" the voltage, he could deliver maximum tone while avoiding feedback and distortion. But this was only one piece of the puzzle. For the guitar, a variety of wood types were tried and tested for the quality of sustain they would bring to the instrument, and the pickups—magnetic poles wrapped in wire coils and housed in those metal or plastic bars that rest under the guitar strings and amplify the acoustic sound of the strings—were broken down and rebuilt to exacting specifications. In breaking apart many store-bought pickups and then reassembling them by laboriously winding the coils on each magnet, the guitarist figured out how to stop the coils vibrating in a way that lent itself towards achieving the favoured "brown sound." He soaked each of the modified pickups in stove-heated surfboard wax—which would solidify when taken off the heat—until he thought they had absorbed an amount sufficient enough to prevent the wire coils from vibrating.[5]

None of these elements on their own, however, would have brought to fruition the sound that emerged, completely realized, from Sunset Sound Recorders in Los Angeles during the sessions for the first *Van Halen* album during the autumn of 1977.

The studio at Sunset Sound had been established in the 1950s by the Walt Disney producer Tutti Camarata, who demonstrated some backyardism of his own in seeing in this property—an auto-repair shop—the perfect acoustics for attaining the quality of sound he required. Its sloping concrete floor, designed to let engine oil and other automotive fluids run into a gutter, along with the dimensions of its interior created a unique reverberation sound field, and turned out to be perfect for capturing a "live" and vibrant sound on tape. This would be the studio where most of Disney's movie soundtracks were created for some time to come.[6] And it was the studio's characteristic 'live' sound which led the four members of Van Halen to record as an ensemble, essentially replicating their stage performance to maximize the ambience of the room.

2

2 Sunset Sound Studios.
Photo by Lucie Baratte.

This made *Van Halen* something of a throwback to the way records had been made up until about a decade before; the band recorded more basically and cheaply than even their punk contemporaries, and using a fraction of the kind of million-dollar budgets that performers such as Fleetwood Mac or Bruce Springsteen were spending at the time. With the band keen to spend as little time in the studio as possible, and in pursuit of a performance spontaneity, a devil-may-care attitude prevailed. The approach, as singer David Lee Roth once said, was to aim for a kind of "hodgepodge" that cut against the overperfection of the studio recordings of the time: "[we] just throw some stuff in and see where it lands."[7] And like the Van Halen live shows, where the songs tended to end rather ragged and chaotic, one quality that characterizes the album is that the tunes, for the most part, don't come to a neat ending or fade gradually. They tend to end with a bang or a crash, a final flash of energy, just as they would do onstage.

In additional to all these ingredients, the sound of Van Halen would benefit from Sunset Sound's famed echo chamber, which the longtime recording engineer Bruce Botnick has spoken of as the source of mysterious powers that could only be put down "longitude, latitude and zenith," and as such, its qualities were entirely unique.[8] It was a space that had been constructed as a more or less rectangular room of non-parallel walls—with the walls and floors at differing angles in order to attain the desired room reverb, created by sound bouncing around off the surfaces—and located on a floor above the performance room that was sealed behind a heavy meat locker door. Inside, nothing but wood was visible, which was the cladding on top of layers and layers of drywall, with, Botnick said, "maybe about twenty or thirty coats of resin over it. So it felt like a wooden room. You could go in there, sit down and turn the light off and think you were in the biggest wooden room you've ever been in."[9]

But it was actually an exceptionally small room and, at it's widest, only a few feet across. Inside was a speaker channelling sound from the performers, and a microphone set up to record the reverb as the sound from the studio reverberated in the small space. On *Van Halen*, this is the echo that adds depth and a quality of airiness to the sound of the guitar, thus maximizing the desired tonal quality. Its effect was employed by others who used the studio and—indeed—can be heard on The Doors' "Light My Fire" (in the crack of the opening snare), and in the bossa nova-style rimshots played by drummer John Densmore at the beginning of "Break On Through."[10]

One of the most singular examples of the sound that resulted from all this was found in track two of the *Van Halen* album, "Eruption". As the title suggests, it approximates, in sound, a force elemental enough that the band's record label, Warner Bros., would take out adverts for the album declaring: "Van Halen—more energy than a nuclear reactor!" What remains remarkable is that this landmark in electric guitar artistry one minute and fortytwo seconds of controlled energy and aggression that pushed the instrument into new sonic territory was that it was only recorded by accident as Eddie Van Halen and his brother, Alex, the band's drummer, were warming up in the studio before a show at the nearby Whisky A Go Go. Up until this point in time, it was merely a couple of minutes of exercises that allowed the guitarist to loosen up his fingers before going on stage. On this particular day, the studio engineer had set the tape rolling in case anything interesting happened while the brothers were warming up, and so what appears on record as a result is the one and only "take." On hearing this explosive, souped-up, baroque hot-rod of a tune—punctuated by the sound of dive-bombs, groans, and barely comprehensible squeals in between passages that soar effortlessly as if they had found a pathway onto the jet stream – the band's producer, Ted Templeman knew in an instant that it had to go on the album.

For five years after that moment, Van Halen continued to make their albums quickly and cheaply—time in the studio was more usually counted in days rather than weeks—and left in the mistakes other artists would take care to remove or overdub. While major success would ultimately change the dynamics of their creative process, the delinquent potential of backyard tinkering still seemed to draw Eddie Van Halen's attention. By 1983, just as some of the Los Angeles studios were slowly beginning to switch to new digital technologies, Eddie could be found rummaging through the junk of some of the most wellknown Hollywood Recording Studios in search of discarded recording consoles to equip the studio he was now building in the backyard where else of his new Hollywood Hills home. It was in this studio that Van Halen's best-selling album, *1984*, was recorded in the spring and summer of 1983, using a salvaged recording console that had previously been used in the United Western studios on Sunset Boulevard. By now a relic of a bygone age, it had the military green look and feel of those metal filing cabinets from the 1950s and 1960s, which were once seen in offices the world over. It looked, Eddie Van Halen later said, like "a piece of shit."[11] But, it had recorded Frank Sinatra, The Beach Boys, Phil Spector, and The Mamas and the Papas—and just maybe, it held the promise of finding that elusive point where latitude, longitude, and zenith intersect, and where the "brown sound" might live.

Endnotes

1 Reyner Banham, *Los Angeles: The Architecture of Four Ecologies* (London: Allen Lane, Penguin Press, 1971) p. 221.

2 Kevin Starr, *Coast of Dreams: A History of Contemporary California* (London: Vintage, 2005) p. 57.

3 See the feature at the Smithsonian Institute: http://tiny.cc/v3of2w

4 Olivia Mattis, "Scriabin to Gershwin: Color Music from a Musical Perspective," in *Visual Music: Synaesthesia in Art and Music Since 1900*, ed. Kerry Brougher, et al. (London: Thames and Hudson, 2005) p. 211.

5 The electric guitar pickup is a device fixed to the body of the instrument beneath the strings that "picks up" vibrations and translates them into an electrical current. The pickup is composed of two main elements that come as stock on most guitars: a coil of insulated copper wire and a magnet, which magnetize the guitar strings. When the strings vibrate—either through picking or strumming them—the vibration causes the flux field of the magnet to move along with the strings. The motion of the flux field creates an alternating current within the pickup's coils. The alternating current then travels from the pickup, through the volume and tone controls, through the output jack, through the cable (or wireless) and finally to the amplifier, where it comes out in the form of tone. Van Halen's painstaking experiments in breaking down and rebuilding stock pickups, as well as the unorthodox use of surfboard wax to prevent excessive vibration in the pickup coil became a key component in achieving his desired, and distinctive, guitar tone.

6 Tim Hollis and Greg Ehrbar, *Mouse Tracks: The Story of Walt Disney Records* (Jackson: University Press of Mississippi 2006) p. 58.

7 Quoted in Geoff Barton, "New Boots and (Stretch) Panties," *Sounds* (28 June 1980): 18.

8 Quoted in William Clark and Jim Cogan, *Temples of Sound: Inside the Great Recording Studios* (San Francisco: Chronicle Books, 2003) p. 49.

9 Ibid. p. 48.

10 James Riordan and Jerry Prochnicky, *Break on Through: The Life and Death of Jim Morrison* (London: Plexus Publishing Ltd., 1991) p. 111.

11 H. P. Newquist, "Edward Van Halen: The Guitar Interview," *Guitar* (March 1995): 121.

HELSINKI SEEN THROUGH THE LENSES OF THE KAURISMÄKI BROTHERS

Tony Mitchell

The opening sequence of Mika Kaurismäki's 1982 film *Arvottomat* (*The Worthless*), his first feature film after returning to Finland from studying film in Munich for five years, is one of the most famous in Finnish film history. We see an aerial view in black and white from a helicopter flying over the Gulf of Finland and into the centre of Helsinki, before we cut to the feet of protagonist Manne (played by celebrated Kaurismäki actor Matti Pellonpää, who died in 1995 at the age of 44) kicking off his boots from the end of his bed as the phone rings (an old-fashioned landline of course, which, out of shot, he drags toward him by the cord). The sequence is accompanied by Sibelius's most well-known composition, the stirringly patriotic *Finlandia*, but something is wrong—there's a chugging prog rock accompaniment to it, with synthesiser, bass, and drums, rearranged by Anssi Tikanmäki, scoring his first film, which strikes a jarring note. Tikanmäki subsequently became celebrated for this Sibelius arrangement, which the Sibelius estate never gave permission for, although Mika Kaurismäki claims they knew about it. The composer went on to score numerous other Kaurismäki films (including Aki's 1999 silent film *Juho*), and his orchestra—which includes two of Tikanmäki's brothers—accompanied the film live at the Berlin Film Festival, and has also accompanied a number of other classic silent films by Dziga Vertov, Eisenstein, Murnau, and Von Stroheim. In 2012, the Tikanmäki Attack and Roope Latvala, a heavy metal

1

guitarist with the group Children of Bodom, released an album *Anthems*, in which eight well-known national anthems are given the heavy metal-orchestral treatment. *The Worthless* also features a live performance by Finnish rock singer Rauli "Badding" Somerjoki—his nickname was derived from Paddington Bear—who died in 1987 at the age of 39. Somerjoki was a master of rock, tango, old waltzes, and *humppa*, which Peter von Bagh defines as "a kind of fox-trot perceived and understood through the Finnish backwoods."[1]

The Worthless announced a new beginning in Finnish cinema: the film was produced by veteran director Jorn Donner, co-written by the two Kaurismäki brothers, and featured Aki Kaurismäki in one of only two on-screen roles; the other was the lead role as a motormouth womanizer in Mika's 1981 graduation film, the fifty-minute short *Valehtelija* (*The Liar*), also set in Helsinki, which tips its hat to Godard's *Breathless* on a number of occasions. Here, Aki plays the same character, Francophile Ville Alfa, also the name of the production studio, and it is of course "Alphaville" reversed. A minor character is even called Anna-Kaarina. We first encounter Ville in *The Worthless* in a very Godardian moment: reading a copy of *Le Monde* in a bar, denouncing it as crap, and throwing it away. The film, which won the Finnish Jussi award for best direction, is a road movie set between Helsinki and Tampere involving a stolen painting, and is heavily influenced by film noir, Godard, and the French

1 *Calamari Union* in production at Vanha kirkkopuisto (Old Church Park) in Helsinki. From left to right: Heikki Ortamo,

Juuso Hirvikangas, Aki Kaurismäki, Pirkka-Pekka Petelius, and Matti Pellonpää (ca. 1985).

Photo by Marja-Leena Hukkanen.

nouvelle vague, but with the Kaurismäkis' characteristic droll, deadpan humour—which partly comes from the use of very formal, deadpan, literary dialogue. The helicopter reappears as an antagonist toward the end of the movie in a direct steal from Hitchcock's *North by Northwest*, where it chases Manne along the road in his car, then crashes and explodes. The opening sequence was described as follows by Pietari Kääppä:

> *The influences contribute a distinctly transnational perspective on Finland, and the genre-influenced emergence of a new generation of film-makers at the turn of the 1980s is evident in the film's opening. The cartographic imagination of the opening moves through the Puonavuori district to Lönnrotinkatu 7, where Manne the protagonist resides. The opening of the film initiates a dialogue with the traditional view of the city (the top of the Senate is visible and acts as a guiding beacon) and the more urbanised view of the nation. Through this, we are provided with an invite to the remaking of Finnish cinema.*[2]

The Senate Square is now also notable for a sound installation by organist and composer Harri Viitanen and technology expert Jyrki Alakuijala, which is a contemporary version of the European glockenspiel and best heard from the middle of the square, at Emperor Alexander's statue, towards which the loudspeakers are pointed. The sound travels from one building to the next and the composition runs for five minutes and eighteen seconds. It is played every day at 5.59 p.m. Senate Square has also been the site of formal New Year celebrations in Helsinki since 1932. It is, of course, also the location for *Total Balalaika Show* (1993), Aki's film about the collaboration between the Leningrad Cowboys and the 200-strong Alexandrov Red Army Chorus and Dance Ensemble, witnessed by 70,000 people on the biggest stage ever built in Finland. The concert blended *Finlandia* with traditional Russian folk tunes such as "Dark Eyes" and "Kalinka," but really came into its own on versions of the Turtles "Happy Together," Wilbert Harrison's "Let's Work Together," Bob Dylan's "Knockin' on Heaven's Door," and Lynyrd Skynyrd's "Sweet Home Alabama." The Leningrad Cowboys celebrated the twentieth anniversary of the film with a tour of Finland—"Red X-Mas Party 2013"—with the Russian Air Force Choir, and promised "more than 60 performers including cossack dancers, circus performers, DJ's [sic] and massive decorations."[3] As Peter von Bagh, Finland's most prominent film critic, put it:

> *Here, in the heart of Helsinki at its loveliest, in its one-of-a-kind Empire centre, a square still displaying the statue of Czar Alexander II (so the past should not be destroyed!), was an encounter with a rare carnival atmosphere in the city that through the Conference on Security and Cooperation in Europe gave its name to hope. The paradoxes of the cold war were still graphically at hand, also lending force to the vast bursts of laughter in the Senate Square—laughter at the medals, at powers that be who have lost their bearings and humanity.*[4]

The Leningrad Cowboys, "the worst rock and roll band in the world," were born from a still-existing rock group called the Sleepy Sleepers, for whom Kaurismäki had made a couple of music videos. They still own the franchise to the Zetor restaurant in Mannerheimintie, one of the main drags in central Helsinki, outside which there are two hideous wooden replicas of the absurdly be-quiffed and pointy-booted clan. Zetor is a Czech brand of tractor, and the interior is decorated like a barn with old signs, two tractors, farm machinery, sledges, and skis hanging from the ceiling and attached to the walls. There is also a dance floor and stage. The men's toilets are adorned with photos of naked women, and the menu comes in the form of a newspaper, and is translated into twenty-five languages. Every table used to have a bottle of flavoured vodka on it—everything from chocolate to lemon—and a kitchen roll in lieu of serviettes. The speciality is traditional Finnish food (suomalainen ruoka), such as sautéed reindeer, Karelian hotpot, and Lapp cheese with cloudberries. It's designed very much for tourists—although lots of locals go there—and has something of a Hard Rock Café feel about it.

Matti Pellonpää played the ongoing role of the greedy, exploitative manager Vladimir of the Leningrad Cowboys, who eventually becomes Moses, leading the band back to their home in Siberia. He went on to act in eighteen Aki Kaurismäki films, as well as appearing in the last sequence of Jim Jarmusch's compendium film *Night on Earth* (1991). Here, he plays the lugubrious taxi driver Mika who picks up three morosely inebriated workers in central Helsinki, one of whom is unconscious. "You called a taxi?" he asks. "No, we called a garbage truck," one of them answers, "but you'll have to do the job." They tell him the unconscious worker has lost his job, had his new car smashed up, his sixteen-year-old daughter is pregnant, and his wife has chased him out of the house with a knife. Mika tells them an even sadder story, about the loss of his premature baby daughter, and they lose sympathy for their comrade. He drops them off in workers' flats on the outskirts of the city, and the two conscious workers go off singing, leaving their unfortunate comrade to pay the fare from his severance pay. "Do you know where you are?" Mika asks him. "Yes, Helsinki," the worker answers, and sits in the snow in the middle of the road, as two workers greet him on their way to work. The sequence conveys a bleak view of the city, which is deserted, snow-bound, and barely visible from the confines of the taxi.[5] Some scenes were filmed around Senate Square, but give the impression that there is a traffic roundabout at the centre.

Pellonpää, famously referred to as a "sad rat" by Aki Kaurismäki and compared to Buster Keaton by von Bagh,[6] was himself a rock vocalist and lyric writer with the band Peltsix, a sextet based on his nickname "Peltsi." The band released two albums, *Liha ja leikkeletä* (*Meat and Cold Cuts*) and *Silkkaa kryptoniittia* (*Pure Kryptonite*) in the early 1990s. The band featured at various times steel guitar, accordion, violin, flute, baritone saxophone, talking drum, and angel choir, and was described thus by Lauri Timonen in his liner notes to a 2010 compilation by Peltsix:

Creative risk-taking and a quite adventurous variety of genres were typical working ways of the band. No idea was turned down outright and the likes of the musicians could be heard well in the hilariously changing tunes. Masculine melancholy and genuine strength originating from life in taverns, more sensitive self-confessional studies of love, and on the other hand, fiercely opinionated stands on uniting Europe lived in the stories played by the band. As a lyricist Pellonpää was a skilful painter of atmospheres: as a singer he was more of an interpreter of the dark tonalities rather than an actual professional musician ... In the end the running of this adult men's musical nursery served its members as psychotherapy and having fun: from the musical perspective, the unrestrained euphoria flooded with ideas and without fear—it was happy times lived full-heartedly.[7]

The band describe themselves as covering everything "from humppa to heavy," and they took a loose approach to their songs, combining elements of tango and *iskelmä* (Finnish Schlager) with Russian drinking songs, rock, and folk. Song titles include "Vahna nainen hautausmaalia" (Old Woman in the Graveyard) and "Viimeinem Valssi" (Last Waltz). There is a definite tongue-in-cheek quality of pure enjoyment about their songs.

In 2011, Pellonpää's old friend from acting school, Janne Kuusi, made *Boheemi Elää* (*Bohemian Eyes*), a documentary about the actor, with music by Pale Saarinen—an accordionist and composer, as well as a band mate in Peltsix—who stated in the liner notes for the soundtrack album:

In our texts Pellonpää dealt with weird dreams, love, longing, fear, pub ambience, as well as Parisian café life and political phenomenons [sic]. The themes were often familiar, but their metaphors and tragicomic world resembled miniature dramas.... In this roots styled film music I've composed, I've tried to bring out Pellonpää's sensitive, comical side. A certain mythology and gloomy nostalgia is there to hear, but also the down-to-earth side, hilarious joy of life and anticipation for reunion just like in those silent movies.[8]

The opening track, "Lonely Man on the Street," is a suitably melancholy, minor key tune; "Volga on My Mind" is a mournful musical saw solo; and other tracks are entitled "Tragicomic Life," "Misery" (a bleak guitar solo), and "The Accordion has been Drinking." "Rocking Peltsi" memorializes him in rock and roll mode, "Circus World" combines accordion and musical saw, and "Funny Friend" is a rollicking circus-styled tune with whistles. The album concludes with "The Bridge of Memories" sung by a female vocalist, Jonsu, which serves as a fitting memorial.

One of Aki Kaurismäki's most notable early films to star Pellonpää was *Calamari Union* (figure 1). This was a 1985 black-and-white film in which sixteen men (all called Frank, after Frank Armoton, the title of a 1981 Finnish crime novel by Martti Innanen; one Frank keeps quoting Robert De Niro from *Taxi Driver*) decide to leave Kallio, a traditional working-class suburb in east Helsinki, and set off on an odyssey to Eira, a wealthy suburb in the south, which they regard as a promised land. At one point in the film, they all appear onstage in a Helsinki club playing guitars in a rock band, singing "Bad boys are coming to break all your toys." In fact most of the actors in the film are from Helsinki rock bands, indeed von Bagh goes so far as to state they are "portrayed by all of the central figures of the Finnish rock'n'roll scene of the mid-eighties."[9] The brothers' first film, *Saimaa-ilmiö (The Saima Phenomenon)* (1981), was actually a rock music documentary featuring Juice Leskinen Slam and Eppu Normali—two key bands from Tampere, where Aki had studied journalism. Just two Franks manage to survive the journey—even though it is little more than a couple of kilometres—only to discover that Eeira is full of factories, building and construction sites, and dead fish along the shoreline of the lake, so after a fight, they decide to take a rowboat and head across the sea to Estonia. Sanna Peden writes of the film: "Widely considered as something of an inside joke by the 'Kaurismäki clan,' *Calamari Union* plays with the conventions and stereotypes of locality and belonging in the city."[10]

The soundtrack includes a song by Olavi Virta, the most popular Finnish iskelmä singer, "the king of Finnish tango," who recorded 600 songs and made several films before he died at the age of 57 in 1972. His career was cut short in 1962 by his arrest on a drunken driving charge, and he died in alcoholic poverty. His music is frequently played in the Elite Restaurant, an elegant 1930s-style art deco restaurant with a classic Finnish menu and an outside terrace, which is a traditional hangout for artists, writers, and bohemians, with paintings on the walls allegedly left by artists in lieu of the bill, and a dish called "Tono Paolo's onion steak" after a legendary Finnish film actor. Matti Pellonpää also has a table there in his honour (he was also featured on a postage stamp in 1996). When I went to the Elite with a Finnish friend, my friend said after the meal, "My compliments to the chef," to which the waiter replied, "So he can keep his job then?"

It was a classic Kaurismäki moment, reminiscent of the 1996 *Drifting Clouds*. Winner of five Jussi awards, the film features a drunken chef, as well as a deadpan tram driver named Lauri and his wife, an equally deadpan head waitress named Ilona, played by another regular Kaurismäki actor, Kati Outinen. On the same day, Lauri loses his job driving the tram and Ilona loses her job at the central Helsinki Dubrovnik restaurant. The Dubrovnik is also the name of a converted cinema-cum nightclub in the basement of the Andorra bar in Helsinki owned by the Kaurismäki brothers, which has a photo of Pellonpää on the wall. Next door to the Dubrovnik in Erinkatu in the Kampi district central Helsinki, there is another Kaurismäki-owned bar, the Moskova, formerly a film set, which is famous for its vodka and specializes in 1970s Soviet Union décor (the window is hidden by a thick pleated white curtain so you can't see inside), and a gruff barmaid, with a record player playing music by Alla Pugacheva and other 1970s Russian pop singers. Its droll, deadpan atmosphere is classic Kaurismäki.

Drifting Clouds was originally written for Pellonpää and Kati Outinen. After Pellonpää's death, Kaurismäki had to rewrite it: he made Outinen the protagonist and cast Kari Vään-änen, whom he has continued to work with, as her husband. With a loan from Ilona's former boss, the couple sets up their own restaurant in Eira, which they call "Work," with former Dubrovnik employees. On opening night, they get a reservation from a Helsinki union for thirty people. The film features more music by Rauli "Badding" Somerjoki, in-cluding the song performed over the opening and closing credits, which provides its title. The film is also dedicated to Somerjoki. And in the scene in which Ilona has a quiet mo-ment next to the photo of the couple's lost child, the photo used was a childhood photo of Pellonpää. *Drifting Clouds* includes another song by Olavi Virta, whose songs are used over a dozen times in nine Kaurismäki films, including his version of "Over the Rainbow" at the end of *Ariel*.[11]

On the role of music in his films, and his tendency not to use specially composed music, Aki Kaurismäki has stated:

> *I have tried to make a clear break with overintrusive film music. I don't want the music to block out the image … For me, music serves somewhat the same purpose as at public dances, where people are too shy to utter a word but the music makes up for the conversation. The muteness of my characters may seem exotic to people abroad, and one they cannot under-stand as they dance ecstatically in their loin-cloths from sunrise to sunset. But there is also a personal reason behind it: when, as a young man, I tried to approach someone at a public dance, the reply was curt and I was left alone with the music.*[12]

Kaurismäki sees dancing the tango as the only chance for asocial, tongue-tied Finns to meet one another and reproduce, and went so far as to make the controversial statement that tango was born in Finland. In 2013, an Argentinian-Finnish documentary film, *Midsummer Night's Tango* (Poski poskea vasten), directed by German film-maker Viviane Blumenschein, premiered at the Espoo Film Festival in Helsinki, challenging Kaurismäki's statement. The film is a road movie exploring the origins of Finnish tango with the Argentinian singer Chino Laborde, the guitarist Diego "DIPI" Kvitko, and the bandoneon player Pablo Greco, who test the accuracy of Kaurismäki's claim. They even interview him, along with several ex-ponents of Finnish tango in the 1960s, such as the eccentric M. A. Numminen, a polymath musician and author who was a key figure in the Finnish underground, a pioneer of elec-tronic music, as well as a jazz, rock, and Schlager musician. He also composed songs based on Wittgenstein's *Tractatus Logico-Philosophicus* and a sex manual. Made in Porteño, Finnish, and English, and set in Buenos Aires and throughout Finland, *Midsummer Night's Tango* goes beyond national stereotypes and explores the viability of intergenerational cross-cultural col-laboration between the two nations. After the screening in Espoo, there was an evening of tango dancing at a local club, which was attended by the film's director and editor. [13]

One of the musical staples of Aki Kaurismäki's films is rock and roll songs by the Renegades, a British beat group from Birmingham, who moved to Finland in the mid-1960s and became almost as big as the Beatles there. Their lead singer and guitarist, Kim Brown, who later formed Kim and the Cadillacs in Italy in 1975, returned to Helsinki in the early 1980s and took up residence there until his death in 2011. They are reputedly Kaurismäki's favourite band. Their most well-known song was their version of British rocker Vince Taylor's "Brand New Cadillac" (1959), which the group shortened to "Cadillac" and credited as their own song.[14] It reached number two on the Finnish charts in 1964, and was included on the 1960s compilation *Finnish Graffiti*. The song has appeared in at least two Kaurismäki films, quite incongruously: *Crime and Punishment* (1983), where it shares billing with Schubert, Shostakovich, Olavi Virta, and Billie Holliday, and *The Match Factory Girl* (1990), a variation on Hans Christian Andersen's "Little Match Girl." In the latter film, the protagonist Iris—played by Kati Outinen—is pregnant, abandoned, lonely, and desolate; she suffers from deep depression, and "Cadillac" breaks the mood drastically and devastatingly. Not exactly "overintrusive," but definitely disruptive. Iris subsequently begins poisoning all the men in her life.

Probably Aki Kaurismäki's greatest musical coup was to coax the 1950s iskelmä singer Annikki Tähti back from retirement for *Man Without a Past*. In the film, she plays the manager of the Salvation Army flea market, and sings her famous 1954 song "Muistatko Monrepos'n" (Do You Remember Monrepos?)—the first gold record in Finland—at the end of the film, as the couple walk off into the night (and are blocked out by a passing goods train in a typical Kaurismäki moment). Her voice is a little shaky, but it certainly evokes memories of the 1950s. Tähti went into retirement in the early 1960s to concentrate on her family, and made a comeback in 1978 before going into permanent retirement.

Helsinki Tourism offers a three-hour tour of Kaurismäki's Helsinki, although it points out that the director has said "every one of our shooting locations has usually been demolished a day or at least a couple of years later." The tour includes following the Franks' quest for Eira in *Calamari Union*, "some interiors that still actually exist," a stop at the scene of the Leningrad Cowboys' *Total Balalaika Show*, and at Mockba (aka Bar Mokova).[15] The geographer Sirpa Tani writes: "Places play a central role in Aki Kaurismäki's films, but they do not necessarily refer directly to the physical reality in which the films were shot.... Easily recognizable landmarks of cities are conspicuous by their absence. They are substituted by side streets, grey backyards, dock areas, and stuffy bars."[16]

Tani suggests three approaches in Kaurismäki's use of Helsinki locations: the antithesis between city and country, banal urban environments as mindscapes, and the relation to public marketing of the city to tourists. In the first instance, this dichotomy is destroyed in *Ariel* (1988), where the protagonist Taisto, a coal miner, experiences "both Helsinki and the desolate countryside … as merciless places" and the film ends with his flight with his new family to an unknown destination (which turns out to be Mexico). Likewise, in *Cala-*

mari Union, disillusionment leads to flight. In *Drifting Clouds*, very middle-class settings in central Helsinki, in which the characters have a tenuous foothold, are linked to the 1990s economic recession. Kaurismäki has said of the film: "I wouldn't have any self-esteem left if I didn't make a film about unemployment right now."[17] *Man Without a Past* is set in a port village constructed from containers and in Alppiharju, a working-class neighbourhood where The Salvation Army is based. But this environment is transformed by the film's lighting and photography into glowing locations that are full of hope, and become beautiful. Thirdly, as a result of Kaurismäki's films, in which a number of characters end up either in prison or fleeing abroad, Tani claims Finns began to think that "foreign viewers would form a distorted image of Finland and Finns." The "Nordic Oddity" tourist campaign, which included recognition of "bohemian Helsinki," came into being in 2005. As a result, Tani concludes, "the Kaurismäkian city has become an attractive object for marketing and a cultural element with which the Finnish people can collectively identify themselves."[18]

A recent colourful brochure published by the Helsinki Tourist and Convention Bureau in 2012 promotes Helsinki as "Nordic Oddity, Alternative, Bliss, Creative," promoting tours of Kallio ("get to know local rock musicians in the Beaver bar"), block parties, flea markets, second-hand boutiques, night clubs, roadside kiosks, ethnic shopping, recycled products, karaoke bars, skateboarding sites, live music venues, jazz and rock festivals, and the annual Night of the Arts on 22 August, when the city is filled with hundreds of musical and theatrical events, as well as the usual shopping centres and restaurants. The Kaurismäki brothers clearly now provide a cool, hipster-ish image with which to attract tourists, even if they are not mentioned in the brochure.[19] The Five Corners, an intersection of five streets in the Viiskulma district, which features in a couple of car chases in their early films, is also mentioned as "famous for its record shops and other interesting boutiques."[20]

In conclusion, although Aki Kaurismäki has taken up residence in Portugal, and his most recent film, *Le Havre* (2011) is set in France, there is clearly much of Helsinki in his films, at least up as far as *Man Without a Past*. Although much of it may be anonymous—like the Baaribar (literally "Bar bar"), Manne's local in *The Worthless*, presided over by Vasili, the droll, wisecracking barman who is concerned about his business dropping off when a saxophone player takes up residence outside—it is generally characterized by bohemian eccentricity. As Sanna Peden notes:

> *There is a curious disjuncture … in Kaurismäki's Helsinki. The anonymity of the places on screen plays an important role in the films' social critique, while at the same time the real-life locations correspond with the protagonists' rising and falling fortune as the films' "local logic" takes advantage of the reputations and identities of specific parts of the city.*[21]

One consistent factor in Aki Kaurismäki's films, including those he made with his brother, is his focus on the underdog, even at the risk of embracing melodrama (as in the *Match*

Factory Girl). Even the upwardly mobile couple in *Drifting Clouds* are struggling, and the emphasis there on work depicts them as proletarian, trying to survive in an increasingly neo-liberal world. The protagonist of *Man Without a Past* finds himself in harmony with the derelict world and the Salvation Army workers he mixes with, and eventually retrieves enough memory to discover that he used to work as a welder. Kaurismäki's characters have been referred to as "losers", at odds with their environment, but most of them have redeeming qualities.[22] And Kaurismäki's Helsinki may be a disappearing city, but it is nonetheless a very memorable one.

Endnotes

1 Peter von Bagh, "The Comedy of Losers," in Marja-Leena Hukkanen, *Shadows in Paradise: Photographs from the Films of Aki Kaurismäki* (Helsinki: Otava Publishing Company Limited, 1997) pp. 14–15.

2 Pietari Kääpä (2013), "The Worthless / Arvottomat (1982)," in *World Film Locations: Helsinki*, ed. Pietari Kääpä and Silja Laine (Bristol: Intellect, 2013) p. 68.

3 http://www.leningradcowboys.fi/read/items/red-x-mas-party-2013.html.

4 Peter von Bagh, (2000) *Drifting Shadows: A guide to the Finnish Cinema* (Helsinki: The Gamut Oy, 2000).

5 At one stage in filming, the cab got stuck on a tram tracks, and the actors thought the end was nigh.

6 von Bagh, *Drifting Shadows* p. 106.

7 Lauri Timonen (2009), liner notes to Peltsix, *Pikku juttu sadan vuoden päästä 1989–1995*, Compilation CD, Poko Rekords, 2010.

8 Pale Saarinen, *Bohemian Eyes—Boheemi Elää*, Original Soundtrack (Vantaa: Running Moose, 2011).

9 von Bagh, "The Comedy of Losers" p. 19.

10 Sanna Peden (2013), "From Hämeentie: The Local Logic of Aki Kaurismäki's Helsinki," in Kääpä and Laine, *World Film Locations* p. 76.

11 Peter von Bagh, "The Musical World of Aki Kaurismäki," in *Jukebox: Music in the Films of Aki Kaurismäki* (Megamania CD, 2006).

12 Ibid.

13 Espoo, a rather characterless suburb outside Helsinki, was also the setting of a teenage "bad girl" film by Hanna Maylett, *The Last Virgin in Espoo* (Espoon viimeinen neitsyt, 2003), about two girls who hitchhike to a rock festival.

14 A copyright claim later ensued, and Taylor's name was added to the credits.

15 http://www.visithelsinki.fi/en/sightseeing-trips-and-guidances/kaurismakis-helsinki.

16 Sirpa Tani, "The Aesthetics of Backyards: Spaces and Places in Aki Kaurismäki's Films" (2007) http://www.orimattilankirjasto.fi/en/aki-kaurismaki-english/viewpoints-to-films-list/144-tani-sirpa-the-aesthetics-of-backyards-spaces-and-places-in-aki-kaurismakis-films.

17 von Bagh, "The Comedy of Losers."

18 Tani, "The Aesthetics of Backyards."

19 The September 2013 issue of the Helsinki-based English language magazine *Six Degrees* contained an article interrogating the hipster phenomenon in Helsinki after the tenth annual 2013 Flow Festival, a rock music festival that attracts many local hipsters. See: Yorrick Iunga (2013), "Keeping Their Cool: A Closer Look at the Hipster Subculture," *Six Degrees*, Issue 7 (September 2013): 8–9.

20 City of Helsinki Tourist and Convention Bureau, *Helsinki Nordic Oddity: Alternative, Bliss, Creative* (2012).

21 Sanna Peden (2013), "From Hämeentie: The Local Logic of Aki Kaurismäki's Helsinki," in Kääpä and Laine, *World Film Locations* p. 77.

22 von Bagh, "The Comedy of Losers."

"THE ECHO OF THE WALL FADES": REFLECTIONS ON THE "BERLIN SCHOOL" IN THE EARLY 1970s

Tim Caspar Boehme

Until today, "Krautrock" has remained a curious cultural outgrowth. During the 1960s and 1970s, German musicians tried to emancipate themselves from the Anglo-American rock mainstream. Initially, this attempt gained little public resonance in Germany, yet over subsequent decades Krautrock extended its international influence as a source of inspiration and has generated distinctive strands of music that remain difficult to classify. These musical currents, as in the case of the duo Cluster, can be thought of as aesthetic reflections on specific topographies, especially when compared to other representatives of the so-called Berlin School. Since Cluster's career has undergone many changes, we first need to address the general background against which we can interpret their music.

A distinction between regional schools is common in the historiography of Krautrock, exemplified by the differentiation between a "Düsseldorf School" and a "Berlin School." On the one hand, it is legitimate to categorize quite heterogeneous musicians by regional criteria subsumed under "Krautrock," an ambivalent term from an artist's perspective,[1] since bands from Düsseldorf—such as early Kraftwerk and Neu!—share stylistic commonalities that distinguish them from the specific idiosyncrasies of their Berlin-Krautrock colleagues Tangerine Dream or Klaus Schulze: "motoric" rhythms for the former; open, spacious sequencer-patterns for the latter. On the other hand, generalizations of this kind may lead to sweeping gestures of incorporation, which ignore artistic as well as local details.

2

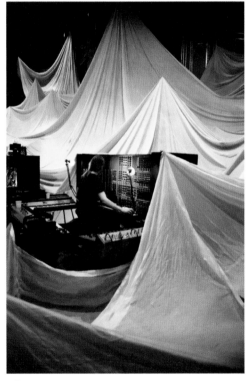

1

1 Tangerine Dream in concert at the Royal Albert Hall, London, June 1976.
Photo: Andrew Putler.
Courtesy of Getty Images/ Referns.

2 Christopher Franke, Peter Baumann, and Edgar Froese in London, January 1974.
Photo: Michael Putland. Courtesy of Getty Images/Hulton Archive.

An amusing example of geographical carelessness is the entry for the "Düsseldorf School of electronic music" in the English-language Wikipedia, which claims that "The Düsseldorf School of electronic music, or just Düsseldorf School, was a development of electronic music in the 1970s, shaped by Düsseldorf-based artists like Kraftwerk, Cluster, Can and Neu!"[2] This would surprise readers from Cologne, since the city's most internationally well-known band, Can, has apparently been relocated about forty kilometres downstream to Düsseldorf—also located on the river Rhine, but for centuries a rival urban centre.

On top of that only about half of the bands mentioned have ever resided in Düsseldorf for a noteworthy period of time. The duo Cluster (composed of Dieter Moebius and Hans Joachim Roedelius), also mentioned in the Wikipedia entry, started in West Berlin in the late 1960s—initially as a trio with Conrad Schnitzler under the name of Kluster. But after their first concert in West Berlin in 1970, a twelve-hour performance in the Galerie Hammer at the Europa-Centre, they left the city—still as a trio—with their post bus heading for West Germany.[3] They played concerts in Düsseldorf and recorded their first three albums in Cologne at the studio of sound engineer Konrad "Conny" Plank, who was responsible for the sound of countless Krautrock records. Shortly after, they split from Conrad Schnitzler, who devoted himself to a chaotic yet productive solo career.[4] Moebius and Roedelius continued as Cluster and toured with their bus for a few years.

Then in 1974, Moebius and Roedelius settled in a village named Forst in the Weser Hills. There they actually came into prolonged contact with the Düsseldorf School. Together with Michael Rother—the guitarist of the influential, but for a long time almost unnoticed, band Neu!—they formed a commune and a short-lived "Krautrock supergroup"[5] under the name Harmonia. During this period, the duo sought to preserve their musical independence and continued to release records as Cluster.

Hence, Düsseldorf was not overly represented in Cluster's history. In comparison, the time in West Berlin was much more formative. Even if it was not until they reached West Germany that Cluster turned into the duo that would emerge as one of the major influences for later artists in electronic music. Cluster's music illustrates that the identification of *regionale Spezifika* (regional specifics) is by no means far-fetched. Their music reveals several characteristic features, which can be read as a response to the historical situation of West Berlin, without automatically ascribing Cluster to a Berlin School. We could argue that Cluster's music, released between 1971 and 1972, reflects some common features of the Berlin School in an exaggerated form.

Yet, we should pause over the expression "Berlin School," which strictly speaking refers to a specific musical development in West Berlin after 1974. The albums *Phaedra* (Virgin 1974) by Tangerine Dream, and also Günter Schickert's *Samtvogel* (self-published 1974) count as the earliest examples. In order to carve out the diverging characteristics of Cluster, we first have to outline some of the typical elements of their West Berlin colleagues as a contrasting lens.

3

The Berlin School, as exemplified by Tangerine Dream's *Phaedra*, is marked by synthesizer sounds that—especially in the title track—slowly progress in repetitively meandering sequencer patterns. The tracks are frequently side filling and refrain from a clear form, yet they reveal a mostly tonal and, to a certain degree, melodic build-up. Moreover, sequencers predetermine a steady pulse as rhythm. It is a form of music that seems to reach into unknown spaces with a *suchende Rastlosigkeit* (seeking restlessness).

Instead of using synthesizers for his debut album *Samtvogel*, Günter Schickert worked with guitar, voice, and echo to create long loops, which can to some extent be seen as the acoustically generated equivalent to Tangerine Dream's sequencer lines. Schickert's pieces, which equally fill complete album sides, revolve more strongly around themselves. With their repetitive set-up, they create an almost claustrophobic atmosphere of being marooned. While Tangerine Dream transgress the boundaries of the Wall, Schickert seems to obsessively pace

3 Tangerine Dream, *Electronic Meditation*, originally released in 1970.

Album sleeve design by Reinhard Hippen, photo by Monique Froese.

4

alongside the oppressive structure. Rhythmically, his music is indeed less clearly contoured. But it still shows rudiments of melody and occasionally even harmony.

None of this applies to the early work of Cluster. There are no harmonies, no melodies, and no recognizable rhythms. Back then, Cluster did not own any synthesizers, even if their music is almost indistinguishable from electronic music. The boundary between *Klang* (sound) and *Geräusch* (noise) is almost dissolved, and elements of their music are constantly in flux, even if at a pace that seems to follow its own rules.[6] The only obvious parallel to the Berlin School, their first album *Cluster* (Philips 1971) consists of three extensive pieces, which Cluster consequently named after their length: "7:42," "15:43," "21:30." This choice of abstract titles reads as a reference to the barely tangible character

4 Cluster performing live (ca. 1971). Courtesy of Metro-nome/Universal.

of their music, whose sounds of seemingly unclear origin slowly move forward and fade away like signals in outer space—even if *Schall* (referring to various types of "acoustic noise") does not exist there.

Cluster created music with extremely simple instruments, such as the guitar and electronic organ, which pushed all boundaries of established rock genres. In their music, which Kraut-rock ambassador Julian Cope described as a "vast weather balloon of sound" in his book *Krautrocksampler*, new arrangements imaginatively emerge from a putative chaos.[7] It anticipates abstract ambient and noise sounds, which increasingly emerged as part of electronic underground phenomena in the 1990s. Their early music as Kluster hinted at the direction Cluster would pursue, but retained isolated instrumental sounds, such as guitar, cello, or organ, and combined these, at least on the first two records, with recited texts.

Such grand gestures, with which all restrictions of rhythm, scale, and chord structures are abandoned, stand in striking contrast with the spatial limitations of the "cartographic cut-out" of West Berlin. Cluster produced these sounds at a time, when they were no longer living in Berlin (only Dieter Moebius moved back to Berlin years later), however, their break with almost all musical conventions can be read as a revolt, echoing the narrowness of the Berlin left behind. It seems as if moving out of the urban enclave set free new energies to assert maximum autonomy over the previous sense of local confinement, yet set within the temporal limits of conventional sound media.

On their second album *Cluster II* (Brain 1972) Moebius and Roedelius resume their strategies of *Geräuschentfaltung* (free sound development), but chose shorter pieces. Now, we can also pick out one or two guitar, organ, and piano sounds. The overall atmosphere is still made of dense, otherworldly sound excursions like "an incessant nightscape: a helicopter ride over miles of countryside, but the lights of the city ever present."[8] Cluster remain abstract and definitely less "musical" than say Tangerine Dream on their album *Electronic Meditation* (Ohr 1970), which was released two years earlier and similarly radical. However, despite all their experimentation, we can clearly identify instruments such as cello, guitar, flute, or drums, and it remains much more conventional in the ways instruments are used: here, musicians who know their craft play conventional but unusually arranged notes. Lacking the necessary technical requirements, Cluster had a certain degree of freedom to override any expectations towards sound generation which may have arisen.

In their collective rejection of existing structure and time, Cluster and the Berlin School display a kind of loose continuity, a form that transcends physical spatiality in a movement towards discretely shaped *Fantasieräume* (fantasy spaces). With Neu! the Düsseldorf School had a perfect realization of "driving music," in which the drums, with their incessant quaver beat, pressed forward like a four-stroke engine (Kraftwerk would score an international hit in 1974 with their programmatic album *Autobahn*). West Berlin music did not have a mechanics drifting by on predetermined tracks. For the Düsseldorf School, however, this could be interpreted as a celebration of a West German industrialized *Nachkriegsmoderne* (post-war modernism), especially in the music of Kraftwerk. The Berliners, by contrast, are either lacking the actively regulative metre completely, as with Cluster, or have yet to find it, as with Tangerine Dream.

We should certainly not overplay the juxtaposition of an open, modern West Germany with a closed-off, left behind West Berlin—which in the case of Cluster, to a certain extent heralds the punk-inspired attitude of refusal of later bands such as Einstürzende Neubauten. A specific detail in Cluster's further development seems to support such a contrasting interpretation: in 1974, after a two-year break, when Cluster lived in Forst together with Neu! guitarist Michael Rother, their album *Zuckerzeit* (Brain 1974) was released. The sounds of Moebius and Roedelius appear to have been completely interchanged: we can hear "programmed," if somewhat stumbling rhythms with a corresponding beat; and though naively twisted, there is even the unmistakeable presence of melodies.

In part, this development can be traced back to the fact that Cluster, once they made music with Neu!'s Rother, had to agree to a certain set of common rules, and thus took up beats and tones in their repertoire. As a precaution, Moebius and Roedelius preferred to use the black keys of their instruments.[9] This novelty can be read as if Cluster had finally arrived in "the West" with *Zuckerzeit*. At this point, however, the Berlin *Freiheitsmodell* (model of freedom) seems very far away as the echo of the wall fades. Meanwhile in the enclave city, the Berlin School further pursued it in varied forms at least indirectly. But its extreme form, as adopted by Cluster in the years of 1971 and 1972, should be considered a particular case.

Translation by Sandra Jasper

Endnotes

1 See, Tim Caspar Boehme, "Pioniere aus Düsseldorf," *die tageszeitung*, 28 July 2009 p. 15.

2 https://en.wikipedia.org/wiki/D%C3%BCsseldorf_School_%28Krautrock%29. accessed 31 August 2013.

3 Kathrin Ohlmann, "Bin ich noch Avantgarde?" *Jungle World*, 40.4, October 2012, http://jungle-world.com/artikel/2012/40/46347.html. Last accessed 12 September 2013.

4 Markus von Schwerin, "Cluster: Die Bildermacher," *Jazzthetik* (3+4) (2010): 79ff.

5 Julian Cope, Krautrocksampler: *One Head's Guide to the Great Kosmische Musik—1968 Onwards*, (Yatesbury: Head Heritage, 1995) p. 45.

6 This semantic distinction between the words *Klang* and *Geräusch* is very subtle, with the former denoting a more aesthetic connotation referring to the harmonic, melodic, and pleasant aspects of sound. The latter indicates more general types of acoustic phenomena that are ordinarily caused unintentionally. The word *Schall*, mentioned in the same paragraph, is a more technical term, which refers to the physics of sound as wave-like vibrations that resonate. Translator's note.

7 Julian Cope, *Krautrocksampler* p. 44.

8 Ibid. p. 20.

9 See, Tim Caspar Boehme, "Märchen erfinden," *De:Bug* (139) (2010): 50.

MARGINS MUSIC: LOST FUTURES IN LONDON'S EDGELANDS

Andrew Harris

In Patrick Keiller's 1994 documentary fiction film, *London*, shot over the course of 1992, the city appears sluggish and defeated. The financial services sector of the City of London is reeling from an economic slump, a massive IRA bomb, and the sudden withdrawal from the European Exchange Rate Mechanism (a precursor to the Euro); there is talk of the City "losing its international position" and a "fear of redundancy in the air."[1] Further east along the Thames, the gleaming new skyscrapers of Canary Wharf are deemed a "failure" and have been placed into administration. The political situation appears moribund with a "civic void" in London's government following the abolition in 1986 of the Greater London Council and a deliberate failure to install a replacement metropolitan administration. A sense of national stasis has meant that, as the film's narrator reports, even the *Financial Times* came out in support of the Labour Party before the general election that year—won for the fourth time in a row by the Conservative Party. Much of London's riverbank is forlorn: the two large, brick power stations at Bankside and Battersea, designed by Giles Gilbert Scott in the mid-twentieth century, lie quiet and empty, as they have since their closure in 1981 and 1983 respectively. At Vauxhall, the only building site visible is that for the new headquarters of the British secret service, MI6.

Keiller's film involves a series of excursions through London by an anonymous narrator, voiced by Paul Schofield, and his friend, the unseen Robinson. Robinson, a part-time teacher in art and architecture at the "University of Barking," has resumed his research on the "problem of London." He is increasingly disillusioned with London's political situation and its seemingly ingrained discomfort with modern city life, claiming "just now, London is all waste, without a future." The film's use of a static camera (apart from one moment in Brent Cross Shopping Centre) and slow sequence between shots reinforces a sense of standstill and inertia. Yet Robinson, and the innovative style and narrative framing of the film, do not necessarily indicate a simple resignation to the state of London in 1992. Robinson reimagines possibilities and scenarios for London, particularly through reference to French writers, such as Rimbaud, Verlaine, and Baudelaire. He speculates that the City of London could be reinvigorated as a new bohemian quarter of artists, although recognizes that "it will be a long time until the Bank of England reopens as a discothèque."[2] Robinson also sees promise and poetry away from London's fossilized and declining centre, suggesting to the narrator that "if we were to find modernity anywhere, it would be in the suburbs."

This essay develops Robinson's assessment that urban modernity in London during this period is to be located at the edges of what had become a fractured and fragile metropolis.[3] But rather than "optimistically" setting out, as Robinson does, to "the suburbs of North West London" and the "Valley of the River Brent," we will travel in an opposite direction to the borders of London with Essex. And whereas Robinson expected to "find new artistic and literary activity emerging everywhere," our emphasis is on some of the musical signals that could be detected. While the only music Robinson seemingly finds on his westward travels is the cheerful strumming of two Peruvian guitarists, Carlos and Aquiles, this essay celebrates two unheralded, experimental guitar bands from the outer edges of East London: Bark Psychosis and Disco Inferno. The music they recorded in the early 1990s was marginal in its position both to the bright lights of central London and mainstream British musical currents. This marginality has been further reinforced by the way, as the cultural studies author Roger Silverstone suggests, "suburbia has remained curiously invisible in accounts of modernity."[4] Yet unearthing and foregrounding their work from East London's edgelands between 1992 and 1994 reveals a music that was furiously modern and breathtakingly futuristic.[5] Whereas Robinson "looked at the surface of the city to reveal to him the molecular basis of historical events, and in this way he hoped to see into the future," we will closely *listen* to the city during this period in the hope of recharting lost urban futures.

Bark Psychosis was started by schoolfriends Graham Sutton and John Ling in Snaresbrook in the late 1980s. They released their first singles on South Woodford's Cheree Records in 1990 when the band members' average age was seventeen; another two singles followed in 1992, including the epic twenty-one-minute *Scum*, while an album, *Hex*, was released in 1994. Their multi-instrumental music, often deploying electronic effects and echoes, deliberately defied and unpicked traditional rock strictures; there were rarely any choruses, while guitars were used as facilitators of timbres, atmospheres, and textures rather than riffs. Although capable of moments of extreme noise, their songs tended to stretch and float, albeit always hinting at a mood of unease and disaffection.

1

Disco Inferno released their first singles, recorded in Leyton, as teenagers in 1991 on an imprint of the same record label as Bark Psychosis. Guitarist/vocalist Ian Crause and bassist Paul Wilmott lived round the corner from each other in Redbridge, while drummer Rob Whatley lived two tube stops away along the Central line at Newbury Park. Between 1992 and 1994, they released five EPs and an album *D.I. Go Pop*, which thrillingly combined the sonic possibilities of sampling with traditional rock instrumentation. Their music was more immediately sharp, tense, and politicized, and was framed through a more pop-orientated format than Bark Psychosis's; a starting template was the post-punk paranoia of Joy Division rather than the English pastoralism of late period Talk Talk. Yet there were similar moments of space and silence in the music; indeed, *From the Devil to the Deep Blue Sky* (1993) was "influenced by the long song structures that Bark Psychosis were putting together at the time."[6] Members of Bark Psychosis and Disco Inferno both grew up in and around landscapes of

1 Bark Psychosis, *Hex* (1994).

interwar, modest, semi-detached houses, and cul-de-sacs, mini-roundabouts, school playing fields, and ribbon developments of shops along arterial roads.[7] These landscapes might be understood as orderly, banal, and drab. But for these two bands, as with the punk contingent of mid-1970s Bromley or the dubstep scene of early-2000s Croydon, the edgelands of London also induced a certain spark, provocation, and hallucination. Bark Psychosis and Disco Inferno sought to warp and weft temporal and spatial understandings of London as a way of shaking out and reclaiming London's future. The narrator in *London* suggests Robinson "seemed to be attempting to travel through time," aiming to fold the eighteenth century back into the city. The much younger Disco Inferno and Bark Psychosis could be understood as impatiently seeking to make London resonate with the "very edge of the future."[8] Robinson summons the lives and imaginative worlds of Romantic French and English writers, all of them with personal connections to London, in an attempt at reimagining and reconfiguring the contemporary city of 1992. Bark Psychosis and Disco Inferno similarly used sampling technology to plug into and rewire the temporary possibilities and burdens of East London. Disco Inferno's music from *Summer's Last Sound* (1992) onwards is a collage of birds, fireworks, clocks, bells, camera shutters, crowds chanting, the crash of cars, lapping waves, and much more—as played by band members via MIDI interfaces. The insistent loop of crowd noise on Bark Psychosis's *Tooled Up* (1992) parallels some of these soundscapes, but otherwise, their use of sampling was less explicit. Yet, all of Bark Psychosis's releases feature sampling and studio innovation, especially in the manipulation and computer editing of their own instruments and vocals. As Graham Sutton commented in 1994, "I'm very much into using technology in ways it hasn't been used before."[9]

This emphasis on sampling was influenced by the new sonic frontiers being pursued in the late 1980s by groups such as Consolidated, the Young Gods, My Bloody Valentine, and Public Enemy. Nevertheless, Bark Psychosis and Disco Inferno's sampling should also be situated within the sonic innovations of rave and hardcore erupting from London's Essex borders during the early 1990s. Samples looped in and out of furious electronic tracks produced by SL2 from Loughton or The Prodigy from Braintree, or on records such as Timelapse's *Sued for a Sample* (1992) released by the Out of Romford label. Ian Crause remembers band members in 1992 listening to "pirate stations broadcasting rave and jungle music around north London, speeding up the rave tracks they'd danced to the night before and sticking their own drums on."[10] In some respects, a tradition for technological modernity and innovation in this part of London was being continued and advanced. Whereas Lea Valley in the early 1890s had spawned inventions of plastic and petrol, these fringe areas of London in the early 1990s forged a crucible for populist experiments with computer-based musical technology that continue to reverberate.

As well as connecting their music to the futurist drive of local rave cultures, Disco Inferno and Bark Psychosis's use of sampling also directly drew on the sound-worlds of these East London edges. Traffic noises and the gentle hum of Stratford can clearly be heard at the start of Bark Psychosis's *Scum* (1992)—recorded in the crypt of St John's Church—which also features a recording of a Pentecostal choir next door.[11] Disco Inferno's use of London's ambient sounds is less direct, aside from a recording of their clearly unhappy landlady at the end of the *D.I.Go Pop* album. But the pavement footsteps, breaking glass, revving engines, police sirens, and squealing brakes of their sample sources noticeably draw and dwell on the everyday noises and emotions of London life. Moreover, their jarring sounds, interwoven with basslines and guitar melodies, evoke the distinct layering and folding of memories and senses of place peculiar to London—a city where the suburb in its modern form was first created. The Eastern edges of London are characterized by a heterogeneous accumulation of land uses and architectural visions: garden cities and municipal estates rub up against new-build housing, industrial sheds meet waste grounds, shopping malls, and nature reserves. Disco Inferno's pile-up of sounds, and frequently buried vocals, capture and respond to this often bewildering enmeshing of landscapes and histories on London's fringe.

As well as the use of sampling to open up the jumbled histories, present-day environments, and technological futures of London's eastern edgelands, the music of Bark Psychosis and Disco Inferno also probed and reflected their position of geographical and socio-economic marginality within the city. The imaginative worlds of these two bands betray a location in a part of outer London possessing particular topographical characteristics and class dynamics, especially in contrast to more congested and wealthier central zones. The cover of Bark Psychosis's 1994 album *Hex* is revealing in this respect. It shows a ground-level view across an archetypal London edge landscape: scrubland, fencing, pylons, an isolated row of houses, distant lights, and tower blocks. There is no one visible apart from some shadows in the foreground, while most of the image is dominated by the bruised, early night sky. Bark Psychosis's soundscapes capture much of this strangely abandoned and disconnected setting: *Hex* begins with the lyrics "you stand apart with the sinking sunlight" and proceeds to refer to "your street deserted"; while space and silence pervade their music with almost four minutes of distant ambient noise tapering away on their (non-album) track *Hex* (1994).[12]

Disco Inferno's lyrical concerns and soundscapes also respond to the specific environment and geographical position of London's eastern periphery. As Ian Crause acknowledges, "we were straight from the A12, close to London but definitely not a part of it—on the outside looking in."[13] *The Atheist's Burden* (1994) celebrates the "deep blue" early morning skies found away from light pollution in the centre; in Ian Crause's lyrics, these provide a glimpse of a future unburdened by the "marks" of the past.[14] The "gulls coming off the coast" to scavenge inland in *Summer's Last Sound* (1992) and the samples and title of *Even the Sea Sides Against Us* (1994) hint at their location close to the wide expanses of the Thames estuary and the faded resorts of the Essex coast; while *At the End of the Line* (1994) mourns not only a sense of social and technological progress but is suggestive of their location towards the end of the Central Line.

For both bands, this sense of being out on the margins was reflected and reinforced by a precarious and uncertain financial position. As Ian Crause intimates in *Even the Sea Sides Against Us*, "We don't expect to be seen/We don't expect to be heard/Money's tight at the moment." Disco Inferno could only afford basic, outdated MIDI equipment in 1992—with this purchase marked by the release of a compilation of their early tracks entitled *In Debt*. Despite signing a new recording contract in 1992, members of Bark Psychosis were on the dole and living in squats.[15] As Graham Sutton almost inaudibly mutters on *Fingerspit* (1994), "Everyday and everynight/streets leave their mark on my skin/This city breaks you down." The national economic uncertainty and political malaise of this period, as documented by Keiller's film, compounded affairs. In *Summer's Last Sound* (1992), a track described by Crause as "about the decay I saw around me in London during the recession of the early 1990s," it is reported that the "price of bread went up five pence today."[16] His lyrics also express a sense of "raw violence" brewing at both home and abroad, with "hushed-up trials" and an immigrant "kicked again today."

One response to this perilous and threatening situation was, like Robinson's expeditions through London, to keep moving. In the Bark Psychosis track, *Big Shot* (1994), Graham Sutton intones, "It's 3 a.m./Don't know where we're going/Just drive somewhere fast." Ian Crause is similarly restless in his "waiting for a future to come along and sweep us away." He is continually frustrated in finding "a rock to cling to," "a safe place to land," and "a corner at the edge of a map."[17] Yet unlike Daniel Defoe's shipwrecked Robinson, Disco Inferno's music remains adrift, and the futures they survey remain frustratingly out of reach despite being "so close" and "in the palm of your hand."[18] In 1995, with much of their equipment stolen, Crause moved to Barking (also location for Robinson's university in Keiller's *London*) and Disco Inferno disbanded. Bark Psychosis split in 1994 with a compilation album released in 1997 called *Game Over*. Frustrated by the regressive ambitions of Britpop and Blairism, Ian Crause and Graham Sutton sought new possibilities in Bolivia and Argentina respectively. Unlike many of their early 1990s contemporaries, such as Blur, there have been no lucrative reunions.[19]

Nonetheless, the foreboding soundscapes of Disco Inferno and Bark Psychosis seem increasingly resonant. Disco Inferno's *A Whole Wide World Ahead* (1994), perhaps conscious of the IRA threat, is eerily prescient of London in July 2005: "Journeys on tube trains/About to explode/As sick, sick people/Unburden their load." London is again afflicted by recession, veering uncomfortably close to a complete financial meltdown. But much of London looks very different to the city of two decades earlier. The empty landscape featured on the cover of *Hex* has now been covered by Olympic stadia and the ArcelorMittal Orbit tower—what the novelist China Miéville calls a "snarled Gaian hernia."[20] To the twentieth-first-century viewer of Keiller's *London*, the sparse, riverside vistas contrast starkly with the garish, luxury apartment blocks, prime "opportunity areas," and high-end cultural consumption that have proliferated across these locations over the last twenty years. Despite recent crises, London appears firmly locked into a new speculative bubble; any alternative visions and imaginations for the city seem squarely blocked and stunted. Perhaps again we will need to listen closely to London's edges and margins in urgent new efforts at mapping a whole wide world ahead.[21]

Endnotes

1 All references to *London* are from the British Film Institute DVD release *London and Robinson in Space: Two Films by Patrick Keiller*. Thanks to Luke Williams and Rosa Appleby-Alis for eastern expeditions that helped stimulate this chapter, and to the comments of Ned Raggett and Kevin Milburn. For a mix of some of the music featured please visit http://www.mixcloud.com/harrisssment/corner-at-the-edge-of-a-map/

2 Although a decade later, Ballard described Tate Modern in the former Bankside power station as a "middle-class disco." J.G. Ballard, *Millennium People* (London: Flamingo, 2003) p. 180.

3 Keiller's first two films, *Stonebridge Park* (1981) and *Norwood* (1983), both dealt with London's suburban landscapes.

4 Roger Silverstone, ed., *Visions of Suburbia* (London: Routledge, 1996).

5 The term "edgelands" is taken from the 2011 book of that name by Paul Farley and Michael Symmons Roberts, although this chapter seeks to chart more geographical and historical specificity to its use through close reference to London.

6 From a 2012 Pitchfork interview by Ned Raggett: http://pitchfork.com/features/articles/8758-disco-inferno/2/

7 Other members of Bark Psychosis were from Stratford (Mark Simnett) and Redbridge (Daniel Gish, who started out in Disco Inferno). Their album *Hex* included drumming from Talk Talk's Lee Harris, who originally hailed from Southend. Disco Inferno's Ian Crause and Rob Whatley grew up just beyond the North Circular road and close to Roding Lee South Pumping Station.

8 Lyric from Disco Inferno's "Even the Sea Sides Against Us".

9 Indeed, Graham Sutton and John Ling formed the drum'n'bass electronic act Boymerang in 1994.

10 2012 Pitchfork interview. The same sentiments seem to be expressed in Underworld's track, *Dirty Epic* (1993): "Ride the sainted rhythms on the midnight train to Romford."

11 Graham Sutton went on to found a studio called Dustsuckersound, hovering up sonic debris much like the sonovac in Ballard's 1960 short story "The Sound-Sweep."

12 Lyrics from "The Loom" and "A Street Scene". In 1994, Graham Sutton suggested "Space and silence are the most important tools you can use in music"—interview with Graham Sutton in *Audrie's Diary*, 1994. Available: http://post-rock.lv/bark2.htm

13 Neil Kulkarni 2011 interview in *The Quietus*: http://thequietus.com/articles/07144-disco-inferno-interview. Ian Crause may be playfully referring to 1988's "Straight Outta Compton" by the gangsta rap act N.W.A. This sense of being detached from central London was illustrated by the use of a 1993 photograph by David Spero on the cover of the *Second Language* EP (1994). This depicts the M1 motorway in Hendon/Brent Cross bypassing and cutting off suburban houses below.

14 Ian Crause speaks about the skies of "north-east London" in the 2012 Pitchfork interview: http://pitchfork.com/features/articles/8758-disco-inferno/4/.

15 1994 interview with Graham Sutton: http://post-rock.lv/bark2.htm.

16 In his 2008 blog entry on this song, Owen Hatherley suggests the line "And we've known all along/That a home can put your life at risk" is a reference to negative equity. I would suggest it is more a reference to how households from particular ethnic or religious minorities can be easily targeted. http://nastybrutalistandshort.blogspot.com/2008/09/every-step-that-we-tread-dead-are.html.

17 Lyrics from "A Rock To Cling To," "Summer's Last Sound," and "Whole Wide World Ahead."

18 Lyrics from "Even the Sea Sides Against Us" and "Summer's Last Sound. "

19 As part of a comeback in 2012, Blur released a song called "Under the Westway." The lyrics from Bark Psychosis's "Big Shot" explored similar themes eighteen years previously: "And below: the Westway reaches out to clutch you back."

20 China Miéville, "Oh London, You Drama Queen," *The New York Times*, 1 March 2012, http://www.nytimes.com/2012/03/04/magazine/china-mieville-london.html

21 Indeed, the last two years have witnessed reissues of some out-of-print recordings by Disco Inferno and Bark Psychosis. *Fields of Reeds* (2013) by These New Puritans, a young experimental guitar band from Southend, is a highly evocative exploration of the estuarine landscapes of Essex, with lyrics such as "there is something there/In crashed cars by the train line" (and is produced by Graham Sutton).

THE SOUND OF DETROIT: NOTES, TONES, AND RHYTHMS FROM UNDERGROUND

Louis Moreno

The music is different here, the vibrations are different.
Sun Ra
We have three natural resources in Detroit: salt, water and techno.
Scan 7
Still you resist …
Céline

Reflecting on the urban crisis of the 1960s and 1970s, certain observers claimed that what was unfolding was an event so vast, and its causes so complex, that it outstripped the "mundane" framework of political analysis.[1] To properly understand the process enabling advanced capitalism to tear up the foundations of everyday life, they suggested some kind of complementary restructuring of the senses was needed. Here, science fiction seemed to provide the tools to track the urban mutations of deregulated capital.[2] The proposition was later refined by the critic Fredric Jameson: the dystopian compulsion to imagine the global destruction of cities was nothing less than the attempt to comprehend capitalism as a totality. But, Jameson added, the inability to think beyond the event of catastrophe diagnosed a state of political inertia.[3] If the *differentia specifica* of the utopian genre was the imagination of a society without private property, then one of the defining political features of the current era might well be a secular decline in the capacity even to fantasize, let alone realize, a world free of the influence of real estate.

1

Perhaps another symptom of this pathology appears in the range of stock images that construct our contemporary sense of "the global." Take, for example, three stereotypes of the contemporary city subject to globalization—each demarcated forms of urban future all circumscribed by the gravitational field of international capital. At the top level, the architecture of the "global city," encapsulates a perhaps now mannered expression of the "future city," a high-rise transnational command structure of financial capital. Bordering this gated community, there is the image of the developing mega-city region consisting of the spatial reflux of a global proletariat in a state of agglomeration. Finally, we have the materialization of Marx's metaphor of "dead labour." Cities defined not simply by vacated structures, but the abandonment of entire infrastructure; whole geographies sinking under the weight of fixed capital now surplus to global requirements. Each of these images respectively encapsulates dominant, emergent, and residual moments of planetary urbanization.

1 Cybotron, *Enter*, 1983, Fantasy Records, published by Deep Space Music. Art direction by Phil Carroll, cover art and design by Jamie Putnam, digital video processing by Ed Tannenbaum and Jim Wiseman.

In the last instance, the case of Detroit is paradigmatic: maintaining a grip on the contemporary imagination as potent as any metropole handling "tier one" capital. And its presence evokes a very specific—almost pedagogical—symbolism. The ruin of a city, which not only unlocked but cultured American capitalism, offers a warning about the mercurial temper of socio-economic forces that can destroy as well as create the conditions of existence. But there are good reasons to be wary of the tragic narrative of creative destruction. As the urban historian Jerry Herron explains, this conceit presents a perspective on Detroit evacuated of political content. Such that when curated into coffee-tabled slabs of "rot, dereliction and decay,"[4] the images tend to stand in front of the social history of an urban system of exploitation. What is left is an ensemble of stylized facts about economic growth freighted with dubious pathos. It is as if the collective memory of Detroit, monumentalized in the beautifully decayed structures of Michigan Central Station, the Packard Motors Plant, and others demonstrates that the social potential of a city is wholly immanent to the requirements of capital investors. And as an "ideological artefact," this fetish could be said to perpetuate what Manuel Castells once called the myth of the urban crisis[5]; that the crises of industrial capitalism are a product of the physical and social structures of a particular city, thereby sanctioning an economic assault on the wages and living standards of a city's people.

This substitution of a cultural sense of the past for a political analysis of the present takes other forms. Recent documentaries on Detroit tend to collapse the city's historical struggles into a narrative of the rise and fall of Detroit's cultural industries. In Julian Temple's documentary *Requiem for Detroit?* (2010), for example, the city's astonishing variety of musical innovations in R & B, soul, and punk help vent the urban explosion of the late 1960s and 1970s. Yet, the union of art and politics is compressed to such an extent that the complex event of the "Great Rebellion" in 1967 ends up appearing simply as a backdrop to a moment of counter-cultural desire. Even when the class and racial dimensions of the rebellion are acknowledged, they appear as a threshold, which like the city's music and car industries, is now the stuff of fond memory. What these perspectives on Detroit's future represent is a view of the contemporary city "expressed" as Raymond Williams said "in an habitual past tense."[6] Caught in the axis of architectural and musical degeneration, Detroit's future is consolidated by the dominant forces of geopolitical economy. Politics becomes modified by meditations on the residual aesthetics of industrial decline. The end point makes Detroit the last stop of late capitalism: offering spiritual redemption either through the neo-pastoralism of urban agriculture, or via urban explorations by "stalkers" into a Zone made radioactive by globalization.

If Detroit represents an image of the future—and much of the interest in the city seems to derive from a growing appetite to explore alternatives to capitalism—it is an image contractually bound to capital. Something revealed by the fact that Detroit's infrastructure is in effect held hostage by abstract creditors. The net result is that the current debate revolving around Detroit—at least as it appears from a distance refracted through images and documentaries—seems wholly inert, almost "contained," separated from wider discussion precipitated by Occupy about how the *total* situation of capitalism can be overturned. The industrialization of exploitation, the urbanization of racism, and the financialization of everyday life all recede from view. And by turning the space of Detroit into a work of "nostalgia art," one side effect is to reassert a perverse form of the American dream, a sentimental yearning—perhaps not unlike that seen in post-Communist societies—for the zombie-like return of the punishing conditions of mass employment shackled to heavy industry.

But is it possible to resist such a grimly retrospective "reading" of Detroit's future? Can we recover a "structure of feeling" from the immense cultural and political material that Detroit created that is not circumscribed by the limits imposed by finance? Here a number of strategies present themselves. The first, already mentioned, is the idea that "the urban" eludes perception requiring a retraining of our sense of what produces and consolidates social space. Another, more distant, starting point is recommended by Futurism, and figures like Luigi Russolo who thought that bourgeois nostalgia could be short-circuited by channelling urban sound. A third strategy is put forward in the extraordinary 1997 film *The Last Angel of History* by Black Audio Film Collective,[7] which suggests that some kind of dialectic between the spatial and the sonic—mediated by the hybrid sonic-fictions of Afro-Futurism—is possible. But, before we consider this and its relevance for Detroit, we shall begin with the sound-sweeps of an earlier generation of Futurists—for no other reason than simple synchronicity. For, just as Russolo was assembling a sonic battery of machines to harness the energy of Milan's factory workers, a more economic mobilization of the body was about to be set in motion in a workshop in Michigan.

When the Model T rolled out of Highland Park on 1 December 1913, what emerged was not the invention of the automobile, but something more far-reaching. Henry Ford's innovation of the moving assembly line would culture a sense of space and time that was manufactured in Detroit. And what distinguished the commercial atmosphere of Detroit, compared to other corporate centres like Chicago and New York, was less the intense verticality of its business district, and more the acoustic tumult of plant life. Diego Rivera's *Detroit Industry Murals* (1933) is perhaps the most well known artistic representation of this experience of "shrieking, hammering ... delirium."[8] Another, smaller, but similarly dynamic illustration, can be found in the famous Detroit episode in Louis-Ferdinand Céline's *Journey to the End of Night* published in 1932. Here, we learn hardly anything of a metropolis whose architecture and urbanism aspire to Second Empire grandeur. Instead, what Céline evokes is a factory town whose booming economy is expressed by convulsions that rent the spirit from the body:

> *Still you resist; it's hard to despise your own substance, you'd like to stop all this, give yourself time to think about it and listen without difficulty to your heartbeat, but it's too late for that.*

This thing can never stop. This enormous steel box is on a collision course; we, inside it, are whirling madly with the machines and the earth. All together.[9]

Céline never worked the line of course, but as a physician employed by Ford he had studied first hand the impact of the assembly process on individual workers. And in a work saturated with resentment, the Detroit episode has an idiosyncratic texture, where the social relations of the city—mediated by forces that work the narrator's body into "lumps of flesh convulsed with vibrations"—culminate in a singular urban impulse: the need to complete the human circuit, the need "to touch a real body."[10] What emerges then is a complex expression of alienation whose industrial structure of feeling is geographically specific: an experience of lives dispossessed by an urbanizing mode of American accumulation.

In counterpoint to this unremitting melancholy, the music of the blues offers something like an existential defence. The blues, the poet and novelist Richard Wright observed, "though replete with a sense of defeat and down-heartedness, are not intrinsically pessimistic; their burden of woe and melancholy is dialectically redeemed through sheer force of sensuality."[11] In a similar vein, Ralph Ellison—reviewing LeRoi Jones's book *Blues People*—argued that what the blues (and its descendants) gave African-Americans were the resources to construct themselves "in the world of sound" in resistance to "the denial of social justice."[12] Later, the ability to musically adapt the lived experience of Fordism famously gave rise to Berry Gordy's own assembly plant of Motown, crafting and redefining the blues into an exuberant soul sound. The blues and soul therefore comprised, what Wright concluded was, "an almost exultant affirmation of life ... no matter how repressive [the] American environment."

By the 1960s, the repression would be intensified on an industrial scale in Detroit's deteriorating plants. Local radicals like John Watson—addressing Italian workers in 1970—described what was unfolding as nothing less than an all out "war going on inside the American factories":[13] a claim substantiated by the fact that by the mid-1960s, "more auto workers were killed and injured each year on the job than soldiers were killed and injured during any year of the war in Vietnam."[14] Echoing Wright's definition, the Detroit sound modulated with the times, taking a harder urban edge—something John Lee Hooker would take to a national level. And Joe L Carter (a bluesman who worked in Ford's Rouge plant) vocalized the blues of absolute subsumption in the lyrics, "Please Mr Foreman slow down your assembly line / No, I don't mind working, but I do mind dyin'."[15]

Joe L's powerful urban blues introduce the 1970 film *Finally Got the News* and inspired the title of Georgakas and Surkin's "study in urban revolution," *Detroit: I Do Mind Dying*.[16] Both track an astonishing period in Detroit's history, when, between 1967 and 1974, a constellation of movements revolving around the Dodge Revolutionary Union Movement and the League of Revolutionary Black Workers attempted to take control of the urban apparatus of power. In a moment—which Jameson doesn't flinch from calling "the single most significant political experience of the American 1960s"[17]—the League laid out an approach that moved on the urban nexus of monopoly capital. Based on a realization that labour resistance inside the plants could only ever achieve partial reforms because the "whole city structure goes into action"[18] against organized labour, the Detroit movement developed an alternative strategy. Their "inventive genius"—mirroring Ford—lay in their understanding that the city's economic power lay in the spatial configuring of a "productive system of incessantly self-refining functionality."[19] This consciousness of the social and spatial basis of power meant, as the League's Ken Cockrel explains in *Finally Got the News*, that any strike had to be backed up by (and in effect scaled up through) a complementary infrastructure. A revolutionary system of collective consumption that could feed and sustain the workforce, whilst simultaneously defending and representing their interests in the law courts and through media. By mapping the circulation of capital through the nodal points of economic, institutional, and informational power they "sought to create" nothing less than "a multilevel power apparatus parallel to the power apparatus of the system it sought to destroy."[20] Urban revolution, the League concluded, was a wholly practical solution to the crisis of Fordism; without it, the city's industry would be given the freedom to continue to run the city's people into the ground.

Supplemented by a later documentary, *Taking Back Detroit*, filmed in 1980,[21] this triptych comprises a sequence of urban analysis whose politics has not dated, for the very reason that its full implications have still to be properly explored.[22] And even in its failure, this movement helps underline a point too often overlooked in the commentary on the organic failure of regional industry. Namely, that the spatial shift towards a "post-Fordist" organization of capital—with its technocratic emphasis on "lean" organizational structures, and the fetishization of intellectual labour—works both in the first instance (such as the unemployment created by plant closure) and last analysis (of the homelessness created by gentrification) to liquidate alternative configurations of sociospatial power.

To illustrate this, we need only look at three of the cultural manifestations of post-Fordism. First, in 1972, Berry Gordy moved the base of operations of Motown Records to Los Angeles, mirroring the wave of relocations that would dismantle the main employment base of the city over the next few decades. Second, when work began in 1973 on the Renaissance Centre, designed by John Portman, it was clear that Detroit's elites intended to avoid dealing with the urbanized injustice revealed by the 1967 rebellion. Instead, power was to be consolidated in a style of postmodern urbanism. Here was the advent of a mode of development that used the pretext of degeneration to justify tax cuts for suburban wealth, whilst turning ownership of the city's central assets over to financial control.

Detroit was at an impasse, the myth of the urban crisis—that labour and social infrastructure are a burden on market expansion—seemed to consolidate a view that historical change can never be constructed "from below." Yet, just as the prospect of a radically different urban future was being shut down, and the message that there is no alternative structuring of society becomes dominant, a third and more renegade response assumed sonic form. As the writer Kodwo Eshun argues in *The Last Angel of History*, something like an epistemological break happens in black music during the 1970s.[23] According to Eshun, the Delta blues contract enforced by the Devil on Robert Johnson is torn up, as musicians mine the possibilities of the recording studio. And in doing so, African, American, and European traditions, musical styles, and production techniques are recombined; new "sound worlds" are assembled, which enable not only reflections on the history but also make the desire for life endemic by projecting this struggle into the future.

Here, two particularly powerful musical currents begin to fuse in Detroit—both inspired by a sense of how the more up-tempo innovations of jazz and soul could be future-proofed. The cosmic and aquatic funk of George Clinton and Parliament-Funkadelic across albums like *Mothership Connection* (1975) and *Motor-Boogie Affair* (1978) offered ways to recharge the circuits of R & B, rock, and soul. Simultaneously, out of Germany, Kraftwerk began to use electro-acoustic instruments and synthesizers, creating records called *The Man Machine* (1978) and *Computer World* (1981), which articulated an aesthetic fascination in the ambiguity of technological change. Interestingly, these synthetic innovations revolved around the same problem. For Clinton, this interest in spatializing funk was a reaction against the "mainstreaming" of black culture, and the normalizing of the James Brown sound.[24] Kraftwerk's sonic curiosity turned on the source of Clinton's unease—could the funky drummer be roboticized?

The results had an immediate impact on industrial centres either in the throes of collapse or experiencing the rush of accumulation. From Sheffield to Tokyo, these experiments opened up new pathways for reinterpretations of the basic blueprints of pop culture. And because this music tended to be instrumental, its conceptual basis—often taking inspiration from the rate of change of music technology itself—could nurture the imagination of writers looking for resources to animate their powers of precognition. In this respect, perhaps the most crucial passage of influence was between Japanese electronic music and American science fiction. Yukihiro Takahashi's 1981 album, *Neuromantic*, evoked atmospheres and environments that William Gibson would interpolate into some of his early speculations on the trajectory of post-Fordist capitalism.[25]

But while the dematerialization of social and economic power to "the scary new networks" of cyber-capital was—as the writer of "The Cyborg Manifesto" said, "a matter of immense human pain in Detroit"[26]—the city's musicians fabricated their own hi-tech mythos. Influenced by the mix of genres broadcast late night by the enigmatic DJ Electrifying Mojo, Juan Atkins and Richard Davis formed the band Cybotron to culture a new style of pure-funk. And with the 1981 single "Alleys of Your Mind," Cybotron constructed a sound that engaged with Detroit's socio-economic reality, but used the freedoms of P-Funk and

Kraftwerk to create something alien to the reflective traditions of the blues: where "P" was played in the key of paranoia, and time and space were bent "out of synch." For example, in "Night Drive (Thru Babylon)" (1985) by Model 500, the passenger is taken on a journey to the centre of the 1980s: but this is Céline as cyborg, kerb-crawling for human contact, and where sexual desire, modulated by the stiletto kick of the Roland TR-808, is mediated via the marauding body of a Porsche 924. And whilst the lyrics describe states of "anti-love"— as robots stare "contemptuously" at the "inferior designs of the outmoded, underpowered and otherwise obsolete life forms"—the landscape is filled with radical possibility. Against the vision of a metropolis rotating on the axis of Fritz Lang's Moloch-Machine, Cybotron envision a different form of urban space. Interviewed by Jon Savage in 1993, Atkins and Davis said that their pivotal track "Techno City" (1985), the one that categorized this sound, attempted to imagine the "workers' city," a utopia worthy of Fourier or Saint-Simon, where "a person could be born and raised:"

> *There would be no Moloch, but all sorts of diversions, games, electronic instruments. Techno City was the equivalent of the ghetto in Detroit, which is overlooked by the Renaissance Tower.*[27]

From the late 1980s onwards, techno globalized, taking on different regional varieties, but within Detroit the spatial dimensions of the sound evolved in a wholly singular way. What distinguished the Detroit style was, to be sure, the geographical conditions of the city, but also something inherent within the music itself. The international extension of the *techno sound* was not just an opportunity to make careers for musicians, certain artists thought that the music carried within it the seeds to propagate the experience of Detroit on a planetary scale. Surfacing in New York and Berlin in the early 1990s, against the backdrop of the LA conflagration, the group/label/social movement Underground Resistance combined Cybotron's vision of urban anxiety and liberation with the seditious rage of Public Enemy. Underground Resistance (UR)—comprising Mad Mike Banks, Jeff Mills, and Robert Hood—channelled the sonic culture of Detroit, incorporated into the Russolian devices of the 808, 909, 303, and a constant stream of 12-inch records, to lay down their "Revolution for Change." The project was elaborated in the track "The Theory," appropriating a sample from Star Trek, UR deterritorialize the myth of urban regeneration: describing a three-stage process: going from studio to studio, city to city, and then from world to world, infusing industrial landscapes with the life-giving properties of Detroit's deep space.[28]

If Utopia is, as scholars tell us, "a socio-economic sub-genre of that broader literary form [of Science Fiction],"[29] then Detroit techno—particularly that of Cybotron, Model 500, and Underground Resistance—occupies a vital point of intersection between narrative and sonic culture. A point Eshun has made when he suggests that what this music does is not so much represent Detroit, but estrange our very sense of Detroit.[30] In this light,

Detroit techno resembles something like "the ansible," that fantastic device of utopian science fiction, which enables instantaneous contact with a multiverse of different worlds and forms of life.[31] In Model 500's "Ocean To Ocean" (1990), the paranoid back alleys of the mind give way to a global horizon of liberation. Drexciya's astonishing body of music submerges Detroit in an aquatic realm populated by those children of "the shipped" thrown overboard on route to slavery. In *The Red Planet* series of releases, the track "Lost Transmission from Earth" suggests the landscape of Mars is populated by the members of the Black Panthers. And back on Earth, broadcasting from low orbit on the space station Mir, UR lay down "designs for sonic revolutions" to resist the racial profiling of mainstream radio and music television. When these different sonic imaginations are overlaid, the word "Detroit," when repeated in Robert Hood's magisterial track "Detroit: One Circle" (1996) becomes a refrain invested with spectral force. If, as the League once said the "whole city's structure" was mobilized against them, this sound converts Detroit into a structure of revolutionary feeling. In a city where space and music have become abundant "natural" resources,[32] the power of Detroit techno lights up a planetary *metroplex* of tonal and rhythmic possibility: a utopia.

For all this, however, a dominant image of Detroit stalks the world today, fortifying a global future emptied of all revolutionary content, consoled by a tragic anxiety about the precariousness of the present and the accumulating losses of the past. The absence of both the people and the future in contemporary representations of Detroit shackles the city to its ruins and rules out the attempt to see beyond the near-view field of the present. The function of such imagery is not so much ideological, but rather the enervation of the imagination. Yet, what I have tried to suggest is that Detroit's underground culture and politics *resists* such sentiment, leaving us with a different kind of anxiety—"an anxiety about losing the future."[33] This way of seeing and hearing Detroit helps us to recover a different type of future shock: the recovery of a utopian impulse that still finds in technology and "the urban" the socio-spatial resources of liberation. Clearly, the predicament of Detroit serves to undermine any attempt to see within this place any kind of future that is highly technological, fully urbanized, politically democratic, and free of capital. But, the very fact that such ideas have been aired, politically as well as culturally, reminds us of the power of the utopian imagination: namely, to subject the normative frame of political economy to "cognitive estrangement."[34] What such a disruption offers, is the ability to, at the very least, imagine the expropriation of the future from the jaws of historical defeat. What remains is an open sense of history, which—for the moment, whilst politically unimaginable—is not necessarily unheard of. Against the spatial ideology of the future city, the sound of Detroit resonates with a different "utopian impulse"—the funk of *futuricity* itself.

Endnotes

1   A mix of all the music referenced in this essay, can be found here: http://www.soundcloud.com/unspecified-enemies

2   The drama of urban accumulation famously gave rise to an extraordinary burst of intellectual creativity in sociology, geography, and political economy in the 1970s—most notably the contributions Henri Lefebvre, David Harvey, and Manuel Castells. But with respect to science fiction (SF), what I have in mind is the more speculative approach of (i) Lefebvre's *The Urban Revolution* (2003) and *The Survival of Capitalism* (1976); (ii) Samuel Delany's own analysis of the urban crisis in *Dhalgren* (1975); and (iii) later Donna Haraway (1991) and Fredric Jameson's sense of the political potential of science fiction vis-à-vis postmodernity. More recently, Andy Merrifield has reasserted the urban SF perspective. But the link between Lefebvre and, especially, Jameson's singular analysis of Utopia provides the conceptual fulcrum for this essay.

3   Frederic Jameson, "Future City," *New Left Review* (2003) p. 76

4   Jerry Herron, "The Forgetting Machine: Notes Toward a History of Detroit," The Design Observer Group (9 January 2012), http://places.designobserver.com/entryprint.html?entry=31848 (accessed 17 March 2014); Jerry Herron, "Three Meditations on the Ruins of Detroit," in *Stalking Detroit*, ed. Georgia Daskalakis, Charles Waldheim, and Jason Young (New York: Actar, 2001).

5   Manuel Castells, *The Urban Question: A Marxist Approach* (Cambridge, MA: MIT Press, 1977) pp. 380–401.

6   Raymond Williams, *Marxism and Literature* (New York/Oxford: Oxford University Press, 1978) p. 128.

7   Made by Black Audio Film Collective and directed by John Akomfrah.

8   Quote from a first-hand report of Ford's Assembly Park in 1914, cited by Herron, "Three Meditations on the Ruins of Detroit" p. 34.

9   Louis-Ferdinand Céline, *Journey to the End of the Night*, trans. Ralph Manheim (London: Calder, 1988) p. 204.

10 Ibid. p. 205.

11 Douglas Henry Daniels, "The Significance of Blues for American History," *The Journal of Negro History* 70 (1/2) (1985): 14–23.

12 Ralph Ellison, "The Blues by Ralph Ellison" *The New York Review of Books* (6 February 1964).

13 Dan Georgakas and Marvin Surkin, *Detroit, I Do Mind Dying* (Cambridge, MA: South End Press, 1998) p. 98.

14 Ibid. p. 96

15 The full lyrics: "Please Mr Foreman, slow down your assembly line / No, I don't mind workin', but I do mind dyin' / Working twelve hours a day, Seven long days a week / I lie down and try to rest, but, Lord knows, I'm too tired to sleep / Please Mr Foreman, slow down your assembly line / I said, Lord, why don't you slow down your assembly line. / No, I don't mind workin', but I do mind dyin'."

16 *Finally Got the News* was filmed by Stewart Bird, Rene Lichtman, and Peter Gessner, produced in Association with the League of Revolutionary Black Workers. See Georgakas and Surkin's text for an account of the film's production.

17 Fredric Jameson, *Postmodernism, or, the Cultural Logic of Late Capitalism* (London: Verso, 1991).

18 From a retrospective interview with the late Ken Cockrel in 1972 in Georgakas and Surkin, *Detroit, I Do Mind Dying* p. 81.

19 Smith (1993) p. 15 cited in, Herron (2001) p. 33.

20 Georgakas and Surkin, *Detroit, I Do Mind Dying* p. 76.

21 Stephen Lighthill's film tracks the organization surrounding Ken Cockrel and Justin Ravitz's campaigns for citywide office.

22 Andy Merrifield, *The New Urban Question* (London: Pluto Press, 2014) pp. 89–101.

23 This argument is developed in Eshun's *More Brilliant Than the Sun: Adventures in Sonic Fiction* (London: Quartet Books, 1998).

24 Interviewed in The Last Angel of History, Clinton says that by "by this time black music [and] 'black' itself had become commercial, you know it's hip to be black, and dance to James Brown and all that, so rock n roll had faded out in 1969 so it was time to make a change … I was always a sci-fi freak so the next record we had to find a place you hadn't perceived black people to be, and that was on a spaceship."

25 As well as inspiring Gibson's 1984 novel *Neuromancer*, the track "New (Red) Roses" is adapted for an extraordinary short story where the ability to conceive and perceive itself becomes corporate stock, and the imagination is subject to hostile takeover by the "corporation as life form": "New Rose Hotel," in William Gibson, *Burning Chrome and Other Stories* (London: HarperCollins, 1995).

26 Donna Haraway, "The Cyborg Manifesto," in *Simians, Cyborgs, and Women: The Reinvention of Nature* (London: Free Association Books, 1991) p. 153. Haraway is a clear influence on *The Last Angel of History*.

27 Jon Savage, "Jon Savage on Song: Cybotron—Techno City," *The Guardian* (15 February 2010).

28 The sample in full: "Stage one of our experiment is conducted in the laboratory. Stage two of the series will be attempted in a lifeless underground. Stage Three will involve the process on a planetary scale. It is our intention to introduce the Genesis device into a pre-selected area of our lifeless space body … matter is re-organised with life generating results."

29 Fredric Jameson, *Archaeologies of the Future: The Desire Called Utopia and Other Science Fictions* (London: Verso, 2005) p. xiv.

30 Eshun, *More Brilliant Than the Sun* (1998).

31 Created by Ursula Le Guin and featured in her novels including *The Dispossessed* (1974).

32 From an interview with the Detroit musicians and UR affiliates Scan 7 in Gary Bredow's documentary *High-Tech Soul: The Creation of Techno Music* (2006).

33 Jameson, *Archaeologies of the Future* p. 233.

34 Ibid. p. xiv.

DANCING OUTSIDE THE CITY: FACTIONS OF BODIES IN GOA

Arun Saldanha

1 Goa, 2006, photo by
Ami Vitale.
Source: Getty Images.

Music has a thirst for destruction, every kind of destruction, extinction, breakage, disloca-
tion. Is that not its potential "fascism"?
Gilles Deleuze and Félix Guattari[1]

The faculty of sight is central to the very concept of tourism. Tourism is defined through photography, ads, museums, "views." But are tourists merely pairs of eyes? Tourists swim, talk, climb, stroll, relax, become bored perhaps, or ill. They taste, smell, listen, dance, get drunk, have sex. Travel involves entire bodies—and *different* bodies. Soundscapes especially warrant a differential and embodied approach. An exemplary place to think about travel as an event involving hearing and movement is the psychedelic rave scene in Goa. My basic argument is that music, through the connections it enables between bodies, things, and physical conditions, *orders* bodies into grids of social difference. In a "Third World" destination such as Goa, this ordering becomes a matter of political and ethical concern.

Towards the end of the 1960s, when India was known in the West as the province of spirituality and authenticity, Goa's secluded beaches were rediscovered by hippies. Life in the village of Anjuna centred around taking drugs, swimming in the nude, and playing guitar and bongo. This counterculture was a quest for a life of drugs and music outside the confines of urban white modernity. The hippies would hold all-night parties on the beach. Parties were intimate and generally held some distance from the village, so the villagers could sleep. Both Goans and older hippies can be quite nostalgic about how the parties manifested a more or less symbiotic relationship between locals and foreigners. But then a charter tourism industry developed in the wake of the hippies. News of white tourists, especially the naked female ones, rapidly spread all over India. By the late 1970s, the majority of tourists were domestic. Since then, the controversies about the cultural, environmental, and economic corruptions of tourism have been endless and the party scene is all but dead.

The music played in Anjuna was always music to get stoned to: Pink Floyd, The Grateful Dead, Bob Marley, The Beatles, The Doors, Led Zeppelin, Parliament. Then, in the mid-1980s, something quite unexpected happened, something shrouded in mythical narratives of origin common in most popular music. The music in Goa started becoming electronic, aimed at dancing for hours. As house and techno were developing in Chicago, Detroit, New York, Ibiza, London, and Manchester, acidheads in Goa started looping the bits they liked by sticking pieces of magnetic tape together, exchanging the tapes with friends and becoming deejays. Under the full moon, on the rim of the Indian Ocean, far away from the city, the Goa freaks felt very much connected and alive.

Back in Europe, travellers tried to make sounds that captured those feelings best. They then brought the resulting tracks to Goa. A rapid circuit formed of music being made in northwestern Europe, but danced to in Goa. By around 1992, ravers were so confident something new was happening they christened their music Goa trance—identified by a punchy kick and swirling, hypnotic, densely textured staccato sounds in vaguely Eastern melodies. Soon you could hear few other genres being played anywhere in Anjuna.

Goa trance raves and club nights are held not only all over Europe, but in Japan, South Africa, Australia, Brazil, and Hungary. For Israelis, Goa became the favourite destination to "lose it" after completion of military service. Young people travelled for music and the music travelled with them. Until the scene imploded from greed and overexposure in the early 2000s, Anjuna was the first and last rave capital of the Third World.

This is what Anjuna was like at its heyday, around 1998. Parties take place on the grounds of restaurants or rented spaces in the forest, on the beach or on hills. The music is loud, you can hear it kilometres away. Imagine going to church on Sunday morning in a little coastal Indian village with psy-trance in the background. But since the locals and seasonal workers living off the raves are mostly poor, they are quite dependent on the very sounds that keep their bodies tossing and turning at night.

Sunset makes you flock from the beach to your favourite bar or shack. This is the time to get some chillums circulating, to socialize, and start nodding or dancing to the music. About 10 p.m. you go for dinner, relax a bit, smoke more chillums. Then the agendas diverge. If you're a Goa freak, you're likely to continue chilling till dawn. If you're a backpacker or domestic or charter tourist, and in Goa for only one or two weeks, you'll be dancing much sooner. The music starts pounding properly by midnight. Between 3 and 5 a.m., the parties are generally at their quantitative peak. Most dancers are groups of young male Indian tourists. You will be able to count the number of dancing Goa freaks at this time on one hand.

For the Goa freaks, the real party starts in the morning. Apart from the profound symbolism of sunrise, they just don't like mixing with the *tourists* who drink and take only ecstasy—or worse, speed—come in taxis and not on their own motorbikes, or don't know much about the music, its philosophy, its rituals. The resentment towards Indians is even stronger. There are disturbances as white and brown bump into each other, especially drunk Indian tourists bumping into white girls. Even if they genuinely enjoy themselves on the music, and many of them aren't out for the white girls, nobody likes "the Indians"—not even the locals.

Charter tourists, non-drug-taking backpackers, domestic tourists, and local boys are the contaminants of subcultural purity. The Goa freaks appear on the dance floor when these contaminants start leaving. Before that, freaks patiently sit out the night on the mats next to the dance floor. At every party, there is an enormous area, the chill-out zone, with hundreds of kerosene lamps making it resemble a huge bazaar. The chill-out consists of *chai mamas* sitting stoically through the night, fighting their sleep, selling tea, coffee, snacks, cigarettes, and fruit, with mats for the customers to sit on. This mat economy is principally why locals will protest against party bans.

Finding parties can be troublesome. This is what you do. Get about ten motorbikes together, drive in the general direction. Everyone stops, switches off the engine, listens carefully. Continue driving in the direction the kick is heard. Nights in Anjuna are continually disturbed by the racket of passing motorbikes, especially Anjuna's old favourite—the 500 cc Royal Enfield.

Upon arrival, more disorienting experiences. Hundreds of bikes, taxis, cars, and jeeps are chaotically parked all over. What is the road, the field, the beach, the ditch, the hedge, and someone's garden? The same problem arises when you need to pee—obviously, no toilets at a party. The problem of darkness persists when you try to get to the party, even at the party itself. Often, you need to work your way through bushes and other obstacles when heading to the source of the music. Prudence is still advised at the party, where irregularities everywhere challenge you to keep balance. The dance floor isn't stable ground in Anjuna.

This is the charm of the scene, its distance from the city, making it all the more exciting and authentic. Any Goa freak will tell you that dancing in Goa is the real thing, the stars and moon above, the ocean breeze, the fluid boundaries of party space. *No roofs, no walls*—how unlike the indoor happenings at home! No entry charge, queues, bouncers, guest lists, surveillance cameras, cloakroom, fire extinguishers, first aid, rubbish bins. This is clubbing in the wilderness.

Heaps of loudspeakers stand menacingly at all four corners of the dance floor. Most of the electric energy goes into the bass, so that just passing in front of the speakers makes your intestines twirl. Then again, you might be one of those freaks on acid who would crawl into the speaker if it were possible. Most of the dancing crowd faces the speakers. The deejay spins from somewhere conspicuous, always with a posse of friends and party organizers. A good psy-trance deejay takes his congregation on a trip through the night and morning, playing specific subgenres at different times.

Sunrise at a party is the essence of Anjuna's music culture. The dance floor has been gradually becoming lighter, you can gradually *see* who's dancing around you, can find your friends again. Once more, the chillums come out, more chemicals are taken, another chai drunk. People prepare for the morning. For most Goa freaks, this is when the party commences. It's been chilly—the temperature can drop quite abruptly during the night—but those first rays of sunlight on your face: that is what many seek in this rave scene. When the sun reaches up, smiles emerge everywhere around you. The music immediately sounds different. If it was monotonous just before, now it gives new energy. If it was gloomy and going nowhere, now it's full of promise. The remaining diehard chillers on the mats finally come and join in. Many people arrive after dawn. For most party animals, it's the time you avoid. It's the stark opposite for the Goa freaks. In Goa, sunrise is the ultimate and magic arbiter.

And so the party goes on. And on. Sense of time lapses, measured only by the sun and the state of your body. When you're exhausted and fully dehydrated and the acid is wearing off, it might be time to leave. The music usually stops around noon, but big parties can go on for several days. Some deejays boast of twenty-four-hour sets.

The sun warms you up quickly, and the light makes your tired eyes squint. You can smell the dancing. The dance floor gets dry, and the feet stamp up clouds of dust, which makes breathing difficult. Local kids are paid to run around and sprinkle water from buckets. There are practically no mats left at this time. The dance floor is still fully occupied, but there are far fewer people, leaving lots of room for dogs and cows to scavenge whatever the ravers have left. If you were so preoccupied that you hadn't noticed during the night, you see in the morning that there are actually quite a lot of poorer Indians around, and not just taxi drivers. In India, the division of labour is usually so elaborate that there are more individuals than prescribed functions. On Christmas morning, Catholic families, nicely dressed up, come and have a look at what is for them a freak show. Try to imagine how other-worldly the behaviour and appearances of the Goa freaks are to most Indians.

Goa is relatively wealthy in India, and doesn't have many beggars of its own. But where there are white people in India, there will be beggars. So beggars were imported to Goa, like the thousands of wage-labourers in the tourist industry. The beggars' tactic at parties is to stand minutes at a stretch in front of someone dancing, and look miserable—not difficult among all these white people enjoying themselves.

Beggars must be the most shocking encounter for the unsuspecting clubber. A more in-your-face reminder of the colonial past and the fact this entire scene is built on top of the poverty of India is hardly imaginable. But they are carefully ignored, like the many vendors who hardly do any business but stubbornly persist. The interaction between spaced-out foreigners and poor Indian people is most interesting to observe: feigned indifference of the former, demand for attention from the latter. Sometimes the beggars and vendors are pushed or barked at, or danced away. Sometimes a Goa freak plays with the kids, hugs the beggar women, or offers them a soft drink. Rare moments of generosity to be cherished.

There are a few things to remember about Anjuna's music tourism, a singular confluence of digital technology and anti-urban Romanticism. First, on its own (even if we could think this), music is meaningless. Sounds mean because they're connected to a range of other entities and conditions: sun, moon, heat, rocks, kerosene, cannabis, sweat, all implicated in the event of Goa trance. Second, obviously the most important connection music makes is with human bodies. Bodies dancing, but also smoking, working, selling, buying, trying to sleep. Different bodies have different relationships to the music, and move around the event in different ways. So, third, there are patterns of spatiotemporal politics. The sounds interact with the sights and the physical layout of the party space to produce *factions* of bodies. Bodies are white or non-white, poor or not. Some bodies dance well and easily, others don't. Some are pinned down: chai mamas. Some have to keep walking around: vendors and beggars. Some appear just before dawn: Goa freaks. Between these factions there are continuous frictions, negotiations, and alliances. This should keep us wary of rave culture's self-proclaimed universalism. At least on this dance floor, it's not so much unity as factions that music and drugs create.

If music gives you a sense of purpose, for others it will be noise. It is precisely the potential for escape that can turn music not only imperialistic, but also into a narcissistic enclave changing nothing in the overall systems of domination. This hypocrisy about hippiedom has been pointed out before—what did Woodstock do about the concurrent riots in America's cities?—but it is crucial to understand why so much of it occurs unconsciously.

Ending on a positive note, Anjuna shows the pleasure of dancing does indeed have the potential to bring together people from astonishingly different backgrounds. One has to blame capitalism, patriarchy, and whiteness, not psy-trance, for these racialized dance floors. Music is probably the form best suited to extract the energies already oscillating in and between human bodies and their surroundings, to *carry them elsewhere.* Music intensely connects bodies to bedrooms, buildings, streets, cities. Music does such a good job in ordering bodies that it travels great distances. Music fixes because it flows, and it flows because it fixes. And whether it turns its bodies into factions or into revolutionary becomings, is entirely up to you.

Endnotes

This is an abridged and revised version of "Music Tourism and Factions of Bodies in Goa," first published in Tourist Studies 2(1) (2002): 43–62.

1   Gilles Deleuze and Félix Guattari, A Thousand Plateaus, trans. Brian Massumi (New York: Continuum, 2004 [1980]) p. 330.

ENCOUNTERING *ROKESHENI* MASCULINITIES: MUSIC AND LYRICS IN INFORMAL URBAN PUBLIC TRANSPORT VEHICLES IN ZIMBABWE

Rekopantswe Mate

This essay focuses on two songs—"Rokesheni" (the locations) and "Mabhebhi ekusabhabha" (babes from the suburbs)—by Winky D (born Wallace Chirimuko), an urban grooves artist whose music I first heard by chance in Harare and Beitbridge in 2009 and 2010.[1] The essay seeks to show dilemmas posed by experiencing music in informal urban transport public transport vehicles (IUPTVs), also referred to as commuter minibuses, emergency taxis (ETs), or simply Kombis.[2] Playing loud music has become a hallmark of IUPTVs in African cities.[3] Not only is loud music in confined spaces uncomfortable and unpleasant, passengers often have no say in the choice of music but endure the acoustic assault as part of the necessity of mobility in urban spaces. The physical discomforts are palpable.[4] The songs referred to in this essay were played repeatedly in IUPTVs—especially on the City-Greencroft and City-Mbare routes in Harare and Beitbridge. The music stood out because of its beat, it being ragga (reggae/dance-hall music), its use of Shona lyrics (one of Zimbabwe's three official languages)[5] laced with slang, and what seemed to me to be coherent rhymes. Composing rhyming lines in vernacular poetry is ordinarily a preserve of accomplished writers. Thus, the allure of the lyrics seems to be the linguistic prowess of the artist. In addition, as part of my fieldwork, I had interviewed in-school youth who mentioned listening to music as a favourite pastime, with local, then budding artists such as Winky D and his urban grooves peers as favourites. Until I finished the fieldwork, I had not made the connection between the name of Winky D and the music that dominated the air in Beitbridge and Harare. I subsequently made the connection while doing research on youth music lyrics.[6] Before getting to the lyrics of songs under discussion, the essay briefly describes the socio-economic set up of the *rokesheni* in popular and formal parlance; followed by a description of the origins of urban grooves as a music genre, and its connection to the rokesheni; IUPTVs as spaces for consuming music; and finally a discussion of lyrics of the two songs.

Like his urban grooves peers, Winky D has produced songs about the rokesheni, an old reference to areas designated as "Africans only" residential areas during the colonial era. Sometimes, these areas are also referred to as "the ghetto" in local slang and urban grooves songs—a term popularized by Jamaican ragga artists[7] and hip hop.[8] Historically, these areas were built to accommodate semi-skilled and unskilled workers in adjacent industrial areas. These residential areas are characterized by small plots of land (around 300 square metres), hence comparatively small houses; originally four rooms or less.[9] In time, these areas became associated with livelihoods based on or augmented with low-end informal sector activities, which officials resent—hence a long history of sporadic and violent confrontations apparently to "restore orderly" urban planning.[10] In this vein, since independence many of the houses have been extended with or without planning permission, much to the disaproval of technocrats. The latter culminated in the controversial Operation Restore Order (ORO) in 2005 in which unauthorized buildings and extensions were destroyed countrywide.[11] Notwithstanding the rationale and impact of ORO, these residential areas continue to experience unprecedented overcrowding due to growing demand for accommodation on the back of urban migration, a mismatch between the demand and supply of housing, as well as endemic unemployment including underemployment which disqualifies some urban residents from owning their own houses. Many unemployed people access urban accommodation through rented rooms that are sometimes partitioned with improvised materials to accommodate multiple households. This not only puts pressure on sanitary facilities; it is stressful to people because of lack of privacy, overcrowding, and inherent low-self esteem due to perpetual indebtedness to landlords.[12]

In post-independence quests to undo colonial legacies, the previously "Africans only" areas are referred to as "low-income residential areas" and/or "high-density suburbs"—different from previously "Europeans only" areas, which are referred to as "low-density suburbs" or "high-income areas." This labelling gives the impression that most urban dwellers live in suburbs qualified only as "high density" / "low income" or "low density" / "high income."

Around the world, suburbia is associated with middle-class existences, health, and wealth. The situation is different for the rokesheni. Since the 1990s, many have been epicentres of public health crises, such as cholera and typhoid outbreaks. Thus, by publicly referring to these areas as "rokesheni" or "the ghetto" artists are being subversive. Although performers rebut some of the negative connotations of the genesis of the rokesheni, they also draw attention to challenges that persist and have worsened over the years. These include overcrowding, limited social amenities, recent urban migrants, and gender tensions—especially the distrust of urban or fashion-conscious women.[13] Hence, these spaces are both stigmatized as poor, but also celebrated as a source of creativity, and as places of origin by artists. Consequently, in the post-independence dispensation, the rokesheni denotes socio-economic inequality among Africans; a reality whose true extent is not well documented in Zimbabwe.

To understand the rokesheni, it is necessary to compare it with the *sabhabha* (suburbs). Following independence in 1980, people with access to mortgage finance and aspirations for a better life moved to residential areas previously reserved for Europeans: the sabhabha. In the colonial era, these areas were referred to as *kumayadhi* (Shona) or *emayadini* (Ndebele, the second official vernacular language) to refer to the larger plots (or "yards") on which the houses were built, and the fact that they had gardens. The houses are larger with at least three bedrooms, and single or double carports. Some have swimming pools, tennis and/or basketball courts. Most have servants' quarters, which in the post-independence era are rented out to people in need of accommodation to augment incomes. Residents in these areas typically employ servants to help with domestic work and yard work outside the house. These residential areas are favourably located vis-à-vis wind direction, the siting of industrial areas, and railway lines. Security is a major concern as seen in barred windows, high security walls topped with electric fences, and/or razor wire. Increasingly, electronic security systems are preferred.

Based on the foregoing, one can say that residential areas encode socio-economic differences among Zimbabweans. For example, the vast majority of Harare's population (about 75 per cent) resides in a small section of the city in areas referred to as rokesheni.[14] The reality of socio-economic difference is seen in popular language in the 1990s, a time when these differences became more pronounced and more people were forced into rooming arrangements because of poverty. Young people raised in the sabhabha, and largely seen as raised in the lap of relative luxury, earned names/labels such as "the nose brigade." The label was applied to young people who attended better-off multiracial schools, spoke English all the time instead of vernacular languages, had accents or elocution that supposedly mimicked the English (or Europeans) who were locally understood as speaking through the nose, hence "nose brigade." Alternatively, these youth were referred to as the "*bhibho* brigade" to refer to their preference for crew cuts inspired by styles seen in music videos of overseas artists.[15] By contrast, their apparently less sophisticated counterparts from rural areas and the rokesheni, who attended comparatively less endowed mission and rokesheni schools, were referred to as SRBs (strong rural backgrounds) thus "country bumpkins."[16] In some instances, they were referred to as "shrubs," another longhand of SRB. The nose/bhibho brigade were clientele of Radio 3, an English-language public radio station mandated to play international music from the US and UK.[17] Through this radio station, the nose brigade listened to jazz, country music, rock, and rap music. By contrast, the SRBs were associated with *sungura* (local music), which was linked to rural-bound buses, farm compounds, rural shops,[18] and predominantly played on Radio 2, a public radio station that used the two vernacular languages. In 2000, when urban grooves emerged, these categorizations were scrambled. Not only did youth from the rokesheni, the erstwhile shrubs, emerge as the dominant artists, they appropriated international music styles such as rap, dancehall, and others with lyrics in the vernacular to comment on life in the rokesheni. Accordingly, urban grooves can be seen as an intertextual performance in which artists rebut some of the implicit and explicit stereotypes and realities of their neighbourhoods—such as poverty/deprivation and assumed lack of exposure. It gives them a platform to talk back and play down the stigmatized images of their neighbourhoods, while also revealing challenges wrought by economic difficulties. Urban grooves controversially gained prominence in the midst of Zimbabwe's economic and political crisis in 2000 as part of a government policy to enforce a policy of 75 per cent local content on public radio, irrespective of a dearth of such content and means of producing it.[19] In a context where Zimbabweans largely frown at performing arts as a livelihood, many artists resort to music as a last resort. Urban grooves lyrics reveal emerging survival strategies in a context of endemic unemployment, emergent masculine subjectivities in the rokesheni, and artists' perceived modes of worldliness. Their lyrics challenge norms about gender and age relations, kinship, and conviviality through bare-knuckle discussions of what they see and hear in the rokesheni. They use vernacular languages, albeit slang variants, making their messages accessible and obscure—especially to those who see slang as an annoying corruption of local languages, culture, and young people.[20] In this respect, youth artists across Africa are ridiculed as being "hooligans,"[21] "mad"/possessed by malevolent spirits,[22] or are simply not taken seriously.

Notwithstanding the foregoing, the ascendancy of hip hop as a music style of choice for unemployed urban youth in sub-Saharan Africa has attracted a lot of attention from researchers who acknowledge that it provides a platform for marginalized young people to speak, call leaders and elders to account, or simply to showcase their consumer capabilities and aspirations.[23] In the case of Zimbabwe, urban grooves was reportedly co-opted into state propaganda between 2000 and 2008 during Zimbabwe's crisis,[24] thus its latitude for commentary is apparently narrow. Notwithstanding this criticism, urban grooves—like other youth music styles across the world—remains a window through which researchers can access realities of young people living in marginalized areas or experiences they observe in these areas.[25]

Anyone who uses public transport in Harare and cities elsewhere in sub-Saharan Africa is familiar with the (ab)use of music in these confined spaces to attract passengers, to show off their music equipment and collections, among other reasons.[26] In Zimbabwe, IUPTVs have become a platform for artists to showcase their music, aided by the admiring crews of these vehicles. When IUPTVs first emerged, they were modes of transport and nothing else. They became commonplace as neo-liberal reforms deepened in the 1990s, leading to the sole urban transport bus company going bust. In time, local entrepreneurs imported second-hand Toyota HiAces from Japan via South African ports, and retrofitted them with radios—and more recently, digital music players and speakers (of which more below)—and chairs so that they seat fifteen to eighteen paying adults (four people per bench/row, four rows in most vehicles, one or two people in front with the driver, the conductor stands or crouches in the vehicle until one passenger disembarks). There are no seat belts for passengers except those in the front seat and the driver. The retrofitted chairs/benches have a foldable section to enable passengers to pass to and from the back. There is limited legroom for most adults. Most people endure this for thirty minutes or so of travel into or out of Harare's city centre. Sometimes, when people with big bodies enter, seating has to be rearranged to allow all passengers to fit on the narrow seats. As a rule of thumb, pre-teens travelling with adults ordinarily do not pay so they sit on adults' laps or sit on any available flat surface. When travelling alone, children pay. Depending on size, luggage is held on the lap, goes below seats, behind the driver's seat (on top of a section of the engine hold that protrudes into the vehicle), behind the back seat, or on the roof of the minibus if it has a carriage. On some routes and depending on crews and the nature of luggage, a fee is levied for excess or bulky items. On the City-Mbare route, carriages are not necessary as self-styled assistants also called touts (in Shona, *mahwindi*) stand by the doorway and simultaneously keep the luggage steady on the roof while the vehicle is in motion.

Retrofitted speakers are installed below the front and/or back seats or on the ceiling of the minibus. In some cases, radios/digital music players are connected to amplifiers or enhanced bass players. Complaints by passengers and businesses near IUPTV thoroughfares about noise pollution abound. These complaints culminated in running battles between and among local authorities, law enforcement, and minibus crews in 2012 and 2013.[27]

As elsewhere in urban sub-Saharan Africa, IUPTVs do not always respect road etiquette and regulations in terms of overtaking other vehicles, road markings, speed limits, and so on.[28] Flouting traffic rules is widely seen as one of the reasons behind the carnage on African roads.[29] Zimbabwean regulations demand that these vehicles be driven by persons over twenty-five years of age with at least three years of driving experience after getting a driver's licence. Yet, anecdotal reports abound that this age limit is not always respected because of pressures of unemployment and kinship considerations in recruiting crews on the part of owners of minibuses.

Flouting rules is sometimes attributable to stiff competition in this business. Crews who are frustrated by long loading queues at official bus termini and/or traffic congestion in the city centre, increasingly load from undesignated areas in the city increasing the risk of accidents and making themselves vulnerable to harassment by law enforcement agencies. In undesignated loading areas (called *mushikashika*[30] in local slang), the crews work with a loose network of friends and assistants who call out the minibus's route, its fares, while they are simultaneously on the lookout for law enforcement agents and warn the driver should any be spotted. Self-styled assistants "load" cars for fifty US cents (or five South African rands): a mandatory tip for crews of vehicles. Thus, the more cars they load, the more they earn. Undesignated loading zones are therefore a hive of activity, noisy, and confusing. While this type of "work" is part of evolving survival strategies in response to the crisis of unemployment, it increases risks of injury or death for motorists and pedestrians.[31] The touting for business, the number of vehicles manoeuvring to park, to load, and to leave—as well as loud music—make for valid complaints that IUPTVs exacerbate noise pollution and are a nuisance in city centres. The noise and defiance of crews leave passengers helpless. Many self-styled assistants are foul-mouthed and their notoriety precedes them. They badger would-be passengers to board their vehicles. When browbeating fails, pushing and shoving is resorted to. Thus, few passengers dare to complain about noise, discomfort from the blocked doorways, or any of their other antics—including misinformation, especially about destinations or routes of the vehicles. As observed and reported by passengers in Nairobi, these vehicles accentuate passengers' sense of vulnerability because of their confined spaces/crowdedness, and if expressed, passenger preferences are openly ignored leading to humiliation.[32]

Music and its volume is one such area of contestation. Touts typically bob along to the beat and/or dance stylistically while shouting for commuters if the minibus is stationary. Passengers with earphones listening to music from cell phones and other devices, remove their earpieces to surrender to the dominance of music in the vehicle. Passengers who receive calls sometimes get a reprieve, as the volume is lowered a notch only to go up again afterwards. General complaints about noise while the vehicle is being loaded are sometimes entertained if complaining passengers threaten to disembark. Once mobile and passengers have started paying, drivers ignore pleas to reduce the volume knowing that if passengers choose to disembark, they will lose their fares. There are no refunds on IUPTVs except in the event of a breakdown. Even then, some crews try to avoid refunds by negotiating alternative transport with their colleagues in other vehicles. In this way passengers are held prisoner to the music and confined space, under the whim of the driver and his conductor until disembarkation. It was while in similar circumstances waiting to board, sitting inside vehicles waiting for them to fill up, or travelling in IUPTVs on routes described above that Winky D's two songs discussed below were forced upon me.

In "Rokesheni," Windy D boasts about being an indigene of the rokesheni and warns his adversaries (ostensibly from the suburbs) saying, "*siyana nesu vekurokesheni*" (leave us [rokesheni guys] alone). He makes it clear that if his warnings are not heeded, persistent pests risk beatings that are easily doled out in the rokesheni. The song talks about the use of violence (brawling) by ghetto (male) youths to create and defend turfs/spaces of autonomy and to gain respect in their residential areas and among peers. Each rokesheni mentioned in the song (Highfields, Kambuzuma, Glen Norah, Chitungwiza, Dzivarasekwa, Mabvuku, and Mbare) is associated with a particular style of violence or is dominated by a colourful character who can be relied on to deal with errant newcomers or outsiders. Thus, in some of these residential areas, there are young men who ride IUPTVs for free simply because they are neighbourhood tough guys and no one dares to demand fares from them. This frustrates IUPTV crews who are presented as weaklings but who need the fares to earn an income. One hears of gangs from Mbare, one of the first and therefore the oldest rokesheni, home to one of Zimbabwe's busiest long-distance bus terminus and first port of call for many urban migrants. It is also home to con artists and petty criminals who prey on unwary travellers, but where one has to be careful not to snitch on these gangs or risk harassment. In High-fields, there is occasional gun violence yet no one is ever arrested; in Dzivarasekwa, there are guys who spend time sitting on street corners plotting ways to make money while engaging in substance abuse. Anyone who disrupts such group bonding sessions is likely to be treated shabbily by the group.

This song shows young men in precarious livelihoods, who are trying to make do and are not broken by unemployment. Their invincibility may be a vain attempt to show masculini-ties of resource-challenged men as compliant and well aligned to hegemonic masculinities,[33] but the resource austerity is also clear. The use of violence shows attempts to restore their dignity and self-esteem as they defend their turf and self-respect. Their individual and group crisis is clearer in the next song.

In "Mabhebhi ekusabhabha" (girls from the suburbs), we are presented with confrontations between Zimbabwean ghetto masculinities and suburban femininities. Ghetto masculini-ties are formed on the basis of a patriarchal drive to subjugate women—a challenging feat for resource-poor men wanting to subjugate women accustomed to comparatively exten-sive material comforts. Ghetto masculinities are hardened by the need to make do and to cope with austerity and limited opportunities in the face of endemic unemployment. The lyrics therefore celebrate poor men making do by not indulging the demands of women's every whim. This is presented as both coping with economic difficulties and disciplining the women. Accordingly, there is an element of misogyny in that women's demands and expectations are subject to caricature and dismissed as misguided and excessive. However, it also points to the economic incapacities of men. The song starts with a rallying cry to "ghetto youths" (presumably males only) to date girls from the suburbs and shock them with realities of life in the ghetto. Girls from the suburbs are presented as soft, preening, and materialistic. They are so wrapped up in their own upbringing as to be unaware of life in the rokesheni hence the rude surprises. The rallying cry goes like this:

Ma-ghetto youths	Ghetto youths
Laina bhebhi rekushabhabha	Get yourself a girl from the suburbs
Woripinza ghetto	Put her in the ghetto
Woti bhebhi pamba pangu apa	Tell her baby here is my place
Pasina window kana burglar bar	Without windows or burglar bars
Achimwa tii tsvuku isina mukaka	Drinking black tea without milk

In the rallying cry, suburban girls are shocked and challenged as the realities and expecta-tions they have taken for granted—such as houses with windows (which could mean either adequate ventilation or openings that are appropriately glazed and secured with burglar bars) and tea with milk. Clearly, these young men are down-on-their-luck lodgers in the rokesheni. Because of unemployment, many young men find themselves in windowless or poorly ventilated dwellings, which is obviously a shock to suburban girls. In addition, drinking black tea is ordinarily seen as a sign of deprivation, because of the lack of fresh or powdered milk. It is inferior to white tea in Zimbabwe.[34]

In different verses, Winky D relates experiences of dating girls from different suburbs in which confrontations between ghetto masculinities and suburban femininities are re-vealed. We also see challenges of social etiquette on the part of ghetto youth. For instance, while visiting the girl from Marlborough whom he visits with a friend, the friend asks the maid out. This is unbecoming and disruptive to the singer's relationship, because no self-respecting girl from the suburbs expects her boyfriend to have a friend who dates neighbourhood maids. He ends up fighting with the friend over the matter. Winky D is candid about challenges of the ideal of the male provider for his lot; for instance, when his alter ego dates a girl from Chisipite (an upmarket residential area) knowing full well that he does not have a car with which to pick her up. There are clear challenges in control-ling the girl because she is forced to hitchhike, exposing her to other men. This threatens the security of his alter ego and the relationship. When the girl from Mandara says she is hungry, the singer's alter ego responds by saying he can provide, but serves her food with soya chunks. In Zimbabwe, soya products are seen as poor people's source of protein—"pretend meat"—when preferences such as beef, chicken, or pork are out of reach. In popular opinion, soya products are yet another indication of relative deprivation.[35] The girl from Greencroft says she needs a wardrobe upgrade and demands a hipster (low waist jeans then fashionable), but he buys her a "petticoat" a slip to wear below her skirts and dresses. In Zimbabwe, these slips are utilitarian and worn daily to counter see-through fabrics. Wearing a petticoat symbolizes "feminine decency" for married women and marriageable girls. It preserves their honour by completely covering up the lower body; although these days, some women get around this by wearing trousers or leggings below their short or see-through dresses, tunics and tops. By contrast, hipsters (like trousers and other trendy fashion items) expose the outline of the body (and body parts) and express urbanity and materialism, which are seen as typical of urban women and an apparent pointer to their non-marriageability.[36] By unilaterally buying her a petticoat he dictates his preferences. Their tastes are obviously different. The girl protests. The girl from Masasa Park, attracted to the singer's ability to speak in patois,[37] started to misbehave by apparently emulating him. He breaks up with her by betting her in an illegal street corner gambling game. This could be metaphorical or literal, pointing to the extent of his disgust at this young woman's audacity, because she is not supposed to emulate him; rather women should maintain a position of respectability as cultural gatekeepers, and speaking patois—even as an expression of comradeship with one's boyfriend—is out of line. The girl from Borrowdale (an upmarket residential area) wanted the singer to shave his dreadlocks, apparently to make a gentleman of him. Dreadlocked men are assumed to be unemployed, addicts, and therefore not ideal as future husbands for girls from respectable backgrounds. He is annoyed with her. The girl from Westgate attempts to get married to the singer, but the singer's alter ego moves to Epworth (an upgraded informal settlement) on the outskirts of Harare. Residences in this area may have numbers, but streets are not well laid out and named as in low-density suburbs. This makes it difficult to find addresses. In addition, it seems only determined girls would tolerate moving from the suburbs to an upgraded informal sector in pursuit of love, so she gives up. This allows the singer's alter ego to run away from his amorous pursuer to the amusement of his confidantes.

We have seen that emerging acoustic cultures such as music played in public transport in urban Zimbabwe may have their uses to artists and crews of IUPTVs but they are a form of abuse to passengers and businesses nearby. Both music production and work in IUPTVs are male dominated and have created spaces in which men try to instil control over their lives and assert their masculinity by subjugating the people they encounter. Passengers are "held captive," and the music imposed upon their senses with no recourse to alleviate the situation.[38] These circumstances allowed me to encounter an artist and his lyrics I would not have encountered if I had used a different mode of transport. I listened to the lyrics and marvelled at them more to amuse myself and pass the time than out of pleasure. Despite unfavourable conditions under which I encountered his music, Winky D's mastery of the Shona language is admirable. His lyrics are controversial for some, but they showcase rokesheni masculinities of young men as invincible, active, and in charge—despite the challenges they face. Encountering them in IUPTVs also shows another layer of patriarchy in operation as male crews ignore pleas of hapless passengers who have no other transportation choice.

Endnotes

1 These experiences were part of my doctoral fieldwork in 2009/10 in Beitbridge on the border with South Africa. I travelled back and forth between and within Beitbridge and Harare using public transport.

2 The term *Kombi* was popularized by the 1970s Volkswagen minibus of the same name, which was made in South Africa. See Mesheck M. Khosa, "Routes, Ranks and Rebels: Feuding in the Taxi Revolution," *Journal of Southern African Studies* 118 (1) (1992): 232–251.

3 See Kenda Mutongi, "Thugs or Entrepreneurs?: Perceptions of *Matatu* Operators in Nairobi, 1970 to the Present," *Africa*, 76 (2006): 549–568; Mbugua Wa Mungai and David A. Samper, "'No Mercy, No Remorse': Personal Narratives about Public Passenger Transport in Nairobi, Kenya," *Africa Today* 52 (3) (2006): 51–81.

4 In Nairobi, pregnant women complained of uncomfortable vibrations in their abdomens because of "thunderous" noise in IUPTVs. See Mutongi "Thugs or entrepreneurs?" p. 557.

5 The other two official languages are English and Ndebele.

6 See Rekopantswe Mate, "Youth Lyrics, Street Language and the Politics of Age: Contextualising the Youth Question in the Third Chimurenga in Zimbabwe," *Journal of Southern African Studies* 38 (1) (2012).

7 See Melanie Newell, "Dancehall Culture and its World: Synthesizing Competing Discourses and Interpretation of Jamaica's Controversial Ghetto Culture," MA in Development Studies thesis (The Hague: ISS/EUR, 2009).

8 See Charis Kubrin, "Gangstas, Thugs and Hustlas: Identity and the Code of the Street in Rap Music," *Social Problems*, 52 (2) (2005): 360–78.

9 For instance, Alison Brown, "Cities for the Urban Poor in Zimbabwe: Urban Space as a Resource for Sustainable Development," in *Development and Cities*, ed. David Westendorff and Deborah Eade (Oxford: Oxfam GB, 2002) pp. 263–281.

10 See A. Y. Kamete, "On Handling Informality in Southern Africa," *Human Geography* 951 (2013): 17–31.

11 This was a controversial crackdown, launched with military precision, to get rid of unauthorized buildings and extensions, as well as informal sector activities in a vain bid to force people to comply with urban by-laws. A lot has been published on the impact and political fallout of this crackdown, the details of which are not discussed here for limitations of scope. For example, see J. Fontein, "Anticipating the Tsunami: Rumours, Planning and the Arbitrary State in Zimbabwe," *Africa* 79 (4) (2009): 368–88, among others.

12 See, for instance, A. Y. Kamete, "In Defense of National Sovereignty?: Urban Governance and Democracy in Zimbabwe," *Journal of Southern African Studies* 21 (2) (2003): 193–213; Rekopantswe Mate, "Stillborn in Harare: Attempts To Privatize Water in a City in Crisis," in *The Age of Commodity: Water Privatization in Southern Africa*, ed. David A. McDonalds and Greg Ruiters (London: Earthscan, 2005) pp. 225–239.

13 See Paula Jean Davis, "On the Sexuality of 'Town Women' in Kampala," *Africa Today* 47 (3–4) (2000): 29–60; Koni Benson and Joyce Chadya, "*Ukubhinya*: Gender and Sexual Violence in Bulawayo, Colonial Zimbabwe," *Journal of Southern African Studies*, 31 (3) (2005): 567–610.

14 A. Brown, "Cities for the Urban Poor in Zimbabwe."

15 See Moses Chikowero, "'Our people father, they haven't learned yet': Music and Postcolonial Identities in Zimbabwe," *Journal of Southern African Studies*, 34 (1) (2008): 145–160.

16 See Rudo B. Gaidzanwa, "The Politics of the Body and Politics of Control: An Analysis of Class, Gender and Cultural Issues in Student Politics at the University of Zimbabwe" *Zambezia* 20 (2) (1993): 15–35.

17 Chikowero "Our people father, they have not learned yet"; Jonathan Zilberg, "Yes It's True: Zimbabweans Love Dolly Parton," *Journal of Popular Culture*, 29 (1) (1995): 111–125; Tawana Kupe, "The Meanings of Music: The Presentation of Popular Music in Zimbabwe," *African Identities* 1 (2) (2003) pp. 145–160.

18 Banning Eyre, *Playing with Fire-fear and Self-censorship in Zimbabwean Music* (Copenhagen: Freemuse, 2005).

19 See Mate, "Youth Lyrics, Street Language and the Politics of Age."

20 See A. Perullo, "Hooligans and Heroes: Youth Identity and Hip Hop in Dar es Salaam, Tanzania," *Africa Today* 52 (4) (2005): 75–101; Marame Gueye, "Urban Guerilla Poetry: The Movement *y'en a marre*

and the Socio-political Influence of Hip Hop in Senegal," *Journal of Pan African Studies* 6 (3) (2013): 21–42; on the use of marginalized languages in music, see Francis B. Nyamnjoh and J. Fokwang, "Entertaining Repression: Music and Politics in Postcolonial Cameroon," *African Affairs* (104) (2005): 252–74.

21 See Perullo, "Hooligans and Heroes."

22 See Gueye, "Urban Guerilla Poetry."

23 See, Perullo, "Hooligans and heroes"; Mate, "Youth Lyrics, Street Language and the Politics of Age"; Gueye, "Urban Guerilla Poetry"; Ruth Prince, "Popular Music and Luo Youth in Western Kenya: Ambiguities of Modernity, Morality, and Gender Relations in the Era of AIDS," in *Navigating Youth and Generating Adulthood*, ed. C. Christiansen et al. (Nordiska: Uppsala, 2005) pp. 117–152.

24 For instance, Katja Kellerer, "'Chant Down the System 'till Babylon Falls': The Political Dimension of the Underground Hip Hop and Urban Grooves in Zimbabwe," *Journal of Pan African Studies* 6 (3) (2013): 43–64.

25 See Newell, "Dancehall Culture and its World"; Robin Weitzer and Charis E. Kubrin, "Misogyny in Rap Music: A Content Analysis of Prevalence and Meanings," *Men and Masculinities* 12 (1) (2009): 3–29; Ernst Morrell, "Toward a Critical Pedagogy of Popular Culture: Literary Development," *Journal of Adolescent and Adult Literacy*, 46 (1) (2002): 72–77.

26 See Mutongi, "Thugs or Entrepreneurs?"; Wa Mungai and Samper "No Mercy, No Remorse."

27 "Council, Police Deploy at Ranks," *The Herald* 10 October 2012. Apparently, the point of this crackdown on IUPTVs was to "bring sanity" to Harare. "Another Kombi War Erupts," *The Herald* 29 March 2013. In the latter, IUPTVs parked in undesignated places were clamped and towed away with owners expected to retrieve the vehicles after paying fines. In both cases, hundreds of touts were arrested for miscellaneous offences including touting and making noise in the city. It is now illegal to tout for any business. Offenders risk stiff fines or six months in prison. However, touts still defiantly do business and IUPTVs still use undesignated loading zones.

28 See Piet Konings, "Solving Transport Problems in Africa Cities: Innovative Responses by Youth in Doula, Cameroon," *Africa Today* 53 (1) (2006): 35–50; Mutongi, "Thugs or Entrepreneurs?"; Wa Mungai and Samper, "No Mercy, No Remorse"; A. Simone, "Urban Circulation and the Everyday Politics of African Urban Youth: The Case of Doula, Cameroon," *International Journal of Urban and Regional Research* 29 (3) (2005): 516–32.

29 In Zimbabwe, there are campaigns to educate passengers on traffic safety. Passengers are encouraged to report wayward drivers of public transport vehicles. However, IUPTV crews routinely ignore passengers' complaints. In incidents reported above, passengers' pleas for the driver to stop and panicked screams fell on deaf ears.

30 The term has no basis in local vernacular languages. It apparently means something that is illegal or illicit.

31 Here are some headlines in local newspapers "Hwindi Runs Over Student," *H-Metro*, 9 May 2012; "Kombi Drivers Jailed for 1 Year," *The Herald*, 3 February 2013, (for injuring a pedestrian in an attempt to flee the police); "Fleeing Kombi Runs Over Pedestrian," *The Herald*, 6 April 2013.

32 For instance, Wa Mungai and Samper "No Mercy, No Remorse" p. 57.

33 See Weitzer and Kubrin, "Misogyny in Rap Music."

34 Full cream fresh milk or powdered versions are preferred.

35 Soya protein is sold dried as "chunks" or "mince" and widely available from the Mbare produce market. It is the most affordable form of protein. It is cheaper than dried freshwater whitebait (fish), which is another source of protein for poor people.

36 See Davis, " On the Sexuality of 'Town Women' in Kampala."

37 This the language spoken in low-income neighbourhoods in Jamaica and globally popularized by ragga and dancehall music. See Newell, "Dancehall and its World." In Zimbabwe, there are DJs who present shows in patois. The extent of proficiency is hard to gauge. While it points to worldliness, its association with dreadlocked men has negative connotations such as laziness, drug abuse, and looking unkempt.

38 Wa Mungai and Samper, "No Mercy, No Remorse."

MUSIC AS BRICOLAGE IN POST-SOCIALIST DAR ES SALAAM

Maria Suriano

In the early 2000s, Dar es Salaam (Tanzania) saw the emergence of a genre known as Bongo Flava, a blend of foreign-derived styles ranging from hip-hop to ragamuffin. Sung in standard and street Swahili and dubbed "the music of the new generation" (*muziki wa kizazi kipya*), this style has become for urban youths the most preferred method of intra- and inter-generational communication. In an influential essay published in 1978, anthropologist Johannes Fabian argued that popular music and performance not only reflect, but may also *affect* the socio-political reality.[1] This essay builds on Fabian's influential insight and on other key scholarly works on a range of Tanzanian musical genres, which have shown that popular music not only mirrors, but also produces socio-political realities.[2] It illustrates that Bongo Flava has been an instrument of social innovation and self-affirmation in a specific African context.[3] Aesthetics, morals, and politics are intimately associated in East Africa, and there exists a long-standing connection between popular arts and the political landscape. The term "politics" is used here in its broad meaning: while in conventional political science, politics can be carried out solely by the state and the ruling party, popular modes of political expression have often been articulated beyond the channels of official politics.[4] The "OPNI" (*objets politiques non identifies*) or "UPOs" (unidentified political objects) possess political potential.[5] However, the relationship between popular culture and prevailing forms of power is quite complex and does not necessarily carry or imply an open challenge.

It is from Dar es Salaam—the main cultural and economic hub of Tanzania, with its four million official residents—that Bongo Flava has been popularized at a national and regional level. The beginning of this music can be traced back to 1991, when Saleh Jaber, a young boy who mastered Swahili and English (an exception at the time), released *Ice Ice Baby, King of Swahili Rap*, the first rap tape in Swahili. Since there were no recording studios in the country, he used instrumental versions of US rap hits (by artists such as Vanilla Ice and Naughty by Nature) and Jamaican reggae as the base for his own Swahili and English lyrics, though at times he sampled phrases from the original raps.

Such an artistic product was made possible by novel economic and political conditions: the free market and the privatization of the media. President Julius Nyerere retired in 1985 when the International Monetary Fund and the World Bank approved the "Economic Recovery Plan." President Ali Hassan Mwinyi brought an end to the famous *Ujamaa* form of socialist policies that had been launched in 1967. He permitted goods such as televisions to be imported; thus images of Western culture inundated the Tanzanian markets like never before. During this time of political reforms and commercialization, African American genres such as hip hop and R&B were broadcast for the first time by the newly opened radio stations; during Ujamaa there was only one (government-controlled) radio station. Since the early 1990s, these styles have become influential in the everyday lives of Tanzanian urbanites—who have since experimented with bass lines, drum beats, and guitar riffs—producing a bricolage of foreign and local elements.

According to reggae singer and music journalist Innocent Nganyagwa, Dar es Salaam-based reggae singers were despised in the early 1990s for playing foreign music. In response, they named their reggae "local flavour" (*fleva ya nyumbani* or *ladha ya hapa*). Sharing with early rap artists the common discrimination suffered, they invited rappers to their performances.[6] Dar es Salaam rappers initially rhymed in English. Journalist Saleh Ally, a former rapper himself, argues that the first to give rise to hip hop were well-off pupils of the International School of Masaki, a privileged neighbourhood; they mastered English and were exposed to foreign genres.[7] However, disadvantaged urbanites did not live insular lives: some shared information and had friendship ties with their wealthier counterparts. Artist Inspekta Haroun contends that in the early days slums such as Temeke, which generated numerous performers, were "thirsty for hip hop."[8]

A significant factor in the popularization of Bongo Flava has been the rise of professional recording technologies: Mawingu, the first studio established in Dar es Salaam in 1993, marked a turning point. It is in this city that most artists, producers, and distributors work, and the most prominent radio stations, recording studios, and television channels are to be found. This does not mean that each style that was incorporated into Bongo Flava over time necessarily originated from Dar es Salaam. Ragamuffin, dancehall, and reggae were popular in the 1990s in urban Uganda and Kenya respectively; they reached Dar es Salaam afterwards. Member of Parliament and early rapper Joseph Mbilinyi, a.k.a. Sugu (stubborn), claims that Kenya is home to East African reggae, Uganda to ragga, but with regard to the issue of hip hop, Dar es Salaam "is like the Vatican in Rome."[9]

Regarding the social configuration of Bongo Flava artists, most are men in their twenties, from diverse social and religious backgrounds, and with some degree of formal education. Initially singers targeted the young majority—according to the 2002 census, over 63 per cent of the country's population was younger than 25.[10] They have subsequently gained a much wider audience, including young townswomen, older individuals, and rural dwellers. Even though some originate from distant places, most of them were born in Dar es Salaam—frequently in its slums—or moved there to gain access to the facilities related to music production. A few are orphaned and have been brought up by other family members.

Since the mid-2000s, Bongo Flava has been ubiquitous in city minibuses and popular venues like bars and restaurants. Artists have taken increasing advantage of the extraordinary diffusion of this music through radio and TV programmes, tapes, CDs, and VCDs, awards, movies (since 2003), and gossip about their lives, loves, fancy cars, and clothes. Swahili and English magazines and tabloids, whose readership is chiefly located in Dar es Salaam, have played a pivotal role in popularizing Bongo Flava. The ample space given to these artists by the local media has enabled some of them to become superstars (*ma-supastaa*), icons of success and lead a better life. Many have also achieved a high degree of financial autonomy thanks to the unprecedented growth of the music market. This has never been the case for any other music culture in Dar es Salaam, let alone in other Tanzanian urban spaces. *Ngoma* (music and dances often accompanied by drums), *taarab* (sung Swahili poetry), and *dansi* (urban jazz), the main popular genres that appeared in the precolonial era (ngoma) and in the colonial period (taarab and dansi), have never obtained such media coverage.[11]

Music skills essential in ngoma, dansi, and taarab are not required in Bongo Flava, because producers record a voice on a pre-recorded backing track. Although performers are often attacked for their inability to play an instrument, it is undeniable that the use of relatively cheap recording technologies has somewhat democratized music making: even artists from slums can have their voices heard. "What's the point of [using] a foreign language in music when Bongo Fleva is best liked in *Uswahilini* (poor neighbourhoods)?"[12] Uswahilini includes the downtown quarter mainly occupied by Africans once known as Zone III and those peri-urban African areas that—in segregated colonial Dar es Salaam—were beyond British control. Primarily meant to condemn artists' use of English words, this comment made by rapper Afande Sele (born Selemani Msindi) also tells us that Bongo Flava is particularly popular in disadvantaged neighbourhoods, whose residents do not speak English. This implies that the genre allows disenfranchised urbanites to acquire a voice and, to some extent, a new dignity and visibility. For example, the 2004 kwaito hit "Hakuna Kulala" (There is no sleep) from the album *Ubin-adam-kazi* by Juma Nature joyfully displayed the social marginalization of Temeke; the video clip unapologetically exhibited its residents dancing and drinking home-made liquor.

While early Tanzanian rappers did not address socially relevant subjects, 1999 saw a shift—locally recalled as the end of the "old school" and the beginning of the "official revolution" (*mapinduzi rasmi*), epitomized by "Chemsha Bongo" (Use your brain) by Hard Blasterz. The new imperative became to "keep it real." Lyrics, now in Swahili, had to reflect the local context and express views on the actual urban living conditions.[13] A poignant example of how the process of localization has taken place is represented by the lyrics of "Darubini Kali" (Sharp binoculars), in which Afande Sele states: "Rap is not telling lies, … [claiming] you have a big car, when you live in a house of clay."[14] As Saleh Ally aptly put it, "You cannot say, 'I have a big car,' while you don't even have a bicycle."[15]

From the outset, Bongo Flava lyrics have appropriated a variety of foreign signs and symbols. Swahili lyrics are often infused with "Swanglish" words (code switching). Sometimes the pronunciation of the letter "r" replicates the English language (*k ribu* instead of *karibu*). Dar es Salaam-based artists have not just adopted Swahilized English terms and Swahili slang—quintessential creations of this city—but have moulded the street language. Newly created words have been extensively appropriated by Swahili tabloids and even by some newspapers.

Young male artists sport extra-large shirts and earrings (in Swahili culture frowned upon). "From the US, we copied the use of socks and coats even though the weather is hot," Saleh Ally ironically says.[16] Rastafarian outfits and hairstyles are also quite influential. Even the body language combines US and Jamaican elements, while female artists make frequent use of familiar cultural references from the Middle East.

It is worth noting that, in line with previous dictates, performers should adhere to a dress code monitored by the Dar es Salaam based Musicians' Union (CHAMUDATA), and by the BASATA.[17] Even if in practice there is no effective regulation, attempts have been made at controlling female artists.[18] In 2005, the Swahili tabloid *Kiu* reported that the previous year "through BASATA, the Government [had] tried to ban the semi-naked dress-style of female musicians when they were performing on stage."[19] In 2005, several tabloids hosted debates over female singers' obscenity.[20]

It should be emphasized that Bongo Flava artists have not built an identity completely breaking with the past, nor do their lyrics appropriate foreign cultures uncritically. Rather, songs are filled with life experience and convey pressing urban issues felt at a local level, from marriage and infidelity to HIV-AIDS, unemployment, poverty, drug abuse, and even bribery.

Despite the existence of lyrics against corruption, artists' attitude towards power—either represented by elders or politicians—is largely ambivalent.[21] Far from ignoring or challenging their elders, Bongo Flava artists often strive to create bonds with them, for example by celebrating the figure of the late Nyerere. This indicates an attempt to connect to the past, but may also suggest an entirely new claim: that wisdom is not just a prerogative of the elders. The ambivalence towards the political establishment is visible during election campaigns, when performers often follow politicians in their countrywide tours and release praise songs (largely for the ruling party) on invitation—and allegedly for compensation. First visible in 2000, this trend was reinforced in the electoral campaigns of 2005 and 2010.

By and large, conventional values are not challenged, but reaffirmed. In "Mwana Mkiwa" (Orphaned child), K. Saul sings about highly valued patience.[22] In "Je, Utanipenda" (Will you love me?), Mike T highlights: "I came to your parents' home with my best man," who is the representative in the customary bridewealth negotiations. The emphasis on marriage and conventional domesticity is a general aspiration among the average youths in Africa, as elsewhere.[23] But in the context of Tanzania, these principles have a specific resonance with postcolonial state policies, when leaders deemed arts educational, and sought to control them. In search of a national identity, Nyerere established in 1962 the Ministry of Culture and Youth, whose primary aim was the use of arts to teach the masses. To quote from one official document: "We will sing about socialism as a means to ending poverty. We will dramatize about a man who is ill and does not go to hospital so that our people should see the importance of going to hospital when they are ill."[24]

Many Bongo Flava singers have embraced the culturally entrenched notion of music as educational. In "Hajazaa" (She hasn't given birth yet), Voice Wonders warns his listeners to use hospitals and avoid traditional healers. If "a good song … has to entertain, … criticise, and … teach, educate,"[25] the social message may serve to please the public. This is how Afande Sele expresses the prevalent audience's expectations: "People do want a message, not [hear artists] boast and celebrate sex and alcohol."[26] In fact, the overwhelmingly young listeners and tabloids targeting townspeople see music as didactic. Columns of Swahili tabloids, where lyrics are scrutinized and explained to readers, praise songs with a message. The hit "Understanding" by Lady Jay Dee featuring TID (Top in Dar) was applauded by Maisha on the grounds that it "teaches us about married life; it stresses the real love and patience within the household, things that make a marriage long-lasting."[27]

Lyrics often draw on a rich repertoire of Swahili proverbs and sayings. Rhymes resonate with Swahili poetry, and also the nicknames given to artists, thereby providing links between music, cultural performance, and social identity, in a practice widespread in different African contexts. Far from being uncritical importations of the rivalries between "East Coast" and "West Coast" US rappers, mabifu ("beefs" or fights) between artists are an enduring feature of Swahili cultural performances. Tunes often borrow from coastal and upcountry local rhythms so that the term "local" encompasses genres with multiple origins: from Egypt to India, from Cuba to Congo, from the US to Jamaica.

The impact of musical genres originating in the US is not simply the result of a growing cultural or ideological influence. Rather, it is the continuation of a long-standing process of adaptation of foreign genres to local aesthetic principles, which constitutes a key Swahili trait.[28] Bongo Flava is the latest Tanzanian urban style that provides evidence of a constant practice whereby "images and sounds that are part of a global stream of popular culture can take on quite different meanings once they get picked up by youth in a particular place."[29]

The visibility of familiar features together with socio-politically engaged lyrics have prompted the older generation to pay attention to the stories the youths have to tell. By the mid-2000s, the whole phenomenon of Bongo Flava had to some extent "captured the thoughts of grown-up people."[30] Yet, for the majority of socially settled individuals, this genre is still largely the "music of chaos" (*muziki wa fujo*). Indeed, this is reminiscent of past generational tensions over the rise of new music cultures. In the 1940s, cosmopolitan dansi, now seen as a typical Tanzanian genre widely popular among adults, was frequently disparaged as a foreign style and was associated with loafers.[31]

Adult disapproval has grown in response to significant changes in the lyrics since the mid-2000s. Hits echoing the emphasis by Jamaican dancehall and US hip hop on urban subcultures focusing on fun have been successful. The tune, more than the lyrics, has increasingly determined the commercial success of Bongo Flava songs.[32] Alcohol, marijuana, money, sex, and the objectification of young townswomen are recurring features. They depict the actual or aspirational lifestyle of a significant portion of urban youths.

The ambivalent reactions to the popularity of these songs—commonly disparaged in local discourses—suggest a long-term pattern of ambiguous relations between artists and mainstream Tanzanian culture. To be sure, the entertainment trend partly stems from the fact that by the early 2000s there was a new album being recorded nearly every week. This made it difficult, if not impossible, to release exclusively socially conscious songs, as this would have generated repetitive and cumbersome lyrics. Yet, the decision not to address educational issues also points to the fact that by ignoring the dictates of former cultural policies, artists have consciously detached themselves from the older generation. More non-committal songs ultimately signal a pervasive and long-standing desire by Tanzanian youths to participate in global cultural trends.[33]

To conclude, by capturing sounds heard on international records and combining them with local conceptions of music making, young artists in post-socialist Tanzania have reshaped foreign influences in a way that is unique to the urban landscape of Dar es Salaam. They have created a distinctive bricolage of global and local references. Bongo Flava artists are complex figures: as children of globalization, they see themselves as citizens of the world and claim universality accordingly. But their allegiances ultimately lie with Tanzanian society: conventionally accepted norms are mostly reaffirmed, often in combination with controversial values, which depict novel metropolitan subcultures and aspirations.

While African youths are often seen as a "lost generation" easily manipulated by their elders,[34] Bongo Flava lyrics, along with artists' and audiences' comments, reveal the agency exercised by Tanzanian urbanites. Regardless of whether songs reassert or dismiss deeply entrenched social norms, Bongo Flava has become a key platform for public debate and for asserting youths' autonomy, through the expression of a plurality of (sometimes contradictory) meanings, continuities with the past, and new identities. If music can be an instrument of expression and socio-political change, Bongo Flava has allowed urban youths to carve out a niche for themselves in the reconfiguration of Tanzanian culture.

Endnotes

1 Johannes Fabian, "Popular Culture in Africa: Findings and Conjectures," *Africa* 48, 4 (1978): 315–334. Key work on popular culture has been conducted by Karin Barber. See her "Popular Arts in Africa," *African Studies Review* 30 (3) (1987): 1–78.

2 Kelly M. Askew, *Performing the Nation: Swahili Music and Cultural Politics in Tanzania* (Chicago: The University of Chicago Press, 2002); Laura Fair, *Pastimes and Politics: Culture, Community and Identity in Post-Abolition Urban Zanzibar, 1890–1945* (Athens: Ohio University Press, Oxford: James Currey, 2001); Susan Geiger, *TANU Women: Gender and Culture in the Making of Tanganyikan Nationalism, 1955–1965* (Portsmouth: Heinemann, Oxford: James Currey, 1997); Werner Graebner, ed., *Sokomoko. Popular Culture in East Africa* (Amsterdam: Rodopi, 1992); Frank Gunderson and Gregory F. Barz, eds., *Mashindano! Competitive Music Performance in East Africa* (Dar es Salaam: Mkuki na Nyota, 2000); Margaret Strobel, "From Lelemama to Lobbying: Women's Associations in Mombasa, Kenya," *Women in Africa: Studies in Social and Economic Change*, ed. Nancy Hafkin and Edna G. Bay (Stanford: Stanford University Press, 1976) pp. 184–211; T.O. Ranger, *Dance and Society in Eastern Africa, 1890–1970: The Beni Ngoma* (London: Heinemann, 1975).

3 This essay draws on empirical evidence, gathered in the course of extensive fieldwork (interviews and informal conversations with more than twenty artists, fans, radio presenters, and journalists were conducted from 2004–2005 and in 2006; performances were attended in Dar es Salaam, Mwanza, and in small towns such as Songea and Mbinga); combined with published and unpublished works.

4 Jean-François Bayart, "La politique par le bas en Afrique noire: questions de métode," *Politique Africaine* (1) (March 1981): 53–82; esp. pp. 65–68. Cf. also James Scott, *Domination and the Arts of Resistance* (New Haven and London: Yale University Press, 1990).

5 Denis-Constant Martin, ed., *Sur la piste des OPNI (objets politiques non identifiés)* (Paris: Karthala, 2002).

6 Innocent Nganyagwa, interview, Msasani, 30 October 2005. All interviews took place in Dar es Salaam.

7 Saleh Ally, interview, Sinza, 8 April 2005.

8 Inspekta Haroun (a.k.a. Babu, grandfather; born Haroun Kahena), interview, Kijitonyama, 10 April 2005.

9 Sugu (born Joseph Mbilinyi), interview, Sinza, 22 March 2005.

10 Government of Tanzania. 2002. Evaluation and Analysis of the Age Structure, 2 http://www.tanzania.go.tz/census/pdf/Evaluation%20and%20Analysis%20of%20the%20Age%20Structure.pdf. (accessed 4 December 2006).

11 Peter Mangesho, "Global Cultural Trends: The Case of Hip-hop Music in Dar es Salaam," (MA dissertation, University of Dar es Salaam, 2003) pp. 62–64. For ngoma, taarab, and dansi, and a discussion of the categories of traditional and modern, see Kelly M. Askew, "As Plato Duly Warned: Music, Politics and Social Change in Coastal East Africa," *Anthropological Quarterly* 76, 4 (Autumn 2003): 609–637.

12 Afande Sele, *Darubini Kali* (GMC Wasanii Promoters, GMC Sole Distributors, Dar es Salaam, 2004).

13 Sebastian Maganga (radio presenter), interview, Clouds FM headquarters, 11 March 2005.

14 Sele, *Darubini Kali*.

15 Saleh Ally, interview. Cf. also Peter J. Haas and Thomas Gesthuizen, "Ndani ya Bongo: Kiswahili Rap Keeping it Real," in *Mashindano! Competitive Music Performance in East Africa*, ed. Frank Gunderson and Gregory F. Barz (Dar es Salaam: Mkuki na Nyota, 2000) pp. 279–294; 285; Alex Perullo, "'Here's a Little Something Local': An Early History of Hip Hop in Dar es Salaam, Tanzania, 1984–1997," in *Dar es Salaam. Histories from an Emerging African Metropolis*, ed. James Brennan, Andrew Burton, and Yusuf Lawi (Dar es Salaam: Mkuki na Nyota, 2007) pp. 250–272.

16 Saleh Ally, interview.

17 John Kitime (dansi musician and former president of CHAMUDATA), interview, Kinondoni, 3 November 2005.

18 For continuities with previous attempts to control young townswomen, see Andrew M. Ivaska, "'Anti-mini Militants Meet Modern Misses': Urban Style, Gender and the Politics of 'National Culture' in 1960s Dar es Salaam, Tanzania," *Gender & History* 14, 3 (2002): 584–607.

19 Na Mwandishi Wetu (by our writer), "Lady JayD, RayC Nusu Uchi" (Lady JayD, RayC Half Naked), *Kiu*, (18–21 April 2005) p. 2.

20 Na Mwandishi Wetu (by our writer), *Amani*, (10-16 March 2005); *Nipashe*, (11 February 2005) p. 3.

21 Achille Mbembe, "Provisional Notes on the Postcolony," *Africa* 62 (1) (1992): 3–37 and 25.

22 Hassan Abbas, *Maisha*, (16-22 February 2005) p. 4.

23 Donald B. Cruise O'Brien, "A Lost Generation? Youth Identity and State Decay in West Africa," in *Postcolonial Identities in Africa*, ed. Richard Werbner and Terence Ranger (London: Zed Books, 1996) pp. 55–74 and 58.

24 Quoted in Elias M. Songoyi, *The Artist and the State in Tanzania. A Study of Two Singers: Kalikali and Mwinamila* (MA dissertation, University of Dar es Salaam, 1988) p. 10.

25 Saleh Ally, interview.

26 Afande Sele, *Darubini Kali*.

27 Jane John, *Maisha* (23–29 March 2005).

28 Askew, *Performing the Nation* pp. 66–67.

29 Peter W. Remes, "*Karibu geto langu / Welcome in my Ghetto*": Urban Youth, Popular Culture and Language in 1990s Tanzania (PhD thesis, Northwestern University, 1998) p. 329.

30 Innocent Nganyagwa, "Dira ya muziki," *Zeze* (24 February–2 March 2005): 10.

31 Cf. Maria Suriano, "Letters to the Editor and Poems. *Mambo Leo* and Readers' Debates on *Dansi*, *Ustaarabu*, Respectability and Modernity in Tanganyika, 1940s–1950s," *Africa Today* 57 (3) (2011): 39–55.

32 P Funk (owner of Bongo Records), informal conversation, Kijitonyama, 23 April 2005.

33 Cf. Andrew M. Ivaska, *Cultured States: Youth, Gender, and Modern Style in 1960s Dar es Salaam* (Durham, NC: Duke University Press, 2011).

34 O'Brien, "A Lost Generation?" p. 55.

SINGING THE PRAISES OF POWER

Bob W. White

In political systems characterized by limited freedom of expression, the links between popular culture and power are particularly complex. In his analysis of the relevance of popular culture to contemporary theory in anthropology, Johannes Fabian points to the distinction between "popular culture" and "culture *tout court*."[1] According to Fabian, popular culture opens up the possibility of a new analytical approach because it is implicated in networks and institutions that transcend the boundaries of culture tout court—not only in its production and distribution, but also at the level of meaning. The integration of popular culture at these different levels allows us to observe the processes that culture tends to ignore or mask: the most obvious examples are the articulation of different sorts of identity (community, regional, and national), the movement of capital (political, symbolic, and financial), and the instrumentalization of culture (whether for commercial, political, or other ends). In other words, popular culture in Africa can be seen as a diagnostic tool for the analysis of power.

The fascination with the notion of "resistance" has already been the object of several shrewd analyses, and the issue of resistance is so central to intergenerational dynamics that the demographic category of "youth" is often commensurate with a position of protest.[2] Ethnographic research in the Democratic Republic of Congo reveals a context where resistance is far from being the norm in practical and artistic attitudes to leadership. More specifically, I have identified three different models of authority employed by Kinshasa bandleaders to manage musical careers: "playing with power," "strategic collaboration," and "putting Kinshasa on your head."[3] However, these models, which represent three different conceptions of authority, cannot be fully understood without deeper consideration of the strategies used to address people in positions of authority outside the context of the music scene.[4] In order to account for this complexity, I outline five strategies used by musicians in Kinshasa to communicate with those in positions of power. *Indifference* can be expressed through silence with regards to political issues (for example, in love songs), or it can be more explicitly articulated, as when an artist responds to a journalist's questions about his political orientations by saying "I don't do politics." *Overt resistance* is rather rare in this context, although there are some well-known examples elsewhere on the continent: Fela Kuti's Afrobeat in Nigeria, Thomas Mapfumo's *chimurenga* music in Zimbabwe, and Tiken Jah Fakoly's Africanized reggae in Côte d'Ivoire. *Derision* can take various forms, from caricature to banalization,[5] particularly in the DRC, where freedom of expression has been severely restricted by successive political regimes. One of the few artists to make systematic use of derision is Luambo Makiadi, known as "Franco," leader of the legendary group O.K. Jazz.[6] *Indirect discourse* often centres on the use of one or more figures of speech (allegory, metaphor, parable) to criticize power without actually incriminating oneself. This strategy allows fans to interpret a song's political content, which is hidden behind lyrics that on the surface seem anodyne or inoffensive. *Praise* is a highly distinctive Kinshasa art form, quite different from the now well-documented griot praise-singing traditions of West Africa or the Sahel.[7] Since the 1980s, techniques for the performance of praise in popular music have proliferated (especially the various forms of *libanga,* see below)—and these inevitably draw on past practices in order to develop appropriate strategies for the present.[8]

In studying popular music in Kinshasa, I have taken a particular interest in praise, not only because its performance challenges conventional wisdom about power dynamics in this setting, but also because the practice of singing the leader's praises occupies an important place in the imaginary of Congolese political culture.[9] Though it was clearly a form of propaganda, the system of state-sponsored singing and dancing promoted by the Mobutu regime in the 1970s and 1980s (referred to locally as *l'animation politique et culturelle*) was justified by referring to an imagined affinity between the people and the head of state: "Happy are those who sing and dance," as Mobutu himself famously said. L'animation politique et culturelle became the cornerstone of cultural policy in the Second Republic and was a prominent feature of the media landscape—especially television—in Mobutu's Zaire.[10] Through l'animation politique, traditional music was systematically refocused on singing the praises of Mobutu, his one-party state, and the MPR (Mouvement Populaire de la Révolution). The influence of animation politique is manifest in popular dance music

1

even today, not only through the integration of certain elements of traditional rhythms and proverbs, but also through the phenomenon of praise-singing known as libanga, which is now an integral part of the sound and structure of Congolese rumba.

Libanga (often used in the plural or *mabanga*) consists of "throwing" (in Lingala, *kobwaka*) the names of friends, acquaintances, or interested parties in return for payments referred to as gestures of "appreciation."[11] For some fans, the phenomenon of libanga is symptomatic of the degradation of classic forms of Zairian rumba, a decline dating from the end of the colonial period: according to these critics, musicians have become specialists in marketing or even masters of illusion.[12] For others, particularly the generation of fans who entered adulthood during the economic crisis of the 1980s, it is only natural that artists should sing the names of the rich, since it is increasingly difficult to earn an income from the sale of records.

1 Luambo Makiadi et le T.P.O.K. Jazz chantet Candidat Na Bisu Mobutu / Luambo Makiadi (Franco) and O.K. Jazz sing the praises of "our candidate" Mobutu, 1984.

In addition to this financial justification, for young people who have become accustomed to the sound of praise, libanga represents a means of gaining social recognition in an increasingly anonymous urban space, not to mention a strategy for getting closer to the "stars."[13] Libanga is a fairly recent phenomenon in Congolese popular culture, but it must be understood in the context of a long history of close links between popular artists and powerful people. Firstly, it should be emphasized that sponsorship has been part of the Congolese music industry since independence, if not before. It can be found not only in the numerous examples of marketing songs, such as Franco's famous "Azda,"[14] but also in the relationships between popular artists and Kinshasa's breweries. For several decades, the sponsorship policies of the capital's major breweries (Unibra with the beer Skol, and Bralima with Primus) have guaranteed a major source of income and visibility for local artists. Constantly searching for links with opinion leaders, companies attempt to associate their products with the popular artists by sponsoring their concerts, tours, and televised shows. The competitive nature of sponsorship agreements with musicians goes some way towards explaining why the superstar Werra Son ("King of the Forest") has appeared in promotional music videos for each of the two rival beers at different points in his career.[15]

The second type of connection between artists and power occurs more intermittently, as it centres around election campaigns. Luambo Makiadi, or "Franco," leader of the legendary O.K. Jazz Orchestra, is probably the artist who most sang the praises of politicians in the Zaire period. Franco composed several songs in honour of post-independence political figures (examples include "Docteur Tshombe" for Moise Tshombe and "Lumumba, Héros National" for Patrice Lumumba) and others dedicated to the Mobutu regime ("Cinq ans ekoki," "Votez vert," and "Mobutu candidat na biso"). He even produced an entire album consisting of various versions of his most well-known "political" songs.[16] Although Mobutu never held democratic elections, his propaganda strategy made use of artists like Franco to create an image of support and solidarity around Mobutu's person. Laurent-Désiré Kabila, who came to power without being widely known to the Congolese population, clearly needed to distance himself from the political culture of Mobutu. With just a few exceptions, musicians immediately felt the effects of this change in power, since Kabila was not nearly as interested as Mobutu in musicians' praise, particularly at the start of his presidency.[17]

The mobilization of musicians in the 2006 presidential contest between Joseph Kabila and Jean-Pierre Bemba did not come as a surprise to anyone. Kabila's series of campaign videos aroused little interest, apart from some comments and rumours surrounding the participation of particular music stars. The videos supporting Kabila represented a veritable who's who of Congolese popular music (Mbilia Bel, Kester Emeneya, J.B. M'Piana, Bozi Boziana, Adolphe Dominguez, Reddy Amisi, Do Akongo, and others), and some of these figures were labelled "collaborators" for working with the Kabila government.[18] Most of these music videos recycled the old familiar formulas of political praise: Joseph Kabila, "builder of peace," "the people's candidate," "brave leader," "let us unite behind him," "our hope for the future," and "guardian of our happiness."

The emergence of the music video in the late 1980s offered new artistic and promotional tools to those working in the music industry. "Bambinga FARDC," one of hundreds of music videos that are produced every year in Kinshasa, is remarkable not only because it explicitly references politics, something which is extremely rare in the popular dance music of Kinshasa. But it is also interesting because it taps into recent traditions of commercialized praise-singing (known locally as *libanga*), without submitting to the authority of the state. In the Congolese blogosphère this music video was accused of being "rumba propaganda," but in Kinshasa the debate around the song raises questions about what happened behind the scenes, revealing a certain inter-generational tension with regards to the equitable distribution of resources by the state.[19] Through a detailed analysis of images and words, it is possible to see that the creative use of generic conventions in popular music videos permits musicians to "hook" youth audiences, especially to the extent that this narrative is able to make effective use of sentiments towards national identity and belonging.

Translation by Caroline George

Endnotes

1   Johannes Fabian, *Moments of Freedom: Anthropology and Popular Culture* (Charlottesville: University Press of Virginia, 1998).

2   Lila Abu-Lughod, "The Romance of Resistance," *American Ethnologist* 17 (1990): 41–55; Sherry Ortner, "Resistance and the Problem of Ethnographic Refusal," *Comparative Studies in Society and History* 37 (1) (Jan. 1995): 173–193.

3   Bob W. White, *Rumba Rules: The Politics of Dance Music in Mobutu's Zaire* (Durham: Duke University Press, 2008).

4   For examples of this issue elsewhere in Africa, see Joyce Nyairo and James Ogude, "Popular Music, Popular Politics: *Unbwogable* and the Idioms of Freedom in Kenyan Popular Music," *African Affairs* 104 (415) (2005): 225–249; Denis-Constant Martin, *Quand le rap sort de sa bulle: sociologie politique d'un succès populaire* (Paris: Seteun-Irma, 2010).

5   Achille Mbembe, "The 'Thing' and Its Double in Cameroonian Cartoons," *Cahiers d'études africaines* XLIII (4) (2003): 791–826.

6   Bob W. White, *Rumba Rules*.

7   David C. Conrad, and Barbara E. Frank, ed., *Status and Identity in West Africa:* Nyamakalaw *of Mande* (Bloomington: Indiana University Press, 1995); Sony Camara, *Gens de la parole: Essai sur la condition et le rôle des griots dans la société malinké* (Paris: Karthala, 1992); Mamadou Diawara, "Mande Oral Popular Culture Revisited by the Electronic Media," in *Readings in Popular Culture,* ed. Karin Barber (Bloomington: Indiana University Press, 1997); Dorothea Schulz, "Pricey Publicity, Refutable Reputations: *Jeliw* and the Economics of Honour in Mali," *Paideuma* (45) (1999): 275–292.

8   Johannes Fabian, *Moments of Freedom.*

9   Lye M. Yoka, "Musique et pouvoir," in *Musique populaire et société à Kinshasa: Une ethnographie de l'écoute,* ed. Bob. W. White and Lye M. Yoka (Paris: L'Harmattan, 2010) pp. 239–256.

10 Bob W. White, "L'incroyable machine d'authenticité: *l'animation politique* et l'usage public de la culture dans le Zaïre de Mobutu," in *Anthropologie et Sociétés,* 30 (2) (2006): 43–64.

11 For a more detailed analysis, see Bob W. White, "Modernity's Trickster: 'Dipping' and 'Throwing' in Congolese Popular Dance Music,"

in *Drama and Performance in Africa,* ed. John Conteh-Morgan and Tejumola Olaniyan (Bloomington: University of Indiana Press, 2004) pp. 198–218; Bob W. White, *Rumba Rules.*

12 Serge Makobo, "Musique de Kinshasa: des artifices qui bousculent les mœurs," in *Musique populaire et société à Kinshasa,* ed. Bob W. White and Lye M. pp. 175–210.

13 Bob W. White, *Rumba Rules.*

14 This was a song sung by Luambo Makiadi, or "Franco," in the 1970s; it advertised the Volkswagen Beetle, which had just arrived in the country (Azda was the name of the dealer).

15 Werra Son, "Tindika Lokito": http://www.youtube.com/watch?v=OlwT gu1ESWc&feature=channel, Werra Son, "Sous sol": http://www.youtube.com/watch?v=QwGFPgQIQ9E&feature=channel

16 It is interesting to note that this album also contains some songs unrelated to election campaigns.

17 Bob W. White, *Rumba Rules.* Under Laurent Kabila's government, a song was released promoting the new national currency ("Franc congolais"); another encouraged patriotic sentiment ("Tokokufa pona Congo"). Despite the appearance of a large number of music stars in the accompanying videos, these two songs were seen as propaganda by most people in Kinshasa. Kabila also enlisted singer-songwriter Jean Goubald to produce an album of "patriotic" songs. According to some rumours, Kabila funded the promotion of this album through a levy on civil servants' salaries (see the following link: http://alexengwete.afrikblog.com/archives/2009/02/03/12341476.html).

18 The PPRD (Parti du peuple pour la reconstruction et la démocratie) is the party created in 2002 by Joseph Kabila, current President of the DRC. To see examples of these accusations against Werra Son, read the comments left in response to the music video at: http://www.youtube.com/watch?v= 1aQSzKauOE&feature=channel

19 The video is available online under: http://www.dailymotion.com/video/x88pc8_rumba-propagande-fardc_music. Elsewhere I have analyzed this video with the help of David Nadeau-Bernatchez in *L'Afrique des générations,* Muriel Gomez-Perez and Marie Nathalie LeBlanc (ed.) (Paris: Karthala, 2012).

4

ACOUSTIC ECOLOGIES

CINEMAS' SONIC RESIDUES

Stephen Barber

1 Sound Mirror, Dungeness,
England.
Photo by Stephen Barber.

The sound of film infiltrates and refigures the city. For many decades, a pivotal experience during the course of urban walking was to pass the foyer or side-doors of a cinema and abruptly hear a blurred cacophony—film-dialogue, noise or explosions from films of conflicts, music—expelled from that space. Especially in summer heat, with the opening of windows, doors, and emergency exits, that sonic eruption into the adjacent urban environment, from cinematic orifices, was accentuated. The walls of a cinema auditorium form the carapace reinforcing the concentrated experience of the film audience, exempted, for a few hours, from the imperatives of exterior urban space; that experience, especially in its corporeal dimensions, was primarily a sonic one, amalgamated from the elements emitted from the cinema's sound-system, together with the voices and noises of spectators, which—in such environments as all-night cult-movie screenings or those occupied by audiences culturally oblivious to any need for spectators to watch a film in silence—formed an incessant counterpoint to film soundtrack elements: voices of seduction, voices of outrage, voices of adulation.

The first auditoria constructed specifically for the celluloid projection of films, from the 1900s (following several years, from 1895, in which film-projection had inhabited the space of pre-existing venues, such as variety halls and theatres), were not conceived as environments for sonic projection, since film itself remained silent, even if the auditorium itself was saturated with multiple strata of noise. But from the late 1920s, cinema auditoria, such as those designed by the influential architect S. Charles Lee in Los Angeles, formed film's acoustic receptacles, intended to transmit sound as immediately and physically as possible to the audiences seated within them. In 1929, the Surrealist film theorist Antonin Artaud underlined that corporeal aspect of film sound in its emergence, together with its active diminution of the film-image: "The image presents itself only in one dimension, it's the translation, the transposition of the real; sound, on the contrary, is unique and true, it bursts out into the room, and acts by consequence with much more intensity than the image, which becomes only a kind of illusion of sound."[1] The pervasive sonorization of film from the early 1930s—resisted only by experimental film movements—consolidated worldwide film industries' vast cultural power, as important instigators of human experience and perception, via the medium of film and through film spectatorship in sound-sensitized cinema spaces, for the remainder of the twentieth century. All technological experiments of the following decades, especially the 1950s and 60s, designed to magnify infinitely the presence and propulsion of sound in enclosed spaces, as with IMAX in Canada and Astrorama in Japan, are simultaneously experiments with space and corporeality. Such experiments, often requiring extravagant and expensive technological specifications, also necessitated the engagement of an urban population attuned to entering specialist auditoria, such as IMAX cinemas or projection spaces created for world's fairs and expositions, primarily to experience the corporeal dimensions of film sound, even in excess of their desire for film's images. An exception to that concentration of film sound within the enclosed space of the cinema auditorium is the phenomenon of open-air film projections, often using the exterior façades or firewalls of buildings as screens, in which the intermediation of the cinema's walls, between urban space and auditorium, is removed, and the noises of the city and the noises of film directly mesh or collide.

In the spaces of abandoned cinemas, sound possesses a unique, spectral and still-corporeal presence, in intimate rapport with the urban space around them. Cinemas have always formed potentially obsolete spaces, from film's origins, imminently subject to being technologically surpassed, or vulnerable to shifts in urban dynamics such as population changes or the transformations of their surrounding districts. To avert urban obsolescence, cinemas were often intentionally constructed in constellations, on avenues such as Lisbon's Avenida da Liberdade or Los Angeles' Downtown Broadway, in sonic competition against one another (through such vocal media as "barkers": figures employed solely to stand outside the foyers of cinemas to lure passers-by inside with high-volume enticements), but architecturally amassed in alliance against the volatile flux of urban space. Even the most immense and technologically sophisticated cinemas—such as New York's Roxy Theatre, constructed in 1927 as a miniaturized city in its own right, with its own restaurants, shops, hotel, and hospital—could be razed without trace after only several decades, as the city mutated around them and rendered them financially moribund. Cinemas that have endured in uninterrupted operation, from the origins of cinematic space in the 1900s through to the contemporary moment, such as Szczecin's Kino Pionier (opened in 1909 and still in operation), form temporal aberrations in their rapport with city space. A special urban entity emerges when a cinema auditorium is abandoned but not demolished, and may be entered, in that state of suspension, either covertly or after negotiation with its guardians. The dereliction of cinema auditoria accelerated worldwide in the 1980s with the onset of home-video consumption and the transferral of cinematic sound into domestic environments; digital media, with the capacity for film sound to accompany its iPhone-wielding, earphoned spectator on traversals of city-space, further accelerated the mass-abandonment of cinematic space from the 2000s, thereby creating new architectural sites, in their disintegration, for the analysis of sonic post-cinematic detritus.

In exploring the interiors of such derelict environments, two divergent sources of noise can be isolated. Firstly, film projection always leaves behind its distinctive, ineradicable sonic residues. These can take the form, among others, of tiers of seating that gradually splinter and sink; projection screens that collapse and disintegrate, eventually subsiding; film projection equipment that, in obsolete cinemas in which it has not been stripped out, gradually corrodes, releasing rivets and screws; discarded film celluloid reels, primarily stored in the cinema's projection-box, which, notably when exposed to extremes of cold or humid heat, release elements of their emulsions, and undergo striations and fissurations; decorative elements, such as chandeliers and mirrorballs, that disintegrate and fall to the ground. Alongside those film-focused sonic components, abandoned cinema interiors

2 London cinema façade,
Bangkok, Thailand.
Photo by Stephen Barber.

remain inhabited particularly by the noises of auditorium-transiting rodents and small animals, and by the traces of ephemeral human inhabitation, in such forms as bottles splintered underfoot. Often, projects to reactivate such cinematic spaces, either for illicit parties and art events or for economically-oriented redevelopments sanctioned by their owners, leave their own intricate regimes of detritus, in the forms of accumulations of debris, materials left behind from interrupted construction works, and generally unidentifiable or unclassifiable artefacts, each of which emits its own sonic traces as it gradually falls apart. Secondly, abandoned cinemas are also inhabited by incessantly shifting sonic presences originating in the urban environment outside the auditorium, able to enter and permeate the cinematic space through their volume and pitch or via the material fragility of that space's residual infrastructure: unhinged exterior doors, broken or left-open windows. That internally-directed sonic infiltration, from the exterior urban environment, forms the contrary one to the experience of hearing, from the outside, the disgorging of filmic cacophonies from the still in-use auditorium.

In the way that the late nineteenth-century science of optography investigated the potential for the final image registered on a human retina (the face of a victim's murderer, for example) to be embedded there, recoverable by dissection and the replication of the resulting eye-image, the final soundscape imprinted into the fabric and infrastructure of a cinema auditorium may also be explored, in its residues and traces, and through the resonance, in that space, of sonic elements infiltrating it from the city outside. In many ways, that optography era's instigators of film—Etienne-Jules Marey with his mobile camera-gun, Eadweard Muybridge with his many thousands of glass-plate moving-image sequences, Louis Le Prince with his first film of spectral figures traversing Leeds Bridge in 1888—experimented with the same preoccupations as Wilhelm Kühne's optography: the registration, on the eye, of death, and death's revivification in the image. Similarly, abandoned cinema spaces form the optimal experimental site in which to map film sound's death, in the digital era, and potentially reactivate its acoustic detritus. All derelict cinemas worldwide, in that sense, form variants of the distinctive constructions known as "sound mirrors," or "listening ears," like those installed in concrete in the 1920s and 30s on the south coast of England, close to Dungeness, in the form of vast lenses for sonic registration, designed to receive and magnify, for the attentive human ear, the sounds of an oncoming enemy invasion; rendered obsolete and consigned to a ghostly, voided status even before their first use, those sound mirrors still listen, in the contemporary moment.

In the auditorium of the abandoned Patria cinema, on the Stefan cel Mare Avenue of the Moldovan city of Chisinau, in March 2013, the soundscape experienced formed an intricate, conflicted one. The ornate cinema building predated film, constructed as a college for women in the mid nineteenth century, before being largely destroyed during successive German and Soviet wartime incursions through the city, then reconstructed as a cinema by German prisoners of war in the late 1940s. It only closed as a cinema a few months earlier

(I arrived expecting it not to be abandoned, but to still be showing films), and the large auditorium, with its banks of plastic seats, had not had time to endure the deterioration prevalent in abandoned cinemas. Its projectors remained intact, and it appeared still to be exhaling its final pulses of sound, along with its own history of destructions. A pizza restaurant had already opened in one of the foyer areas, and the sounds of patrons' voices and clanging cutlery entered that space, along with police sirens from the avenue outside, punctuated by burnt-out buildings from Chisinau's 2009 episode of urban unrest; the cinema was situated directly alongside the Russian Embassy, and police vans had parked in rows outside, as though the cinema were a riotous source of revolutionary turmoil.

In the auditorium of the abandoned London Theater, on Sukhumvit Road in Bangkok, in June 2012, the detritus of cinematic sound was overlayered, again, by restaurant noise. The 1960s neon signage above the cinema's foyer remained intact, but the auditorium itself, while still occupying its former parameters, had been comprehensively gutted; the space improvised into rows of packed tables for the restaurant's fast-moving clientele, evidently preoccupied with inhabiting the auditorium for the most abbreviated possible interval, and saturating the space with maximal vocal content, in contrast to its previous cinematic clientele's durational experience and relative silence. That vocal sound itself formed a subsidiary stratum to the incessant noise from the gridlocked avenue outside, overseen by vast digital-animation corporate screens. The London cinema was one of several named after European and North American cities, constructed along Sukhumvit Road and the now-demolished Washington Square in the 1960s and 1970s, for US soldiers on leave from the Vietnam war; the London cinema aberrantly survived, while most other cinemas of that era vanished, razed without trace, or transformed into sex venues, or, as with the Siam cinema, burned down in a frenzy by street-protesters in the Bangkok unrest of 2010.

In the auditorium of the abandoned Alcazar cinema, in the medina alleyway area of Tangier, in May 2013, the residues of film formed a phantasmatic presence, among the dust-encrusted rows of seats facing a long-collapsed screen. The cinema was built in the late 1920s, in the style of a Paris neighbourhood cinema, such as the Studio 28 in Montmartre, where Artaud delivered his Surrealism-era lecture denouncing film sound. It had been abandoned for exactly twenty years, according to its guardian; before that, its full-on sound-system had propelled cacophony into the surrounding nocturnal alleys at maximum velocity, as I remembered from my last visit to that cinema, in 1990. Through apertures of broken windowpanes in the auditorium's façade, the dense soundscape of the alleyway outside entered the auditorium, in an intermeshing of city-noise and residual cinema-noise. Its sign was intact but the foyer had been shuttered and its projectors already stripped out, along with the speakers once affixed at either side of the screen; even so, the infiltrated noises of the city—fragments of music, chants, sudden eruptions of voices, the gratings of machines—appeared capable of conjuring elements of a cinematic soundtrack, and film images to accompany that sound were then only a hair's-breadth hallucination away.

In the auditorium of the Volksbühne—not a cinema, but a theatre, and not abandoned, but in active use—in Berlin, in November 2012, the film director Werner Herzog gave a performance that marked the release, thirty years earlier, of *Fitzcarraldo*, his film, shot in the Peruvian jungle, about film's own seminal hallucinations and obsessions. But the film itself was not projected, or even present in any way; instead, Herzog projected pre-cinematic magic-lantern glass slides from the end of the nineteenth-century, of luridly-coloured, European-imagined jungle landscapes; intermittently, he read extracts from the journals he kept at the time of the film's shooting (journals focused on his incessant travels and incidental encounters, rather than on the film-making process itself), or stood alongside vocalists from Sardinia and Senegal, as they improvised chants of loss.[2] In such a performance, the entity of film—at least, film as it had been conceived in the era of *Fitzcarraldo*—is irreparably gone, supplanted by the digital, or else propelled backwards in time, beyond its mid-1890s origins, into the media of glass slides, whose capacity for mutation into moving-image sequences, for projection to spectators in auditoria, preoccupied Marey, Muybridge, and Le Prince (along with the Skladanowsky Brothers, who shot Berlin's first cityscape, from a Prenzlauer Berg rooftop close to the Volksbühne). All that remained of cinema, in that auditorium, denuded of filmic images, was Herzog's own body, surrounded by a wailing vocal soundscape, performing corporeal gestures of film's detritus.

Film, sound, and the auditoria for film's conjoining with sound, always inhabit liminal zones of disjuncture, most intensively so with the abandonment of film's distinctive spaces of projection. But, from those disjunctures, and their detrital traces, new experiments with sound and image emerge. David Lynch shot the Club Silencio sequence of his 2001 film *Mulholland Dr.* in the auditorium of an abandoned cinema on Los Angeles' Broadway: the Tower cinema, constructed by S. Charles Lee in 1927 as the first cinema in Los Angeles (and one of the first, worldwide) to be equipped for sound synchronized with film projection. In that sequence, film has vanished and the cinema auditorium's screen is gone, but an audience has gathered, to experience a performance. The vocalist Rebekah del Rio, performing the song "Llorando," at the site where the cinema's screen had been located, abruptly collapses, and is carried unconscious from the auditorium, but her voice endures beyond her disappearance, in a sonic hallucination or ineradicable spectral residue of film, still inhabiting that space.

Endnotes

1 Antonin Artaud, lecture on film sound given at the Studio 28 cinema in Paris, 29 June 1929, *Oeuvres complètes*, volume III (Paris: Gallimard, 1968) p. 377.
2 Herzog's journals were published as *Conquest of the Useless* (New York: Ecco Press, 2004); in his previous published journals, *Of Walking in Ice*, 1974, film is similarly absent.

ACOUSTIC ECOLOGY: HANS SCHAROUN AND MODERNIST EXPERIMENTATION IN WEST BERLIN

Sandra Jasper

1 Philharmonie under construction.

Photo by Reinhard Friedrich. Courtesy of the Baukunstarchiv, Akademie der Künste, Berlin.

2

2 Philharmonie aerial shot
(1963).
Photo by Reinhard Friedrich.

Die Stadt kann ja nicht als eine Insel im Meer existieren, darf sich nicht isolieren.[1]
Hans Scharoun, 1945
Gehemmter Fortschritt bei gefördertem Rückschritt! (Berliner Bonmot!)[2]
Martin Wagner, 1957

On first encountering Hans Scharoun's newly opened Philharmonie, visitors expressed a sense of disorientation. In 1964, *The New Yorker* correspondent Joseph Wechsberg described the building as "a strange, naked-looking tent-like structure, painted an ugly yellow and devoid of any discernible geometric pattern, it seems to defy one's instinctive sense of order. To make things worse," Wechsberg continued, "the surroundings are desolate, consisting mostly of weed-sprouting ruins and empty fields that were once the verdant Tiergarten." Far away from the city's buzzing new centre along Kurfürstendamm, the concert hall was disconnected from public transport, with barely any street lights and "not a single café, restaurant, or *Weinstube* in the neighbourhood for the elated listener to relax in after a concert."[3]

Hans Scharoun designed the Philharmonie in 1956. He realized the moulding of urban space into a technically sophisticated state-of-the-art concert hall between 1960 and 1963. Built in the midst of West Berlin's largest inner-city *Brache* (wasteland), which stretched from Tiergarten to Kreuzberg and Schöneberg, the auditorium was surrounded by bombed-out plots, the ruined villas and embassies of the former Diplomatenviertel (diplomatic quarter), and the skeletons, shacks, and rusty metal of the abandoned Anhalter and Potsdamer railway stations. Land banking, protracted geopolitical negotiations, slow economic recovery, and zoning plans that kept open the possibility of reconnecting the city, left these spaces irreclaimable for West Berlin's official urban development plans for the next three decades. The Philharmonie and a range of state-funded museums, libraries, and auditoria of the newly built Kulturforum (cultural forum) remained exceptions. From the 1960s onwards, this unusual inner-city area in Tiergarten emerged as a unique laboratory, allowing a diverse range of distinctive spaces and intellectual ideas to flourish, with music culture, sonic experimentation, and design innovation playing key roles.

The term "acoustic ecology" first appeared in the mid-1970s, in the context of the World Sound Project at Simon Fraser University in Vancouver, Canada.[4] It was broadly defined as a field exploring the role of sound in mediating human-environment relations.[5] If we consider the word "acoustic," one of the definitions given in the *Oxford English Dictionary* relates to architectural space: "acoustic—the properties or qualities of a room, building, or other place in transmitting sound, esp. with respect to reverberation time." However, surprisingly, acoustic ecologists have largely neglected the "making" or "design" of sonic spaces, compared to their in-depth studies of outdoor spaces. One exception is a short passage in R. Murray Schafer's *The New Soundscape* (1969) that links increasing ambient noise levels in cities to the emergence of the urban auditorium, where "music may be affectionately placed in a container of silence."[6]

Schafer's simplistic view of the city—a source and site of noise, a "sonic sewer"[7] or "pandemonium"[8]—being screened off in concert halls, which function as substitutes for outdoor life and counterpoints to the deleterious processes of modern urbanization, overlooks how concert halls are themselves part of the technological modernization of cities. If we expand the interdisciplinary terrain of "acoustic ecology" to encompass a more nuanced understanding of the multiple links between the physical spaces of the city, the human body, and sound, the field carries the potential to develop a historically and materially grounded conception of sonic space that counter-balances the prevalence of ahistorical phenomenological approaches and anti-representational theories of sound, which tend to overstate ideas of virtuality, downgrade the material realm, and emphasize a dichotomy between visual and sonic culture.

West Berlin's period as an island city, which lasted from 1961 until 1989, has yet to be critically reassessed for its cultural and intellectual achievements.[9] The divided city of Berlin has long been viewed as the symbolic stage of the Cold War, with its cultural output interpreted through the lenses of two competing ideological systems.[10] Recent studies in art and architectural history have argued that instead of the advent of post-modernism, we can observe a Berlin-specific renewal of the legacy of modernism in the decades after the Second World War.[11] One of the less studied aspects of West Berlin's cultural transformation is the place of sound in architecture and urban design. Sonic spaces played a pivotal role in the cultural and material reshaping of the city. In order to consider the precise ways in which West Berlin played a key role in the persistence of specific aspects of twentieth-century modernism, we need to address how this urban enclave was sustained—both economically and culturally—during the Cold War years.

By the 1960s, the city had long been established as a subsidized enclave. While the Berlin Wall cemented its island status in 1961, its economic isolation had begun much earlier. From 1949 onwards, following the Berlin Blockade and the loss of the city's capital status, its commerce, and its industries, the federal government kept West Berlin alive with direct subsidies that "in some years amounted to over half the [city's] budget."[12] West Berlin's *Wunderwirtschaft* (miracle economy),[13] as former Weimar *Stadtbaurat* (building commissioner) Martin Wagner referred to the city's economy, created a context in which municipal urban planning "obstructed progress" by subsidizing regress,[14] a process that had started with the dismissal of Hans Scharoun from his position as Stadtbaurat.

During his short-lived appointment from 1945 to 1946, Scharoun had worked across intensifying geopolitical divides to develop a comprehensive rebuilding plan for Berlin as a modern metropolis with *Weltstadtcharakter*[15] (cosmopolitan spirit). Scharoun and members of the *Freitagsgruppe*[16] saw a chance for political change and hoped to realize ideas developed previously during the interwar years, such as implementing economic and legal reforms to abolish property ownership and prevent "land speculation [which] stands in the way of a natural and healthy development of the city."[17] With municipal elections ahead, the Social

Democratic Party (SPD) opposed the group's work on the *Kollektivplan* (collective plan) as "utopian plans creating confusion"[18] and asked Scharoun to resign. The administrative split of the city in 1948, West Berlin's increasing significance as a strategic geopolitical space, personnel continuities with those architects and planners active under the Nazi regime,[19] and a US-oriented and strictly anti-communist SPD in the municipal government created a constellation in which progressive voices were increasingly marginalized.[20]

Shortly before his death in 1957, Martin Wagner wrote a fierce critique of West Berlin's urban planning programmes and those avant-garde architects involved in highly state-subsidized municipal housing projects.[21] The Hansaviertel (1953–1960), a costly housing project not affordable for the average West Berliner, celebrated architecture's International Style by including numerous high-profile architects. For Wagner, these 48 architects had composed "48 petty scores" creating a "*Mißklang* (discord) typical of almost all municipal teamwork of our times" celebrating "orgies of directionlessness with its orchestral cacophonies of drums against trumpets and basses against violins."[22] Wagner emphasized the dangers of reducing the modern movement to an aesthetic style in the absence of any consistent and radical po-

3

3 Philharmonie interior design (1981).
Photo by Reinhard Friedrich.

Courtesy of the Baukunstarchiv, Akademie der Künste, Berlin.

sition on housing provision and land reforms. His sober critique of West Berlin's municipal urban planning and subsidy economy foreshadowed apparent inequalities in the level of modernization across the city, which would culminate in the desperate shortage of low- to medium-income housing and the resulting housing battles that took these problems to the streets twenty-five years later.[23] Governmental tax incentives supported private landlords in speculating with property and resulted in the deterioration, demolition, and contested reconstruction of West Berlin's *Mietskasernen* (rental barracks), especially in the working-class district of Kreuzberg.[24]

Hans Scharoun's "organic modernism" has recently been revisited in the context of a growing interest in ecological approaches in architecture, which range from discussions about sustainability to the use of nature-based metaphors in urban design.[25] Considering him an "outsider of modernism,"[26] architectural historians have struggled to classify his body of work, which draws on expressionist, organic, and New Objectivity-inspired design elements. Rather than the straightforward mimicry of natural forms, the "organic" element in his approach reflects a rejection of technocratic or functionalist standardization, and is based on the idea of a processual architecture in which design unfolds from a building's specific purpose and locality. The underlying design principle for the Philharmonie was to place music in the centre of the audience against a tradition of picture-frame stages. This idea can be traced back to Scharoun's utopian architectural vision of the interwar period, inspired by expressionist designs such as Bruno Taut's *Stadtkrone* (city crown). In his watercolours of theatres and cinemas, which he painted as a member of *Die Gläserne Kette* (the glass chain), the artistic performance erupted from the centre of the architectural space.[27]

Scharoun's modernist experiments with sound and architecture combined political and aesthetic dimensions of design to dismantle social hierarchies and musical conventions. The auditorium retained material and theoretical links between the sonic and visual realms and provided technical and spatial facilities for new forms of experimental composition.

The design of the concert hall was not primarily geared towards achieving the highest quality room acoustics—Scharoun had been advised by acoustician Lothar Cremer to alter the circular layout in preference to a more conventional stage to achieve a better sound quality—instead, his aim was to build a space that emphasized the social aspects of collectively experiencing music for a "community of those who listen." The pentagonal concert hall placed the audience around the performers in order to create a spatial arrangement in which "'producer' and 'consumer' are not facing each other."[28] The circular seating plan also enabled a more equal and intimate visual and acoustic quality in all the seats. Thus, the conventional hierarchies of this "space of social differentiation"[29] were dismantled.

Scharoun's idea of placing the music in the centre rather than using a traditional picture-frame stage required a number of innovative acoustic design solutions to be developed, in collaboration with physicists and engineers specialized in sound and room acoustics. The

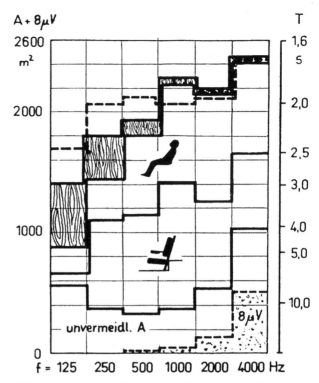

Bild 7: Graphische Addition der Beträge zur äquivalenten Absorptionsfläche.
(Die gestrichelte Linie entspricht den aus Nachhallmessungen errechneten Werten.)

4

lack of sound reflecting surfaces—supplied in traditional concert halls by the walls framing the stage and the decorative historicist ornamentation typical of Art Nouveau and late-romantic architectural styles [30]—resulted in the creation of new design elements, including curved, sound-dispersing wooden panels (or clouds) hanging over the stage, and geometrically shaped triangular diffusors attached to the ceiling (figure 3).

The idea of "organic design" takes on a distinctive meaning that goes beyond simplistic analogies drawn between the human body and architectural space. The body became a central "organic" element in the acoustic design of the auditorium. The tent-like roof structure with its great height and convex shape is a further design peculiarity, which was necessary to guarantee a large enough interior air volume for the desired reverberation time of two seconds. At 26,000 cubic metres, the Philharmonie concert hall held the largest interior air space of any European concert hall. This volume was based on the number of listeners predetermined in the architectural bid for a space with 2,000 seats. As architectural critic R. S. Lanier elaborates in his essay for *Architectural Forum*:

4 Sound absorption diagram
Source: Lothar Cremer, *Die Schalltechnik*, Issue 57, 1964.

The absorption of the audience itself, the main element decreasing the reverberation time, is fixed. Thus a rough formula for reverberation time can be based on volume per member of the audience. Cremer decided that he needed 11 cubic meters (385 cubic feet) for each listener.[31]

If we understand the interior of the concert hall as a space that binds bodies, ideas, materials, and technologies together, an analysis also uncovers how the listeners' bodies became part of the acousticians' detailed mathematical formulae. Not only did the audience's ears perceive the musical performance but their bodies became actual material to absorb specific frequencies, a precondition on which any symphony came to "sound." Unlike cinema or theatre spaces, the physical presence of the audience fundamentally altered the sonic space, so that for rehearsal periods, recording sessions, and varying audience numbers, the shapes and upholstery of the chairs were designed to imitate human bodies in their absence (figure 4).

Instead of decorating the auditorium with historicist ornamentation, heavy curtains, statues, or other sound diffusing elements typical of traditional concert halls—a conception of interior design generally rejected by modernist architects for its distracting and reality-distorting effects[32]—Scharoun created aesthetic designs for new functional elements. Geometrically shaped diffusors, slanting backrests, and wooden building materials reflected Scharoun's differentiation between "organic" and superfluous aesthetic elements. Furthermore, the speakers, cables, and studios—the "sonic infrastructure" of the auditorium—remained transparent to the audience. For composer David Prior, the circular seating makes the apparatus that supports the performance visible, unlike the hidden "infrastructure of film studio, recording studio or darkroom,"[33] which disguises the production process. Thus, the acoustic design of the auditorium became central to the visual experience of the architecture. This ontology of retaining material and theoretical links between the sonic and visual realms is reflected in the visual impact of contemporary concert halls.[34]

The 1950s and 1960s saw a new phase of innovative sound interventions. Scharoun's state-of-the-art concert hall paralleled or even pre-empted experimental sonorizations of enclosed spaces exhibited at World Fairs and Expositions, such as the Philips Pavilion at the Brussels World Fair in 1958 and the *Kugelauditorium* (spherical auditorium), the German Pavilion at the 1970 World Exposition in Osaka.[35] Scharoun explored the possibilities of an urban auditorium, not only designed for orchestral music, but also for presenting contemporary developments in New Music, electronic, electro-acoustic, and computer music, which had emerged since the 1950s. He worked in close collaboration with a group of experts based at various research institutes in West Berlin, such as the Heinrich Hertz Institute, the Institute of Technical Acoustics, and the Department of Musicology at the Technical University of Berlin, as well as with specialized audio manufacturers, such as Georg Neumann GmbH, which had remained in West Berlin. Neumann, who in the 1920s had foreseen "mass-producing microphones"[36] and had become Germany's leading microphone manufacturer, reopened his company in Kreuzberg at Checkpoint Charlie, within sight of the border. Neumann manufactured studio microphones, disk-cutting equipment for records, and mixing consoles, which would not only be used in the Philharmonie, but also in the city's radio stations and recording studios.

These collaborations with scientists and technical experts resulted in a number of innovations altering the technological, spatial, and corporeal dimensions of traditional concert hall design by providing the technical means to amplify and spatialize sound in innovative ways. Facilities including a four-channel mixer in the main studio along with ten loudspeakers attached to the ceiling and fifteen speakers on the back walls of the concert hall allowed for the transmission of special stereophonic performances and electronic music. Three galleries offered the potential for *Raummusik* (space music) with instruments or choirs spread out around the hall. Apart from the main studio for radio transmission, three studios for recordings and one studio for electronic music were also included in Scharoun's original plans.[37]

In *Noise: The Political Economy of Music*, Jacques Attali suggests that with the increase in perfection of sound recording technologies, live performances started to be evaluated against the radio broadcast and the record, which as a result became "the driving force of the economy of music."[38] While it is generally argued that concert halls were built to shield urban audiences from corrosive urban environments, such as the noise caused by air traffic from the nearby Tempelhof airport, the high level of sound proofing in the Philharmonie exceeded human listening capabilities. As acoustician Lothar Cremer explains: "The microphone—or rather the person purely listening to the speakers—reacts more sensitively, because he lacks the visual aids for concentration that listeners in the hall have, giving sight and direction."[39] These sensitive technical recording devices picked up sounds only listeners at home would be able to hear. Triple soundproofing shells were needed because of the concert hall's function as a recording studio for radio broadcasts and recordings by Deutsche Grammophon, which held a monopoly on Philharmonie concert releases.

The Philharmonie's doors remained largely closed to avant-garde composers, such as Karl Stockhausen or Luigi Nono. Works such as Stockhausen's *Gruppen* (1955–57) and *Gesang der Jünglinge* (1956) were ideally suited for this specific space: the auditorium was designed with such experiments in spatializing sound in mind.[40] Tensions arose between Scharoun's vision and the role of the Philharmonie as a flashpoint for cultural politics intended to re-establish West Berlin's role as a centre for the high arts. While the auditorium's sophisticated technical facilities were used to increase the commercial success of the orchestra—the Philharmonie was to become a multimedia concert hall equipped with studio recording and transmission facilities for radio and television broadcasts—the development and presentation of contemporary avant-garde compositions remained a rarity. Despite the available spatial and technical facilities, institutional support of "compositional diversity" was limited. Experimental sonorizations of space were not considered commercially viable for a mass urban public, so the auditorium's specific facilities were left dormant.

Scharoun's work in post-war Berlin elucidates the ambivalences of a locally specific *Nach-kriegsmoderne* (post-war modernism). Amongst the more radical exponents of the architectural avant-garde, who aimed to address broader structural inequalities in their pursuit of rebuilding Berlin as a cosmopolitan metropolis, he quickly fell between the cracks of ideological divides driven by increasing geopolitical interest in the city. His experimental design for the Philharmonie, however, reveals the persistence of a modernist belief in the potential of design and technological innovation to bring about cultural and social change, build new links between sound, music, and architecture as different strands of modernism, and transform the sensory experience of space. Scharoun counteracted persistent anti-urban sentiments not only in his modernist rebuilding plans for Berlin, but also in his auditorium design which challenged a scepticism towards technologically modified spaces, and prevailing notions of acoustic authenticity in music. Financed in part through federal subsidies and funding schemes enabled by the European Recovery Program (ERP), the Philharmonie revealed the political importance and the on-going tensions of keeping the urban enclave not only economically, but also culturally sustained.

As the historian Emily Thompson has pointed out, the building of concert halls since the nineteenth century has been closely linked to the auditorium's role as a sonic refuge from increasing ambient noise levels in cities, thus connecting the design of interior spaces with broader processes of urbanization.[41] However, as concert halls mould urban space, they not only transform the sensory experience of space, but they also alter the material fabric and "political ecology" of cities. The Philharmonie was constructed in the midst of what emerged as West Berlin's largest inner-city area of interconnected ecological field sites. In the mid-1980s, urban ecologists were working in forty-five sites surrounding the concert hall and had listed over 250 rare or endangered species.[42] Although Scharoun and his colleagues could not realize their radical plans for Berlin as a modern *Großstadt* (metropolis), a "cosmopolitan sensibility"[43] prevailed and found its ultimate expression in the field of urban nature.

Endnotes

1   "The city cannot exist as an island in the sea, it must not be isolated." Hans Scharoun cited in Peter Pfankuch, "Kollektivplan- Halbjahres-bericht zum Wiederaufbau, 23.12.1945," in *Hans Scharoun: Bauten, Entwürfe, Texte*, ed. Peter Pfankuch (Berlin: Gebr. Mann Verlag, 1974) p. 155 [my translation].

2   "Obstructed progress and subsidised regress! (Berlin bon mot!)" Martin Wagner, *Potemkin in Westberlin* (Berlin: City-Presse, 1957) p. 21 [my translation].

3   Joseph Wechsberg, "A Letter from Berlin," *The New Yorker*, January 18, 1964: 69.

4   Hildegard Westerkamp, "Editorial," *Soundscape: The Journal of Acoustic Ecology*, Vol.1 (1) (2000): 4.

5   In contrast to the word "soundscape," which has generated theoretical reflections, the conceptual discussions of the phrase "acoustic ecology" have been largely limited to a few general definitions or models, for example in Barry Truax, *Acoustic Communication* (Norwood: Ablex Publishing, 1984) p. 11.

6   R. Murray Schafer, *The New Soundscape: A Handbook for the Modern Teacher*. (Scarborough, Ontario and New York: Berandol Music Limited and Associated Music Publishers, 1969) p. 9.

7   R. Murray Schafer, "The City as a Sonic Sewer," *Vancouver Sun* 11 March 1969: 61.

8   Schafer, *The Soundscape* p. 103.

9   The field of urban ecology pioneered by Herbert Sukopp in West Berlin in the 1960s has been recently rediscovered, see, for example, Jens Lachmund, "Exploring the City of Rubble: Botanical Fieldwork in Bombed Cities in Germany after World War II," *Osiris* (18) (2003): 234–254; and Matthew Gandy, "Marginalia: Aesthetics, Ecology, and Urban Wastelands," *Annals of the Association of American Geographers* Vol. 103, (6) (2013): 1301–1316.

10 See, for example, Philip Broadbent and Sabine Hake, ed., *Berlin Divided City, 1945-1989* (Oxford/New York: Berghahn Books, 2010); Stephanie Barron, Sabine Eckmann and Eckhart Gillen, ed., *Art of Two Germanys—Cold War Cultures* (Los Angeles: Abrams, 2009); Irit

Rogoff, ed., *The Divided Heritage: Themes and Problems in German Modernism* (Cambridge: Cambridge University Press, 1991).

11 On architecture see, for example, Francesca Rogier, "The Monumentality of Rhetoric: The Will to Rebuild in Postwar Berlin," in *Anxious Modernisms: Experimentation in Postwar Architectural Culture*, Sarah Williams Goldhagen and Réjean Legault, ed., (Cambridge, MA: MIT Press, 2000) pp. 165–189; Greg Castillo, "The Nylon Curtain: Architectural Unification in Divided Berlin," in *Berlin Divided City, 1945–1989* pp. 46–55. On art, see, for example, Greg Castillo, "Exhibiting the Good Life: Marshall Plan Modernism in Divided Berlin," in *Cold War Modern: Art and Design in a Divided World, 1945–1975*, David Crowley and Jane Pavett, ed., (London: Victoria & Albert Museum, 2008) pp. 66–72; Maike Steinkamp, "The Propagandistic Role of Modern Art in Postwar Berlin," in *Berlin Divided City, 1945–1989* pp. 23–33; Claudia Mesch, *Modern Art at the Berlin Wall Demarcating Culture in the Cold War Germanys* (London: Tauris Academic Studies, 2008); Rosalyn Deutsche, "Representing Berlin," in *Evictions: Art and Spatial Politics* (Cambridge, MA: MIT Press, 1996) pp. 109–159; Andreas Huyssen, "German Painting in the Cold War," *New German Critique* (37) (2010): 209–227.

12 Richard L. Merritt "Living with the Wall" in Richard L. Merritt and Anna J. Merritt, ed., *Living with the Wall: West Berlin, 1961–1985* (Durham: Duke University Press, 1985) p. 194.

13 A pun on the term *Wirtschaftswunder* (economic miracle), Wagner, *Potemkin in Westberlin* p. 20.

14 Ibid. p. 21.

15 Hans Scharoun cited in Pfankuch, *Hans Scharoun: Bauten, Entwürfe, Texte* p. 268.

16 Literally "Friday Group": a collective of former CIAM members, who met secretly until 1945. Its members, Selman Selmanagić, Luise Seitz, Wils Ebert, Ludmilla Herzenstein, Reinhold Lingner, Herbert Weinberger and Peter Friedrich worked with Hans Scharoun on the Kollektivplan.

17 "Die Bodenspekulation stand einer natürlichen und gesunden Entwicklung der Stadt im Wege", H. Scharoun, "Zur Berliner Ausstellung," *Der Bauhelfer* (5) (1964): 5 [my translation].

18 "Stellungnahme der SPD- Utopische Pläne stiften Verwirrung," *Der Sozialdemokrat*, 1946, cited in Pfankuch, *Hans Scharoun: Bauten, Entwürfe* p. 169.

19 In 1946, Karl Bonatz, who had previously designed bunkers under Albert Speer, was appointed as Scharoun's successor.

20 In 1950, Hans Scharoun also lost his commission for "Wohnzelle Friedrichshain" a housing project in East Berlin.

21 His ten letters, later published in "City-Presse," were directed at four of the most influential politicians in West Berlin, namely Willy Brandt (SPD), Franz Neumann (SPD), Carl-Hubert Schwennicke (FDP), and Ferdinand Friedensburg (CDU).

22 Wagner, *Potemkin in Westberlin* p. 13 [my translation].

23 Ibid. His economic principles of post-war urban planning were published as Martin Wagner, *Wirtschaftlicher Städtebau* (Stuttgart: Julius Hoffmann Verlag, 1951).

24 Richard L. Merritt, "Living with the Wall," in *Living with the Wall* pp. 191–218.

25 See, for example, Deborah Gans and Zehra Kuz, ed., *The Organic Approach to Architecture* (Chichester: Wiley-Academy, 2003); Colin Porteous, *The New Eco-Architecture: Alternatives from the Modern*

Movement (London: Taylor & Francis, 2002); Elke Sohn, *Zum Begriff der Natur in Stadtkonzepten: anhand der Beiträge von Hans Bernhard Reichow, Walter Schwagenscheidt und Hans Scharoun zum Wiederaufbau nach 1945* (Münster: LIT Verlag, 2008); Elke Sohn, "Organicist Concepts of City Landscape in German Planning after the Second World War," *Landscape Research* (32) (2007): 499–523; David Pearson, *New Organic Architecture: The Breaking Wave* (Berkeley: University of California Press, 2001).

26 Eberhard Syring and Jörg C. Kirschenmann, *Hans Scharoun, 1893–1972: Outsider of Modernism* (Cologne: Taschen, 2004).

27 Achim Wendschuh, 1993, *Hans Scharoun: Zeichnungen, Aquarelle, Texte* (Berlin: Akademie der Künste, 1993).

28 Hans Scharoun cited in Pfankuch, *Hans Scharoun: Bauten, Entwürfe, Texte* p. 279.

29 Jacques Attali, *Noise: Political Economy of Music* (Minneapolis: University of Minnesota Press, 1985).

30 Fritz Winckel, "Die besten Konzertsäle der Welt," *Baukunst und Werkform* (120) (1955).

31 R.S. Lanier, "Acoustics in-the-round at the Berlin Philharmonic," *Architectural Forum* (5) (1964): 100.

32 Debates on ornamentation were sparked by cultural critic Adolf Loos in his lecture "Ornament und Verbrechen" (Ornament and Crime), published in *Der Sturm*, 1910; for a discussion on its impact, see Reyner Banham, "Ornament and Crime: The Decisive Contribution of Adolf Loos" *Architectural Review* (121) (1957): 85–88.

33 David Prior, 2007, "A Space for Sound: The Rise, Fall and Fallout of the Concert as a Primary Space for Listening," in *In the Place of Sound: Architecture | Music | Acoustics*, ed. Colin Ripley, Marco L. Polo and Arthur Wrigglesworth (Newcastle: Cambridge Scholars Publishing, 2007) p. 130.

34 Examples include Herzog & de Meuron's Elbphilharmonie, Hamburg (planned for 2014); Renzo Piano's Parco della musica, Rome (2002); OMA's Casa da Música, Porto (2005); Snøhetta's Opera House, Oslo (2007).

35 Composer Karl-Heinz Stockhausen designed the *Kugelauditorium* in collaboration with West Berlin-based architect Fritz Bornemann and sound engineers from the Technical University, including Fritz Winckel, advisor for the Philharmonie.

36 Anselm Roessler, *Neumann: The Microphone Company: A Story of Innovation, Excellence and the Spirit of Audio Engineering* (Bergkirchen: PPVMedien, 2007).

37 The studio for electronic music was never realized.

38 Attali, *Noise: Political Economy of Music* p. 85.

39 Lothar Cremer, "Raum- und bauakustische Maßnahmen bei der Berliner Philharmonie," Scharoun archive, Academy of the Arts, Berlin, 1959.

40 Edgar Wisniewski, *Die Berliner Philharmonie und ihr Kammermusiksaal. Der Konzertsaal als Zentralraum* (Berlin: Gebr. Mann Verlag, 1993) p.130.

41 Emily Thompson, *The Soundscape of Modernity: Architectural Acoustics and the Culture of Listening in America, 1900-1933* (Cambridge, MA: MIT Press, 2004).

42 Herbert Sukopp, unpublished map, (ca. 1982).

43 Matthew Gandy, "Marginalia" pp. 1301–1316.

STEREO CITY: MOBILE LISTENING IN THE 1980s

Heike Weber

1 Young people with a cassette player, West Germany (1980).
Source: "Billige Kombis für junge Hörer" (cheap combinations for young listeners), Test Radiorecorder
(Mono), *Test*, No. 12, 1980.

In the early twenty-first century, tuning in into one's mobile music has become a prevalent means to get some distraction, entertainment, or inspiration on the go, and nearly all digital gear has integrated a radio or stereo function to do so. Listening to music when on the move has taken manifold forms and meanings: teenagers crank up the loudspeakers of their cell phones while waiting at the bus stop; tired travellers relax by wiring themselves to their personal stereo; boom boxes are taken along to accompany a picnic in the park, or to deliver the music for amateur dancers who meet in public to pursue their hobby. For those particularly sensitive to noise, industry even offers noise-cancelling headphones to silence the noise of the city. Others use mobile stereos to shape new forms of mobile urban music cultures. Berlin, for instance, has attracted mobile DJs who play their stereos here and there to gather a local crowd, before moving on to prevent an intervention by the police. In almost any bigger city, silent discos are organized through social media and people come together to dance to the sounds of one's individual MP3 player.

Music has always been a means to claim power or mobilize followers, to create emotions or maintain feelings of familiarity, be it the case of march music, the sounding organs of churches, or the loudspeakers of current public rallies. When music became available through records and radio, it was also soon taken along and used in "mobile" ways. Early record players and radios operated without electricity and hence, were in some ways "wireless" though they could not be operated on the go. But even if their mobility was quite restricted, urbanites of the 1920s and 1930s took music playing technologies to outdoor locations such as garden allotments or on summer picnics, as portrayed in Robert Siodmak's film *Menschen am Sonntag* (1930), a cinematic reflection on the leisure activities of young people in Weimar-era Berlin.

But it was not until the widely-used portable music players of the second half of the twentieth century, that mobile sounds invaded the city and its periphery. In the hand of individual users, such equipment has enabled urbanites to reappropriate public spaces and their soundscapes.[1] Portable radios, tape recorders, and later digital players became a means of creating a personally controlled auditory sphere when away from home, during holiday travels, or on the way to work, on the subway, or while shopping. Moreover, the appearance of the sound-enhanced individual in public space led to new configurations of the city: the conjunction of urban masses with shrinking portable devices, and even wearable technologies, resulted in changing patterns of how to move around urban space and encounter others.[2] Transistor radios became available to mass consumers in the late 1950s, followed by portable recorders in the 1960s, and radio-recorders in the 1970s. But it was in particular during the 1980s, when urbanites explored new forms of mobile music listening through the widespread appropriation of stereo boom boxes and headphone-equipped Walkmans. Most notably, young users explored the mobile potentials of their "object nomads"[3] and thereby formed both new cultures of mobile stereo listening, and novel ways to appropriate urban soundscapes. While the boom box listener adds the personal sounds to the public sphere—which could be described as a kind of "additive" acoustic interference—the Walkman listener substitutes the public sounds with his or her personal music, while restricting the sonic participation of co-present others to the fizzling of the headphones: a kind of "substractive" interference. At first, both ways of mobile stereo listening yielded public agitation and resulted in renegotiations of norms and forms of public behaviour, before finally forming significant elements of urban culture.

In the 1980s, more and more consumer electronics entered the private home: next to radios, televisions and hi-fis, consumers appropriated video recorders, CD players, personal computers, and video games; satellite television became widespread and MTV began broadcasting pop music video clips, first in the US (1981), and then in Europe (1987). The growing diversification of private entertainment equipment was complemented by an array of portable versions, which reacted to a rising urge for mobility, flexibility, and individuality. Such portables could be taken along to the park, the weekend cabin, or the second home, but they were also found in stationary situations on the kitchen shelf, in hobby rooms, or in children's bedrooms. At the end of the decade, most teenagers owned a cassette recorder and even preschoolers regularly listened to cassettes.

Media and other technology are not passively consumed, but actively appropriated by their users; the "domestication" concept emphasizes that users "tame" technologies according to their needs, their wishes, their rituals, and routines, while also shaping new meanings and cultures through their usage.[4] This also means that despite globally distributed designs and music tunes, users might create locally distinctive patterns of appropriation: boom boxes and Walkmans are good examples to demonstrate this, as we will see in the case of West Germany and the US.

While portable electronics were domesticated inside the home quite inconspicuously, once carried outdoors, they easily turned into "unruly" sound technologies. Public mobile listening represented an individual, self-determined "domestication" of the acoustic environment, commonly defined as shared and public. To avoid complaints about loud music, some swimming pools and public transportation companies had already banned music listening from their premises during the 1960s and 1970s. However, in West German cities of the 1980s, it was less this loud listening mode that caused trouble, but the silent version: the wiring of urbanites to headphones.

When Sony's engineers combined a small pocket recorder with stereo headphones to create the first Walkman model TPS-L2 in 1979, they crossed over two previously distinct listening cultures: the personalized stereo headphone listening as practised by the stationary domestic hi-fi listener, and the mobile listening to audio portables.[5] The distinctiveness of Sony's Walkman was its restriction, namely to a wearable, play-only unit for headphone listening, while omitting radio, recording, or loudspeaker functions.[6] Headphones privatized music listening,[7] but before their appearance, the urban sociologist Georg Simmel could describe the human sense of hearing as "supra-individualistic"—sounds were intrinsically "democratic" and to be shared commonly, or in the words of Simmel: "simply everyone present must hear what occurs in a room, and, what is perceived by one person, is thereby not taken away from the other."[8] The Walkman, however, replaced the acoustic sensation of the environment with self-chosen sounds, and simultaneously reduced perception of this space to visual stimuli. For first-time users, this often resulted in odd and novel sensations, and personal stereos have been described as "perception prosthetics."[9] Some users compared this experience to a cinematic film in which they would both act as the hero and provide the accompanying music score.[10] Previously, only car drivers who listened to music had perceived similar impressions, but they had been separated from their environment by the shell of their car.

In West Germany, the Sony Walkman was introduced in 1980, and was soon followed by similar portable recorders produced by other companies. The enthusiastic early adopters were mainly teenagers and members of a new social stratum of young, urban professionals, who would later come to be known as "yuppies". These early users were to be seen with their Walkmans while shopping, strolling, biking, skating, or commuting. By 1984, 30 per cent of the twelve- to fifteen-year-olds in West Germany owned a Walkman. This proportion shrank to 5 per cent in the twenty-five- to twenty-nine-year-old segment.[11] An audio journal defined the Walkman as "a technology for a generation who has nothing to talk about any more," and a leading German news magazine pictured teenagers eating and shopping with their friends while also listening to their Walkmans.[12] Critics placed the Walkman in the context of the then frequent debates about trends towards individualization and the urban "single," as well the *"Null Bock"* (can't be bothered) generation that seemed frustrated and appeared to lack any motivation for social engagement. Inside, stereo headphones were regarded as tools to enhance one's concentration on the music as well as a means to listen without annoying family members. But worn while on the move, headphones disarranged contemporary regimes of how to listen and to listen or gaze in public. For one, the mobile headphone listener obviously closed off his or her ears from co-present others; for another, many Walkman users stared in irritating ways while being immersed in their chosen tunes. Their expressions seemed paralyzed and blank—quite comparable to the "blasé" attitude that Simmel had described for the urbanites of the early twentieth century, which compensated for the excessive human encounters in their urban lives with looks that became indifferent to others.[13] In his famous ethnographic study on Parisian metro commuters, Marc Augé also notes this new and irritating figure in the urban realm: a Walkman listener who indulges in his or her music, and whose body seems to move in time to the beat whilst the facial expression appears distant and paralyzed. For these detached figures, attention is now directed towards an acoustic realm that is separate from their immediate environment.[14]

According to the contemporary observer Volker Gransow, the Walkman also changed the relations between public and private since it disassembled "actions, which are constitutive of the public realm such as hearing, seeing, and personal interactions"[15] and rearranged them in new, technically mediated ways. Walkman users became bricoleurs who could combine previously separated activities such as learning languages while shopping, listening to music while changing subways, or while being in the doctor's waiting room.[16] Such a bricolage also meant controlling one's emotions and embellishing annoying urban soundscapes by tuning in to one's own music.

In West Germany, teenagers—through their ubiquitous wired appearance—paved the way for adults to also wire themselves to mobile headphones music while on the move. "Granted, it takes a bit of courage to appear as a no longer young person with a cassette player and mini-headphones in the street or in public transport," an electronics journal still declared in 1984 in its initial consumer test of pocket stereos.[17] By the end of the decade, however, Walkmans were seen as adequate tools of the urban commuter or pedestrian to blend out unwanted urban soundscapes and to carve out a sphere of privacy and homeliness while outside. The urban jogger, still a rare figure around 1980, became the icon of the late 1980s, condensing the by now positive meanings of mobility, flexibility, individuality, and sportiveness, and this person would most likely wear headphones to stimulate the bodily movement. In the case of female users, headphones also served as a means to shut off potential harassments while travelling alone.[18] Ultimately, private stereo listening while on the move alleviated the feelings of alienation, which anyone can suffer in urban transit places, public transport, or shopping malls, and other places characterized by accidental encounters with strangers.

"North Americans may well be the only people in the world who go outside to be alone and inside to be social,"[19] the media theorist Marshall McLuhan wrote in 1976; they wished for "privacy out-of-doors." While his statement might be too general, such cultural differences on privacy and sociability also show up in the domestication of boom boxes and Walkmans. In the average American city of the early 1980s, Walkmans were already a common sight. They were "seen on countless people in innumerable pedestrian pursuits—from early morning joggers to weekend gardeners, from students between classes to messengers en route between destinations."[20] While West German contemporaries were most likely to consider mobile headphone listening as antisocial, the contrary was the case in the US. The dominant white American discourse defined the personal stereo as a tool of social respectability, even more so since it was contrasted with the contemporary boom box and its loud public use as practised in many African-American communities. The Sony Walkman figured as the "middle- and upper-class answer to the box," as "one of the hottest new status symbols around," and "a civilized alternative to the portable radio-cassette players that blare on streets and subways."[21]

Shared music consumption on the street was practised in many multi-ethnic American neighbourhoods, so that neighbours might participate in the tunes. In 1980, the African-American magazine *Ebony*, a well-established journal aiming at middle-class black readers, reported that "the portable radio-cassette is no. 1 with the young," as everybody from twelve to twenty-five seemed to carry them along, namely "on buses and subways, while shopping downtown, on the beach, and even while roller-skating and riding bikes."[22] By then, the boom box had also become a central technological element in the hip-hop culture initiated by youths in the South Bronx, Harlem, and other economically deprived multi-ethnic urban ghettos.[23] In her study on the emergence of rap in New York, Tricia Rose describes hip hop as the attempt "to negotiate the experiences of marginalization, brutally truncated opportunity, and oppression within the cultural imperatives of African-American and Caribbean history, identity, and community."[24] The early rappers and DJs initiated spontaneous public parties to reclaim the streets, and they often did so by connecting their turntables and speakers to any available electrical source including public streetlights. DJ sounds were disseminated by copying locally produced tapes, for instance, with double cassette decks or boom boxes with two drives, and by playing them publicly on large boom boxes. Breakdancers reclaimed street corners by setting up their portable stereos and dancing; others carried their sound around, and they did so in a demonstrative way by carrying the boom boxes on their shoulders. In this subculture, for many African-Americans, the boom box was thus a political statement, and to "pump up the volume"[25] also meant an acoustic domestication of public spaces and a protest against race and class oppression.

White Americans, on the other hand, have tended to restrict the outdoor use of boom boxes to explicit leisure settings like the park or the holiday beach.[26] No wonder then, that the racially segregated cities of the 1980s were the setting for sonic conflict around the question of loud mobile music listening. In these, white Americans interpreted boom boxes as "weapons to infuriate the staid and proper,"[27] while for young urban African-Americans, they were a means to express their identity and reclaim a place in society. Spike Lee's movie *Do the Right Thing* (1989) would later capture the clash of cultures around mobile boom box listening. The film begins by depicting a hot day in a Brooklyn neighbourhood and its Italian-American pizzeria, which functions as a social meeting point. At the end of the day, a riotous mob has destroyed the restaurant. The outbreak of violence has been induced by a racial conflict between three black customers and the restaurant owner who destroyed their roaring boom box.

In New York, the increase of public music consumption led to several sanctions. For this city, the media scholar Gary Gumpert identifies a "radio war" during which the "auditory aggression" turned into a "subject of police officials."[28] Boom boxes were confiscated, and in some areas of Central Park and Coney Island, music-free zones were installed. In its report on the issue, *The Washington Post* actually interviewed some beach goers and boom box lovers and quoted one of them, Dolores Vitella, with the following statement which tells us a lot about unequal power relations: "I'm sitting here worried that someone will steal my hubcaps. The beaches are dirty, and there aren't any restrooms. And Koch [the then mayor] worries about radios? Give me a break."[29]

Hip hop had started as a subversive urban culture of the American ghetto, based on mobile, low-tech audio equipment, but would soon be globally commercialized. By the early

1980s, it had moved on to West German cities: in pedestrian zones, youths appeared as breakdancers equipped with boom boxes. [30] With global pop culture channels like MTV still missing, the transfer of hip hop was improvised. Early hip-hop movies emphasized the connectedness of graffiti, DJ-ing, rapping, and breakdancing. Accordingly, West German urban youths began to spray trains and walls, to scratch records, and to form bands. The few hip-hop pioneers met on weekends in party rooms and youth clubs and did rap, at first mostly in English, later on in German as well as other native tongues such as Turkish or Greek. But even if some of them addressed the problems facing *Kinder mit Migrationshintergrund* (children with immigrant backgrounds) born in West Germany, the racial and social explosiveness was muted in comparison with the cities of the United States.

While West Germans would typically call the boom box a "ghettoblaster," its common domestication inside and outdoors was less wild and unruly. Like portable radios, boom boxes were taken along to picnics, sport, or parties; they were essential equipment for any school trip, and some youngsters would also shoulder them through the streets like hip-hop stars. Again, teenagers clearly mobilized music consumption more extensively than adults. Already in the 1950s and 1960s, portable record players and radios had been used by urban—and in particular male—youths at their public hangouts; by tuning in to youth-specific broadcasts, they purposefully claimed parts of the public sphere for themselves. [31]

Endnotes

1 Heike Weber, *Das Versprechen mobiler Freiheit. Zur Kultur- und Technikgeschichte von Kofferradio, Walkman und Handy* (Bielefeld: transcript, 2008); Heike Weber, "Taking Your Favorite Sound Along: Portable Audio Technologies for Mobile Music Listening," in *Sound Souvenirs: Audio Technologies, Memory and Cultural Practices*, ed. Karin Bijsterveld and Jose van Dijck (Amsterdam: Amsterdam University Press, 2009) p. 69–82; M. B. Schiffer, *The Portable Radio in American Life* (London: Routledge, 1991); Michael Bull, *Sounding out the City: Personal Stereos and the Management of Everyday Life* (Oxford: Berg, 2000). For the term "soundscapes," see R. Murray Schafer, *Our Sonic Environment and the Soundscape: The Tuning of the World* (Rochester: Destiny Books, 1994).

2 See also: Michael Bull, "Sound Connections: An Aural Epistemology of Proximity and Distance in Urban Culture," *Environment and Planning D: Society and Space 22* (2004): 103–116.

3 Jacques Attali, Bruits. Essai sur l économie politique de la musique (Paris: Fayard, Presses Universitaires de France, 2001 [1977]), 199.

4 Roger Silverstone and Eric Hirsch, ed., *Consuming Technologies. Media and Information in Domestic Spaces* (London/New York: Routledge, 1992); Thomas Berker et al., ed., *Domestication of Media and Technology* (Berkshire: Open University Press, 2006).

5 On the Walkman, see also: Paul du Gay, Stuart Hall, Linda Janes, Hugh Mackay, and Keith Negus, *Doing Cultural Studies: The Story of the Sony Walkman* (London: Sage Publications, 1997).

6 See also Hosokawa, who described this as a "technical devolution": Shuhei Hosokawa, *Der Walkman-Effekt* (Berlin: Merve, 1987) pp. 14–15.

7 On headphones cf: Heike Weber, "Head Cocoons: A Sensori-Social History of Earphone Use in West Germany 1950–2010," *The Senses and Society 5* (2010): 339–363.

8 "Was in einem Raume vorgeht, müssen eben alle hören, die in ihm sind, und daß der Eine es aufnimmt, nimmt es dem Andern nicht fort." Georg Simmel, "Exkurs über die Soziologie der Sinne," in *Soziologie. Untersuchungen über die Formen der Vergesellschaftung*, Georg Simmel (Frankfurt a. M.: Surkamp, 1992) pp. 722–774, here 730,

[translation by Sandra Jasper].

9 See Frank Schätzlein, "Mobile Klangkunst. Über den Walkman als Wahrnehmungsmaschine," in *Radio-Kultur und Hör-Kunst. Zwischen Avantgarde und Popularkultur 1923–2001*, A. Stuhlmann (Würzburg: Königshausen & Neumann, 2001) pp.176–195.

10 Schätzlein, "Mobile Klangkunst"; P. Glaser, "10 Jahre Walkman. Rock Around the Block. Nichts hat unser Leben so verändert wie der Walkman. Eine Festschrift zu seinem zehnten Geburtstag," *Tempo* (June 1988).

11 See Rainer Schönhammer, *Der "Walkman". Eine phänomenologische Untersuchung* (München: Kirchheim, 1988) p. 64.

12 See *Stereoplay*, No. 2, 1981, p. 13; "High und fidel," *Der Spiegel* (8 June 1981): 210–213.

13 Georg Simmel, "Die Großstädte und das Geistesleben," *Die Großstadt. Vorträge & Aufsätze zur Städteausstellung. Jahrbuch der Gehe-Stiftung Dresden* (9) (1903): 185–206.

14 Marc Augé, *Ein Ethnologe in der Metro* (Frankfurt a. M/New York: Fischer, 1988) p. 51.

15 See Volker Granow, *Der autistische Walkman. Elektronik, Öffentlichkeit und Privatheit* (Berlin: Verlag Die Arbeitswelt, 1985) p. 97. The original citation reads "für 'Öffentlichkeit' konstitutive Tätigkeiten wie Hören, Sehen, Sich-Begegnen" [translation by Sandra Jasper].

16 See Theodor T. Heinze, "Spektakel unterm Kopfhörer. Zur Psychologie collagierten Klanges," *Psychologie und Geschichte 2* (1991): 150–158, here 153.

17 See "Gebrauchstest: tragbare Kassettenspieler. Jeder ein Meister auf seine Art," *Funkschau*, No. 16, pp. 29-31, here p. 29.

18 Bull, *Sounding out the City*.

19 See Marshall McLuhan, "Inside on the Outside, or the Spaced-Out American," *Journal of Communication* No. 4 (1976): 46–53, here p. 46. McLuhan sees evidence for this in literature, film, and technical objects like the car.

20 See the article "Walkaround Stereos," *Consumer Reports*, vol. 49, part 1985 Buying Guide (Dec. 1984): 278–82, here p. 278 (condensed from *Consumer Reports*, Nov. 1983).

21 See "Hey, Man! New Cassette Player Outclasses Street People's 'Box,'" *The Wall Street Journal*, June 23, 1980, p. 25; "Private Music and Public Silence," *The New York Times*, April 17, 1981, p. B 4.

22 See "Taking Your Music With You," *Ebony* June 1980, pp. 134–138.

23 Tricia Rose, *Black Noise: Rap Music and Black Culture in Contemporary America* (Middletown: Wesleyan University Press, 1994); Iain Chambers, *Urban Rhythms: Pop Music and Popular Culture* (New York: Palgrave Macmillan, 1985).

24 Rose, *Black Noise* p. 36.

25 This is also a title of a movie from 1990.

26 Up to the 1980s, audio journals routinely connected "portable pleasures" with the holiday season. "Going to the beach without music is like watching a ball game without beer," for example, begins a report in *Rolling Stone* on "Summer sounds to go" (July 21 / Aug. 4, 1983, pp. 105f).

27 Quote from a market study: International Resource Development Inc., ed., *Personal Portable Consumer Electronics Markets* (Norwalk, Connecticut, Report Nr. 587, Jan. 1984), p. 92.

28 Gary Gumpert, *Talking Tombstones & Other Tales of the Media Age* (Oxford: Oxford University Press, 1987). See especially chapter 4 "Walls of Sound."

29 "American Journal: New York City Lowers the Boom," *The Washington Post*, Aug. 2, 1985, p. A3).

30 Paul Karlstetter, *Breakdance, Rap und Graffiti: Ein expressiver Jugendstil? Ursprung, Entwicklung, Rezeption in der BRD und sozialpädagogische Umsetzung* (Landshut 1984, Thesis in Education); *BRAVO*, April 1984 (special issue on breakdance); Sascha Verlan, ed., *Rap-Texte* (Stuttgart: Reclam, 2003); Heide Buhmann and Hanspeter Haeseler, ed., *HipHop XXL. Fette Reime und Fette Beats in Deutschland* (Schlüchtern: Rockbuch Verlag, 2001).

31 D. Siegfried, *Time Is on My Side. Konsum und Politik in der westdeutschen Jugendkultur der 60er Jahre* (Göttingen: Wallstein, 2006).

ACOUSTIC MAPPING: NOTES FROM THE INTERFACE

Gascia Ouzounian

PRODUCING A CONTINUOUS
SOUND COMPOSED OF
48Hz
191Hz
239Hz
279Hz
335Hz
384Hz
479Hz
575Hz
958Hz

There is something about mapping that seems almost antithetical to sound. The idea of mapping stems from our desire to know where we are going. In order to orient ourselves, we need to create grids and boundaries. But boundaries don't apply to sound. Unlike maps, sound does not rely on surfaces or depths; rather, it penetrates them.

Steph Ceraso[1]

The interactive sound map is a relatively recent invention, having emerged at the intersection of soundscape studies, acoustic ecology, and sound art practices in the late 1990s. New mapping technologies like Google Maps and social media websites such as Facebook, Twitter, and AudioBoo have significantly impacted how sound maps are developed and understood; so have licensing agreements including Creative Commons "ShareAlike," which permits people to freely share media including audio recordings, with the right to copy, distribute, transmit and adapt the recordings for non-commercial purposes if they are credited to the author and attributed in the manner the author or licensor specifies.[2] Such innovations helped facilitate projects such as the British Library's UK Soundmap (2010–2011), to which over 350 people submitted approximately 2,000 recordings over the period of one year, tagging field recordings onto a Google Map of the UK, and sharing uploads and commentary through their social media accounts.[3] The same technologies and licensing agreements underpin numerous other online and interactive sound mapping projects, many of which share the aim of popularizing the concept of soundscape.[4] What is more contested is the effectiveness of sound maps in transmitting information about the acoustic environment in meaningful ways, and indeed the very notion of the sound map itself. Some, like cultural theorist Steph Ceraso, regard sound maps as oxymoronic, bringing an ephemeral, three-dimensional, dynamic, and "boundless" medium (sound) into dialogue with a tool (maps/mapping) that has historically evolved in two-dimensional and static terms, and that generally aims to establish boundaries that are understood as being fixed. Others see sound maps as a means to "control" sound. One blogger writes, "reducing sound to a visual field is a bit awkward—do we really hear better while looking at a two-dimensional picture on a screen than we would if we were actually in the space being represented? Maybe not, but the general desire to control sound is very strong, and what better way to control something than to pinpoint it?"[5] In what ways do sound maps succeed, and in what ways do they fail? How do they change the ways in which people

1 A tagged electrical box on Annandale Embankment in Belfast as part of the project *X Marks the Spot* (2012–ongoing) by Matilde Meireles. The poster indicates the frequencies of the different tones that are being emitted by the box (48 Hz, 191 Hz, etc.). The relative lightness or darkness of the numbers corresponds to their relative amplitudes, with darker numbers corresponding to louder tones. In this case, the most prominent tone is 239 Hz. Below the list of frequencies is a QR-Code or Quick Response Code that, when read by a smartphone, will load the project's Web site, xmsbelfast.com.
Photo by Matilde Meireles.

engage with the sonic environment, and in particular the urban soundscape? Are sound and mapping indeed antithetical, or can they come into dialogue in ways that critically alter our understanding of soundscape and its representation?

In *Favourite Sounds*, a project started in London by artist and musician Peter Cusack in 1998, which currently covers over a dozen cities, contributors are invited to respond to the question "What is your favourite [Name of City] sound and why?"[6] Cusack started the project in order to initiate conversations about urban sounds, "to try to get people talking about the way they hear everyday sounds and how they react to them, or what they think they feel about them, and how important (or not important) they are."[7] Initiating dialogue about soundscapes and bringing new voices into this dialogue are at the heart of many sound mapping projects. Max Stein and Julian Stein, the creators of the Google Maps-powered Montréal Sound Map, claim that their project:

> *offers an interface for users to explore and listen to the city with a purposeful and special attention that is rarely given to the sounds of the environment. We aim for people to continue this attentive listening and experience the complexity and lure of the soundscape first-hand. This promotes a more optimistic approach to acoustic ecology, encouraging listeners to lend a musical ear to the soundscape.*[8]

Developing a positive approach towards acoustic ecology is an important idea, which diverges from many historical soundscape projects that document noise pollution and other undesirable aspects of the acoustic environment—exemplified by the early work of R. Murray Schafer and the World Soundscape Project.[9] The idea of "lending a musical ear to the soundscape" is also compelling, as it invites contributors and users of the sound map alike to experience the urban soundscape in aesthetic terms. On the website, uploaded field recordings can be played back in a random order, forming a kind of indeterminate soundscape composition that listeners can stream at any time. On occasion, the "musicalization" of the sound map is literalized. For the event *ABC:MTL* (2013), at the Canadian Centre for Architecture in Montréal, two local sound artists—Lisa Gamble (aka Gambletron) and Jen Reimer—streamed recordings from the Montréal Sound Map as part of their project *Silent Montréal*.[10] The map was projected onto a wall, and listeners were given cordless headsets; they could choose which part of the map they wanted to hear, and the associated field recording was played along with recordings of music curated by Gamble and Reimer. According to Max Stein, on this occasion the musical qualities of the soundscape recordings were brought to the foreground in much the same way as they are on the Stockholm Soundmap, where field recordings tagged to a Google Map of Stockholm are played together with music by a collective of local composers.[11] In curating music for *ABC:MTL*, Reimer says that she and Gamble:

wanted to find music that was sensitive and could combine aesthetically with the field recordings. Most of the music chosen had an ambient atmospheric quality and rhythms were sparse in order to not interfere with the field recordings. Sometimes the music would be so subtle in combination with the field recordings that it was difficult to know which was which.[12]

Reimer's statement shows both the influence that soundscape composition has exerted on musical practices (especially in music that is typically described as "minimalist" or "ambient"), as well as the changing perspective of listeners, who might hear soundscapes as music more readily today than they did in the early- to mid-twentieth century, when composers working in experimental music traditions first put pressure on blurring the boundaries between "musical" and "real-world" sounds.[13]

In addition to promoting new dialogues and creative listening experiences of soundscapes, another way in which sound maps most obviously succeed is in facilitating collective ideas about soundscapes. Many sound mapping projects are collectively created, facilitated by network technologies and share-alike licensing agreements, or by inviting public participation and contribution in other ways. For the celebrated sound recordist Chris Watson's installation *Inside the Circle of Fire: A Sheffield Sound Map* (2013), the Millennium Gallery in Sheffield invited Watson to create a sound map of Sheffield, his hometown. Over a period of eighteen months, Watson collected sounds of the city, "charting its boundaries on the edge of the Peak [River] and travelling its waterways to the bustling heart of the city:"[14]

Sheffield is a city built on rivers ... water is the reason the city's there. It's driven the industry and it's nourished the population, both culturally and in terms of the water supply. So I chose waterways as a way to navigate my way through the city, and then stop off in various places that I thought had particular and signature soundmark—both the built environment and the natural geography of the place.[15]

Thus, *Inside the Circle of Fire* illustrated a specific geographical and cultural history of the city through its particular sonic mappings, and, through its multichannel installation in the Millennium Gallery made this history both sensorial and immersive.[16] In developing the project, Watson invited the public to contribute recordings of Sheffield. He incorporated all public submissions into the gallery installation, and undertook soundwalks with interested participants, during which time he also made recordings:

the whole aim ... was to make a piece which makes people think about the sounds of their city.... Listening to something is quite a creative act. It's not passive. And actively listening, you can decide what you like, and what you don't like, and then you're in a position to start thinking about how you might change the sounds or acoustics of what you don't like.[17]

Thus, Watson not only sought to create an installation that immerses listeners in a sound map of their city, but also to empower people to engage with their acoustic environments in a critical way. Such projects diverge in important ways from historical forms of soundscape composition, which typically put forth a single artist or composer's view of a soundscape, and are often experienced or consumed in a passive way (similar to a concert), without necessarily bringing audiences/participants into a critical dialogue or active engagement with their sonic environments.[18] It is notable that, in the first month of its opening, the installation had over 23,000 visitors, many of whom have reported emotive and powerful listening experiences.[19] The Belfast-based sound artist Matilde Meireles's *X Marks The Spot* (2012–ongoing) is another recent sound mapping artwork that evolves through listener participation (figure 1). For this project, Meireles tagged street-level telecommunication boxes throughout the city of Belfast with posters that showed the frequencies and relative amplitudes of electrical hums that the boxes were emitting. The posters contained QR codes (Quick Response codes) that, when unscrambled by a smartphone, launch the project's Web site.[20] There, visitors can suggest further electrical boxes for tagging, listen to compositions created from recordings of tagged boxes, and find maps of tagged boxes that they can search for while undertaking a "sound hunt":

The tagging process aims to engage people with the space around them. To understand how sound shapes our experience of the city. For obvious reasons I started mapping places closer to me. Places I pass by daily and therefore have a closer relationship with or remember vividly. By inviting other people to participate in the process, this activity is designed to spread throughout Belfast, creating a stronger connection with the city.[21]

Again, the participative, collaborative and open-ended nature of the project distinguishes it from historical forms of fixed, single-authored soundscape composition (as exemplified by electro-acoustic soundscape compositions heard in concert settings). The social dimension of sound mapping—whether through online interactions, or through in-person interactions with artists, designers, or other contributors in the context of listening walks, collective recording sessions, participative artworks, and so on—provides a basis for integrating sound mapping into various kinds of shared experiences of city life.

Another area in which sound maps succeed is in developing rich and easily accessible archives of sound environments. Between 2010 and 2013, the sound historian Emily Thompson, working in collaboration with designer Scott Mahoy, developed *The Roaring 'Twenties,* a media-rich rendering of New York City's soundscape in the late 1920s and early 1930s that focuses on the city's then emerging problem of noise pollution.[22] Published as an interactive website by the multimedia journal *Vectors, The Roaring 'Twenties* collects approximately 1,000 documents related to noise: 600 unique noise complaints culled from the Municipal Archives of the City of New York; 50 clippings of news reels loaned by the Fox Movietone News Collection; and 350 newspaper and magazine clippings. These documents—each meticulously captioned, catalogued, and organized—can be navigated temporally, via a timeline interface that organizes documents by year and month, and spatially, via a high-resolution, digitized map of New York City from 1933, which appears over a contemporary, zoomable Google Map of the city. Thompson introduces the project by writing, "The aim here is not just to present sonic content, but to evoke the original contexts of those sounds, to help us better understand that context as well as the sounds themselves."[23] Among other things, the project enables audiences to discover how concerns about urban noise have changed over time, what kinds of noises were historically considered undesirable (and why), and what the urban soundscape actually sounded like nearly a century ago. Assembled as they are on the web site, the documents further reveal how dialogues about sound and noise have been critical to negotiations of private and public space in the city, and the extent to which these dialogues inform and imbue individual and collective experiences of city life. In the case of *The Roaring 'Twenties,* network technologies facilitate the storage and distribution of a vast quantity of information and media relating to an historical soundscape. Notably, Thompson does not provide any interpretation to the documents she collects in the project. Rather, she acts strictly as archivist, collector, and cataloguer, presenting data that only becomes meaningful through the visitor's engagement with it.[24]

Contemporary sound maps can also function effectively as archives. The creators of the Montréal Sound Map, for example, write that their project "allows users to upload field recordings to a Google Map of Montréal. The soundscape is constantly changing, and this project acts as a sonic time capsule with the goal of preserving sounds before they disappear."[25] Visitors to the Montréal Sound Map can click on individual audio icons to listen to sound files; or, they can choose "Autoplay" or "Shuffle" functions which, respectively, play back all the sound files in alphabetical order (by name of location), or at random. Individual sound files can also be downloaded. A "Sound Browser" allows visitors to search or sort sounds by location (boroughs, neighbourhoods, municipalities, suburbs); date (year, time of day, month, seasons, day of the week); tags (human, mechanical, natural, societal, music, noise); or by the name of the contributor. When selected, an audio file is accompanied by notes on the equipment used in making the recording (e.g., "Olympus LS-10 & OKM Binaurals"), as well as a description of the sounds (e.g., "Standing underneath the Charlevoix Bridge, there is an interesting mixture of traffic above, passing bikes/inline skates/runners, and birds").[26] Contributors also have the option of uploading a photo of the location where the recording was made. These features have become standard elements of online, interactive sound maps, and can be found on the Belfast Sound Map, the Inukjuak Sound Map, the Toronto Sound Map, among others. Most recently, the software programmer Julian Vogels has been developing an iPhone app for the Montréal Sound Map that will allow contributors to make recordings on their iPhones and automatically tag them to the web site. These new technologies will extend the sound map's reach into everyday spaces, and make the sound map increasingly accessible and ubiquitous, as part of everyday experiences of the city. This will potentially alter not only the demographics of the sound map's users/contributors but also the map's content, as mundane and "personal" activities may become increasingly highlighted through frequent and ubiquitous use.

Some sound mapping projects, like Ian Rawes's *London Sound Survey*, archive historical as well as contemporary sound environments, and offer new ways of representing sound-scapes. Rawes describes the project, which he started in 2008, as "a collection of Creative Commons-licensed sound recordings of places, events and wildlife [in London]. Historical references are also gathered to find out how London's sounds have changed.'[27] Rawes acts as sound recordist, archivist, mapper, and designer for the project. He records London sound-scapes (several hundred of his recordings can be heard on the website), collects soundscape recordings by others that are licensed under the Creative Commons agreement, gathers documents relating to historical sounds of London, and invents ways of visualizing and organizing this data. Historical features range from a database of radio location recordings from the mid-twentieth century, to written descriptions of sounds of London that date as far back as the tenth century. Rawes has also created sound maps of London for the website: a Day Sound Map and Night Sound Map, a Waterways Map, and an Estuary Map—all of which collect soundscape recordings tagged onto historical and contemporary maps of London—and a Grid Map that depicts these soundscapes using only graphical icons.[28] As a visual map of sounds, the Grid Map is particularly effective in transmitting a large amount of sonic information in a way that can be quickly digested. It is immediately apparent, for example, that there is a predominance of sounds of road traffic, aircraft, fixed machinery, and tools and plants across the city, while the sounds of people and birdsong are relatively less prominent, and are generally clustered in specific regions. About 5 per cent of the map is marked "inaccessible," forming a kind of sonic no-man's land on the outermost edges of East London. A blog post by Rawes discusses the legal limits that field recordists might encounter, shedding light on these inaccessible zones:

> *Those of us recording the sounds of urban environments in particular might run into prob-lems similar to those besetting photographers, with overzealous officials and others claiming that recording in such-and-such place is illegal, that it infringes someone's human rights, and so on.*
>
> *There's also the growing habit of bringing words like "terrorism" and "security" into play as an attempt at shut-up-and-do-as-you're-told, but as we'll see there are few situations in which such claims have any legal, let alone rational, substance.*[29]

We learn that there are few places in the UK where making an audio recording is specifically prohibited: courts, prisons, nuclear power plants, military bases, and electronics communications providers. It is also, unsurprisingly, illegal to use audio recordings for the purpose of espionage, and against the objections of private property owners.[30] What is more problematic is the blurring of private and public space. According to Rawes, "More and more of what appear to be public spaces are, in fact, privately owned. Shopping centres, many newly-built squares and plazas, and that slender corridor of possession between the side of a building and the row of brass studs set into the pavement are all private property."[31] There are also laws that apply to making recordings of copyrighted material and private conversations. Rawes indicates that he never focuses on private conversations and ensures that specific people cannot be identified in his recordings. These issues shed light on some of the particular challenges sonic cartographers face in documenting the sonic environment, as well as the content of urban sound maps, which typically focus on outdoor locations and spaces that are understood to be public spaces, and which rarely focus on social interactions like conversations or private social occasions.

Although sound maps can serve multiple functions and can do so effectively, they have been criticized for failing to put forth cohesive ideas of soundscape, and for not providing enough context to enable meaningful interpretation. Barry Truax, an influential soundscape composer and researcher, and a founding member of the World Soundscape Project, has said that he finds the sound map "useful to orient people who are unfamiliar with the soundscape concept to the idea that soundscape recordings are markers of place. However, lacking any coherent temporal perspective, and usually lacking any interpretative analysis, the listener is left trying to imagine what has been recorded and what significance it has."[32] Truax's criticism can be especially applied to sound maps whose temporal or geographical reach is so broad or disconnected that any meaningful engagement beyond "listening to field recordings tagged on a map" is effectively extinguished for some audiences. The soundscape composer and theorist Jacqueline Waldock has also questioned whether sound maps are able to effectively realize their aims, and reminds us of the hierarchies, fractures, and divisions that can arise even when projects are well intentioned. For Waldock, some projects have unrealistic goals. She describes the aims of Sound Seeker, an online sound map of New York City that claims to "[reach] across geographical, economical, educational, cultural and racial divides," for example, as "extravagant."[33] Waldock also points out issues of unequal access, asking, "will [sound] maps exclude the sounding worlds of those who cannot afford smart phones? And: have the makers taken into account the recording culture and norms that are produced and reiterated by these maps?"[34] In terms of the latter question, Waldock is especially concerned that sound maps reproduce dominant divisions of "gender, domestic and public, private and collective, poor and well-resourced."[35] On a more basic level, the merging of sound with mapping has also been problematized. Ceraso describes the ephemerality of sound as a feature that puts it into contradiction with conventional ideas of mapping, and argues that the dynamism of the sonic environment is not effectively translated via static recordings of place.[36] For listeners like Ceraso, sound maps fail to capture the "embodied experience of encountering sound in its original environment."[37] Such criticisms will be important for sonic cartographers to consider as the genre matures. At the same time, it should be acknowledged that urban sound maps can and already do reflect a variety of interests and concerns, from archival, historical, and cultural studies of cities to socially-oriented and networked mapping projects, to creative works that bring sound mapping into dialogue with artistic traditions. They also have realizable aims like inspiring attentive listening in others and generating critical dialogues about soundscapes. While still an emerging genre, sound maps have already offered new ways of conceptualizing and representing the urban soundscape—especially in the context of collectively created, interactive, and participatory works. These features position sound maps to be deployed in domains like urban design, city planning, and architecture in new ways that might positively impact urban communities. Udo Noll, the founder of radio aporee, one of the most extensive online sound mapping projects, has written that:

> the whole aporee soundmap thing began as a reaction to the lack and loss of sense of place, the personal experience of decreasing sensitivity for things "in between," the absence of resonance in my relationship to the surrounding world…. i understand that some feel uncomfortable with the amount of contributions, in all their different qualities, the flattening perspective of the map maybe, and insist on distinction, for whatever reason. zoom in, go to the details, listen to the individual sounds, that may change your perspective.[38]

By inviting people to experience, document, and share ideas about soundscapes in ways that were previously unimagined, sound maps have fundamentally altered perspectives on sound as it evolves in relation to space and place, our connection to sound in its environmental and spatial forms, and the many "resonances"—social, cultural, historical, and aesthetic—of these relationships.

Endnotes

1   Steph Ceraso, "The Site of Sound: Mapping Audio," Blog post at Humanities, Arts, Science and Technology Alliance and Collaboratory (HASTAC), 5 October 2010. http://www.hastac.org/blogs/stephceraso/sight-sound-mapping-audio (accessed 25 December 2013).

2   See Creative Commons "Attribution-NonCommercial-ShareAlike 3.0 Unported," http://creativecommons.org/licenses/by-nc-sa/3.0/ (accessed 7 January 2014).

3   See UK Soundmap, http://sounds.bl.uk/Sound-Maps/UK-Soundmap (accessed 28 November 2013).

4   Not all sound map designers are keen to build their projects using "brand name" technologies with corporate interests in their users—like Facebook, Twitter, or Google Maps—but do so out of necessity. Udo Noll, the founder of the global sound mapping project radio aporee, writes, "i don't like [Google Maps] but there's no alternative so far on that scale and detail." See Udo Noll, "sound, place and global reach," Blog post on radio aporee, 2 December 2012. http://radio-aporee.blogspot.co.uk/2012/12/sound-place-and-global-reach.html (accessed 8 January 2012).

5   Anonymous, "Atlas Sound: A Typology of Sound Maps," Blog post on Weird Vibrations, 10 January 2012. http://www.weirdvibrations.com/2010/01/10/atlas-sound-a-typology-of-sound-maps/ (accessed 8 January 2014).

6   See Peter Cusack, Favourite Sounds, http://favouritesounds.org/ (accessed 25 December 2013).

7   Zuzana Friday Prikrylova, "'You learn a lot about the city by asking about its sound': Peter Cusack Interview, Sounds," Create Digital Music, 21 May 2013. http://createdigitalmusic.com/2013/05/you-learn-a-lot-about-the-city-by-asking-about-its-sound-peter-cusack-interview/ (accessed 28 November 2013).

8   See Max Stein and Julian Stein, Montréal Sound Map, http://www.montrealsoundmap.com/. Last accessed 25 December 2013.

9   The World Soundscape Project itself emerged out of Schafer's course on noise pollution at Simon Fraser University in the late 1960s and early 1970s, "as well as from [Schafer's] personal distaste for the more raucous aspects of Vancouver's rapidly changing soundscape." See Barry Truax, "The World Soundscape Project," http://www.sfu.ca/~truax/wsp.html. (accessed 7 January 2013).

10 "2013 Nuit blanche à Montréal at the CCA." Announcement on

Canadian Centre for Architecture (CCA) Web site, 2 March 2013. http://www.cca.qc.ca/en/education-events/1952-2013-nuit-blanche-a-montreal-at-the-cca. The description of Silent Montréal reads: "The silent disco in the Rotunda melds the sounds of the city with electronic music. Cordless headsets will be distributed to participants."

11 Gascia Ouzounian, Unpublished email correspondence with Max Stein, 18 November 2013. The Stockholm Soundmap—Soundtrack is online at http://oljudsthlm.se/soundmap/soundtrack.php. (accessed 28 November 2013).

12 Gascia Ouzounian, Unpublished email correspondence with Jen Reimer, 8 January 2014.

13 For a discussion of twentieth-century experimental music traditions that draw upon "real-world" sounds, see Michael Nyman, *Experimental Music: Cage and Beyond* (Cambridge: Cambridge University Press, 1999 [1974]). Nyman's discussion touches on influences as varied as the burgeoning industrial soundscape in the case of the Futurist composers' use of *intonarumori*, noise-making instruments; the French composer Erik Satie's idea of *musique d'ameublement*, an early precedent for "ambient" music as popularized by Brian Eno; the early American experimentalist Charles Ives' Postface to *112 Songs*, which describes "someone sitting on a porch … looking out over the landscape, sitting there doing nothing and 'hearing his own symphony'" (Nyman, *Experimental Music* p. 41); the work of musique concrète pioneers Pierre Schaeffer and Pierre Henry; and, crucially, John Cage's invitation for listeners to hear any and all incidental sounds as music, widely considered the premise of his "silent" composition *4'33"* (1952).

14 Gascia Ouzounian, unpublished interview with Chris Watson, Belfast, 25 October 2013.

15 Ibid.

16 Most of the recordings in *Inside the Circle of Fire* were made by Watson using a SoundField microphone, which records sound in three dimensions. Inside the gallery, the sounds are projected over a system of twenty loudspeakers: "twelve loudspeakers in the horizontal, four beneath the floor level, and four in the ceiling. The idea is that you create a sphere, effectively, and the listener is towards the centre of the sphere" (Ibid.). Watson tells me that the SoundField ambisonic recording system is especially well suited to sound mapping, it allows people to "hear the space" (Ibid.).

17 Ibid.

18 This discussion does not intend to diminish the value of single-authored, fixed soundscape compositions (or works intended for concert listening), but rather seeks to highlight the participative and collaborative basis of many sound mapping projects, including those that evolve as artworks. In terms of historical precedents, the "soundwalk"—exemplified by the early listening walks of American sound artist Max Neuhaus in his project *LISTEN* (late 1960s) and the soundwalks of the World Soundscape Project (WSP)—is perhaps equally important to sound mapping as soundscape composition. Hildegard Westerkamp, a central figure in the WSP, has written that, "[soundwalking] can be done alone or with a friend…. It can also be done in small groups, in which case it is always interesting to explore the interplay between group listening and individual listening." See Hildegard Westerkamp, "Soundwalking," 1974 (revised 2001) http://www.sfu.ca/~westerka/writings%20page/articles%20pages/soundwalking.html. See also Max Neuhaus, *LISTEN*, 2004. http://www.max-neuhaus.info/soundworks/vectors/walks/LISTEN/LISTEN.pdf. Last accessed 8 January 2014. A more contemporary project that illuminates the social aspects of soundwalking is Andra McCartney's Soundwalking Interactions, http://soundwalkinginteractions.wordpress.com/. (accessed 8 January 2014).

19 Gascia Ouzounian, Unpublished interview with Chris Watson, 2013.

20 See Matilde Meireles, *X Marks the Spot*, 2013. http://matildemeireles.com/portfolio/x-marks-the-spot. (accessed 7 January 2014).

21 Ibid.

22 Emily Thompson and Scott Mahoy, "The 'Roaring' Twenties: An Interactive Exploration of the Historical Soundscape of New York City," in *Vectors* 4/1 (Fall 2013). Online at http://vectorsdev.usc.edu/

NYCsound/777b.html. Last accessed 28 November 2013.

23 Emily Thompson, "Author's Statement on *The Roaring 'Twenties*," in *Vectors* 4/1 (Fall 2013). Online at http://vectors.usc.edu/projects/index.php?project=98&thread=AuthorsStatement. (accessed 28 November 2013).

24 Some sound map designers let the audio data they collect "speak for itself," while others, including those for UK Soundmap, Favourite Sounds, Montréal Sound Map, and Belfast Sound Map, include scope for commentary and descriptions. The Belfast Sound Map (www.belfastsoundmap.org) further permits contributors to submit texts that describe "a sound experience"—i.e., verbal commentary without audio files. At times, commentary on sound maps has a personal or critical scope, touching on personal experiences, local politics, ecology, and other issues that are highlighted through "listening to place"; in other cases, commentary consists of matter-of-fact descriptions of what has been heard or experienced. For the project Sounds Around You (http://www.soundaroundyou.com/), contributors are asked to rate the quality of soundscape recordings they upload (on a scale "bad–good," as well as other features of their uploads ("unpleasant–pleasant," "uneventful–eventful," "chaotic–tranquil"); they are also asked to describe "positive" and "negative" sounds that feature in their recordings. Such features enhance the subjective and personal aspects of sound maps, and provide arguably important context for sounds that might otherwise hold little meaning for listeners; at the same time, listeners might want to hear a recording that is "unadulterated" by commentary, in order to experience it on their own terms, without reference to the recordist's intentions or reflections.

25 See Max Stein and Julian Stein, Montréal Sound Map, http://www.montrealsoundmap.com/. (accessed 25 December 2013).

26 A 7:09 recording contributed by Max Stein, "Charlevoix Bridge (under)," posted May 04 2009 on Montréal Sound Map.

27 See Ian Rawes, London Sound Survey, http://www.soundsurvey.org.uk/. (accessed 28 November 2013).

28 Ian Rawes, "Grid Map," London Sound Survey, http://www.soundsurvey.org.uk/index.php/survey/grid/. Last accessed 25 December 2013.

29 Ian Rawes, "Sound and the Law: What are the limits on recording?" Blog post on London Sound Survey, 13 October 2013. http://www.soundsurvey.org.uk/index.php/survey/post/sound_and_the_law/. (accessed 25 December 2013).

30 As Rawes describes in "Sound and the Law," these laws include: Section 1 of the Official Secrets Act of 1911, which prohibits the use of audio recordings for the purpose of espionage; Section 34C of the Prison Act of 1952, which prohibits audio recordings and transmissions from inside prisons; Section 9 of the Contempt of Court Act 1981, which makes it illegal to record audio in court without permission; the Official Secrets (Prohibited Places) Order of 1994, which prohibits audio recordings from a number of nuclear installations and military bases; and Schedule 17 of the Communications Act 2003, which adds electronic communications stations and offices to the list of prohibited places. Article 8 of the Human Rights Act (1998) protects the privacy of individual homes and personal correspondences, and the CCTV Code of Conduct (revised 2008, by the Information Commissioner's Office) declares that "CCTV must not be used to record conversations between members of the public" (Ibid.).

31 Ibid.

32 Barry Truax, "Sound, Listening and Place: The Aesthetic Dilemma," *Organised Sound* 17/3 (2012): 1–9. Accessible online at http://www.sfu.ca/~truax/OS8.html. (accessed 28 November 2013).

33 Jacqueline Waldock, "Soundmapping: Critiques and Reflections on this New Publicly Engaging Medium," *Journal of Sonic Studies* 1/1 (October 2011). Online at http://journal.sonicstudies.org/vol01/nr01/a08. (accessed 28 November 2013). See also Soundseeker, http://www.soundseeker.org/. (accessed 7 January 2013).

34 See Waldock, "Soundmapping."

35 Ibid.

36 See Ceraso, "The Site of Sound."

37 Ibid.

38 Udo Noll, "sound, place, and global reach."

THE SPACE BETWEEN: A CARTOGRAPHIC EXPERIMENT

Merijn Royaards

It is Russia, 1916, at the height of summer. Denis Kaufman, a young student at the Petrograd Neurological Institute sits down by a lumber mill on the Eastern edge of Lake Ilmen, where he has arranged to meet his girlfriend. In the hours that pass before she arrives, he listens to the sounds of the old mill, the lake, and the rolling hills in the distance.[1] With closed eyes, Kaufman transcribes the waves that settle on his eardrums into unseen, unspoken words; and a stream of aural consciousness blackens his notebook with phonetic fragments. As his hand traces time and sound, touching at the end of language and reaching the limits of its bandwidth, Kaufman marks the beginning of both sound-art and graphic notation.[2] Back in Petrograd, he founds the Laboratory of Hearing, where he experiments with the reorganization of his transcriptions into new sonic landscapes. He will reflect years later that he was struggling on two fronts: first, with the lack of suitable equipment to record sounds rather than describe them; and second, with the enormity of the project itself. It's a battle Kaufman retreats from eventually in 1918, when he steps onto the platform of Moscow's Central Station, overwhelmed by the density of its soundscape, and convinced of the futility of his method: "I must get a piece of equipment that won't describe but will record, photograph these sounds. Otherwise it's impossible to organize, to edit them. They rush past like time."[3]

The inability of Kaufman's era to record sounds the way a movie camera could capture images as frames would prove fateful: today Denis Kaufman is best known as Dziga Vertov, the revolutionary film-maker and pioneer of cinematic montage.

There is a melancholic dimension to the story of Kaufman, who may be credited with the invention of sound-art as we now understand it, but whose acoustic imagination was far ahead of his own time. The Russian avant-garde of the two decades, between the October Revolution and the Great Terror of the 1930s, pushed the possibilities of sound, performance, and film well beyond the state of the art of the period. The new ground that was broken in the process is only recently being uncovered from beneath the bloodstained dust-sheet of Stalinism.

At the First Discussional Exhibition of the Union of Active Revolutionary Art, held in Moscow in May 1924, Solomon Nikritin presented his "tectonic research," a laboratory of process, a map of creative flows expressed through texts, photographs, sketches, and sculptures without resolution; art as pure method.[4] Nikritin was the founder of a group of artists and intellectuals named after its modus operandi, The Method. The concept of method, or process as a dynamic system that drives new ideas and complexity, immediately explodes into a spectrum of thought from Whitehead to Duchamp and beyond, but Nikritin's process-philosophy was of a particular kind, which he dubbed "Projectionism" (from *proiectus*, to throw forward).

Nikritin, who embraced the post-revolutionary drive for a new art to signal a departure from existing religious and bourgeois values, envisaged "a universal science of organization and analysis through a search for structural similarities in all spheres of knowledge."[5] In Nikritin's philosophy of art, the organization and graphic representation of matter and phenomena was the method through which creative energy was transformed into new developments.[6] The Projectionists' task was to sculpt the future out of transliterations of the present; their art was based on a transcription of the world into a schemata comprised of dynamics, streams, and densities that excavated its underlying structures and forged new meanings.

Among his many experiments, Nikritin combined biomechanical principles with music theory and acoustics to develop "temperaments and scales for body movements."[7] He drew diagrams that mapped the relation between colour and sound sensations, and established the Projection Theatre, a place where "the most complicated scores of sounds, gestures, movements and emotional states" were created in pursuit of a new art, a "new man."[8] The Method *was* graphic notation, the transcription of body, resonance, and mind into marks that formed a connective tissue between past, present, and a better future.

Stripped from their utopian idealism, the projectionists were pioneers of scoring the world, and they understood the essence of their process not merely as a conversion of the ephemeral into the fixed, or the folding of four dimensions into two, but as an interface between different states; as the creation of a space between immensities, not as a negation of that vastness, but as the superimposition of unknown territories to try and understand their possibilities.

The Method thus led graphic notation onto forking paths; the projection of ideas and the transcription of etherealities. These paths, however, would interweave throughout the twentieth century, and through their collected intersections appears an image of both the limits and potential of drawing sound. Predicting a first such crossing, the composer Arseny Avraamov had proposed in 1916 to analyze and categorize "the curve structure" of sound grooves on gramophone records to allow for sound synthesis.[9] It was a bid, reiterated by Moholy-Nagy in 1922, which was realized, albeit in a different form, with the invention of sound-on-film, and the graphical- or drawn-sound technology of the late 1920s.[10] In Russia, under the influence of film-makers such as Vertov and Sergei Eisenstein, a contrapuntal approach to this technology intersected sound transcriptions with cinematically expressed[11] ideas that gave light, quite literally, to some of the "masterpieces of early sound art."[12] By "projecting the method," the Projectionists themselves anticipated another intersection of transcription and projection where "even faults and paradoxes gained a new constructive sense and value."[13]

More than thirty years after the Projection Theatre's experiments were cut short by the totalitarian state, this concept would be reformulated by John Cage as "experimental action,"[14] and branch out into the routinely indeterminate *event* or *verbal scores*[15] of the second half of the twentieth century. The reason that notational systems have increasingly become an exercise in the staging of chance operations not only precedes John Cage, it is a direct result of their reductive and paradoxical nature: graphic scores can be viewed as deterministic, for they fix a moment in time (or time as moments); they mark the preliminary end of a thought, however abstract, as pigment on paper; they plot the edges of a question and indicate the parameters of a system. On the other hand, this determinism is subverted by the technique; the compression of a field into a frame, the mapping of time and space as an image that may be (mis)interpreted, the aberrations of subjective "lensing."

Chance is thus intrinsic to notational systems as much as structure and clarity of thought are, and the non-intended acts as a filter through which ideas flow towards possibilities, marking the beginning of a set of new thoughts and actions in the space between direction and misdirection. The twentieth century is littered with conceptual probes dispatched to explore the limits of notation, and we keep sending them up into orbit, penetrating some of its edges, while ricocheting off others. However, as Solomon Nikritin would have it, the "cartogram of the program," the score of the score, remains seductively incomplete.

By way of a conclusion to this brief essay, and as an extended reflection on the themes raised, I have set out in the following pages a selection of my own work with some accompanying remarks. These works in progress hold up a two-way mirror, illuminating some of the limits and possibilities of acoustic notation systems within a wider context of debates over the aesthetic legacy of twentieth-century modernism. We hear in sound as we see in light, and to try and see through sound, or hear through light is to reverse the order of things: to break down, if only conceptually, the perceptual dominance of one sense over another. When notational systems are maps of physical space as an image of its sounding, the field of investigation they unfold is of an architectonic space that "amplifies its own perceptual spectrum," becoming a vision of sound as much as it is a vision of form.[16] The points, lines, and planes draw maps of architecture's own negative space in time. They silently, and visually, extend architecture into its auditory shadow, and in doing so collapse two disciplines into a paradox, a graphic score: a space between.

1

2

1 Beirut: Green Line (May 2010).
An imaginary staging of sniper fire, sound chases light through the rubble. A space between sound and silence, the end and the beginning, the city and its architecture.

2 Acoustic Operation 12 (January 2012).
The staging of a differential. A fictional intervention that feeds distant points-of-audition into a proximate point-of-view. Here, a prosthetic architecture, a vision of form, induces a form of listening. From across the city, sonic fragments ricochet through a network of steel and concrete cylinders. They converge as a soundscape at one of these operations, a montage of urban acoustics and different impulses superimposed onto a cityscape.

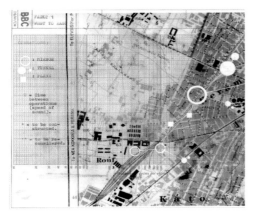
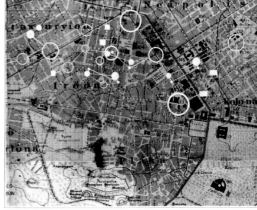
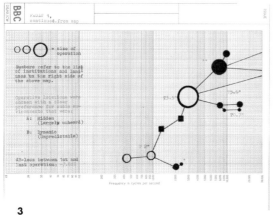
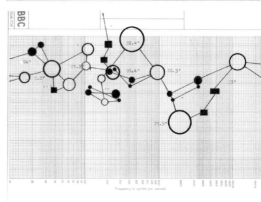

3

3 Sonic Operations, Athens (March 2012).
A map showing the different acoustic operations as they would be spread over the city. The architectural components are tunnel, (sound) mirror, and plane. Tunnels here are the channels through which urban sounds are redirected and recomposed. Sound mirrors are focusing devices, collapsing an auditory spectrum onto a single point-of audition, desynchronized from its corresponding point-of-view. Planes are acoustic reconfigurations of architectural space, a technique of echoic montage.

4 Architecture of Time and Frequency (March 2012).
A transcription of sound from a single point-of-audition in Omonia, Athens, in 2012. Measured frequencies were plotted against their approximate direction and temporal occurrence. The possibilities laid bare by this abstraction are both compositional and architectural: the performance of the score unravels the recorded soundscape as an interplay of pure pitches configured as sonic structure in space.

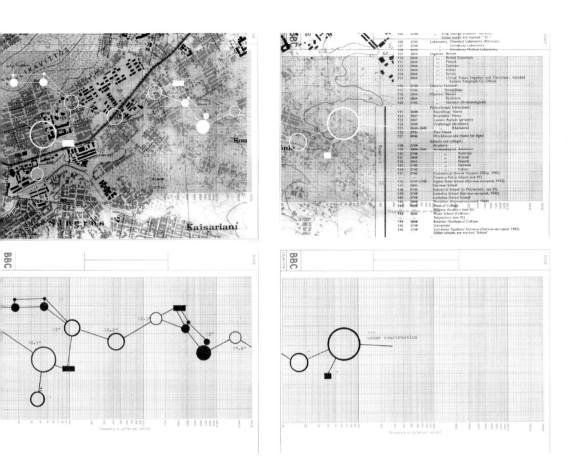

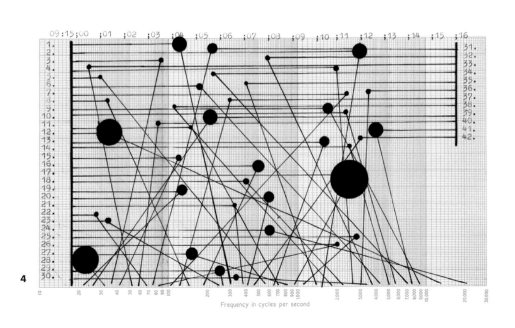

4

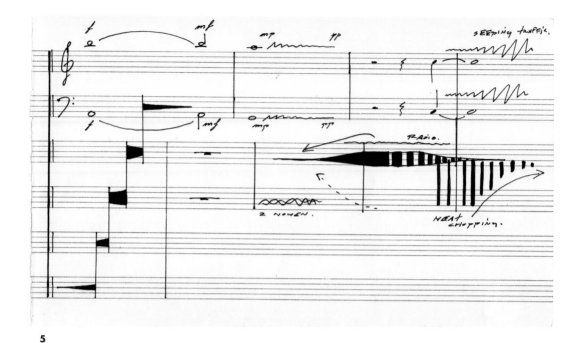

5

January '12
09;36;24- 09;37 01

18Khz- rev.T:
          00.0012
950Hz- rev.T:
          00.0007

4-6Khz- 01.34
11Khz- 00.92
-20Hz- 03.01

7Khz- 00.02
20Khz- flutter

350Hz- nil
8Khz- 00.56
18Khz- 01.84

90Hz- multiple r
14Khz- nil

600Hz- 00.49
16Khz- 00.24

-20Hz- 3.14
23Khz- unsound.
4Khz- slow flutt

6

7

5 Hong Kong, Narrow Passage (December 2011).
A notated fragment of footage shot in Hong Kong alleyways in January 2011. The recorded soundtrack here is transcribed as pitches, timbres, and rhythms without any attempt to organize them. The intrinsic distortion of musical notation is used as a montage technique; the soundtrack was reassembled using its scored-out image.

6 Acoustic Score (July 2012).
This notation maps the interrelation between the acoustics of a railway arch in North West London and a moving point-of-audition. The experience of echoes, especially flutter echoes, is exclusive to the location of the listener. Resonating sound here transforms geometry, a visual parameter of space, into something more visceral, musical. A montage of viewpoints in an echo-filled space will exponentially increase its sonic complexity.

7 Score of a Sound (July 2012).
A sound, a kind of whistling, rises above the background noise. Clear and articulate, it pierces through the heavy blanket of city sounds. It is a single point in a featureless expanse, then a line, then a plane, and finally an idea for a script.

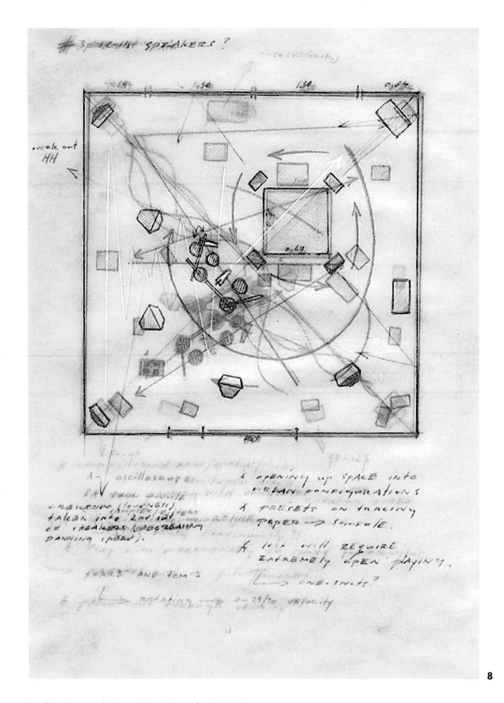

8 Superimposed Transcription (September 2005).
This is a vertical notation of a sound installation. Electronic percussion pads were used to trigger sampled acoustics of the Bibliothèque Nationale in Paris (see figure 9). These triggers were set up in the middle of a gallery space, and could be played with sticks or hands. The resulting sounds would travel across the space in different configurations according to performance parameters such as velocity, the struck surface, and rhythm. The transcription shows the different sonic pathways these parameters would allow for, as well as the placement of the interface and the position of the twenty speakers used in the installation.

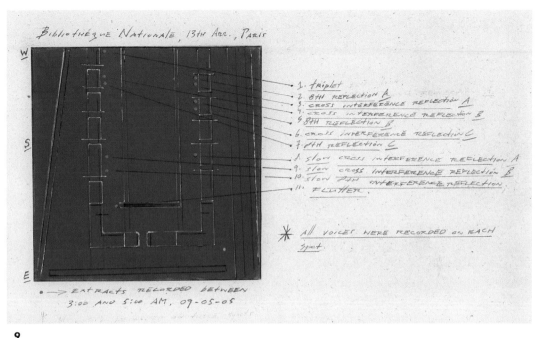

Bibliothèque Nationale, 13th Arr., Paris

1. triplet
2. 8th reflection A
3. cross interference reflection A
4. cross interference reflection B
5. 8th reflection B
6. cross interference reflection C
7. 8th reflection C
8. slow cross interference reflection A
9. slow cross interference reflection B
10. slow pin interference reflection,
11. flutter.

* All voices were recorded on each spot.

→ Extracts recorded between 3:00 and 5:00 AM, 09-05-05

9

9 Audio Map 3, Postmodern Polyrythms (January 2005). Paris, 3th arrondissement, 5.00 am. Four dark extrusions rise from the Seine. Timber-clad stairs lead up to a platform, a labyrinth of vanishing points, a vision of aluminium and glass. Though a terrifying example of post-modern architecture, the Bibliotheque Nationale François Mitterand, completed in 1996, is acoustically one of the most exciting spaces in the city. This map shows the location and rhythmic signature of several recordings made with percussion instruments before dawn one morning in 2005. The recordings were sampled and used in a sound installation, which allowed participants to rebuild and reconfigure this architecture acoustically inside a gallery space.

All figures by Merijn Royaards

Endnotes

1 Andrey Smirnov, *Sound in Z: Experiments in Sound and Electronic Music in Early 20th-Century Russia*, ed. David Rogerson and Matt Price (Köln: Walther König, 2013).

2 Luigi Russolo's manifesto "The Art of Noise" as well as his "Intonarumor" and accompanying graphic scores were conceived in 1913, thus preceding Kaufman's experiments by three years. Russolo however, advocated an expansion of musical sound, and thus may be regarded as a forerunner of music concrète rather than sound art.

3 Andrey Smirnov, *Sound in Z* p. 26.

4 Liubov Pchelkina, "Treasure Hunters of the 1920s," in *Sound in Z, Experiments in Sound and Electronic Music in early 20th-Century Russia*, ed. David Rogerson and Matt Price (Köln: Walther König, 2013).

5 Liubov Pchelkina, "The Biomechanics of Voice and Movement in Solomon Nikritin's Projection Theatre (1920s)," in *Electrified Voices: Medial, Socio-Historical and Cultural Aspects of Voice Transfer*, ed. Nils Meise and Dmitri Zakharine (Göttingen: V and R UniPress, 2012) p. 151.

6 Ibid.

7 Liubov Pchelkina, "Treasure Hunters of the 1920s" p. 15.

8 Ibid. p. 16.

9 Andrey Smirnov, *Sound in Z* p. 29.

10 László Moholy-Nagy, "Production-Reproduction," in Krisztina Passuth, *Moholy-Nagy* (London: Thames and Hudson, 1985 [1922])

11 Sergei Eisenstein, Vsevolod Pudovkin, and Grigori Alexandrov, "Statement on Sound," in *The Film Factory, Russian and Soviet Cinema in Documents 1896–1939*, ed. Ian Christie and Richard Taylor (New York: Routledge, 1994 [1928]) pp. 234–35.

12 Andrey Smirnov, *Sound in Z* p. 155.

13 Liubov Pchelkina, "Treasure Hunters of the 1920s" p. 16.

14 John Cage, *Silence* (London: Calder and Boyars, 1968) p. 69.

15 For an in-depth analysis and historical context of verbal scores see: John Lely and James Saunders, *Word Events: Perspectives on Verbal Notation* (New York: Continuum, 2012).

16 Brandon LaBelle, *Background Noise: Perspectives on Sound Art* (London: Continuum Press, 2010) p. 91.

5

THE POLITICS OF NOISE

MACHINES OVER THE GARDEN: FLIGHT PATHS AND THE SUBURBAN PASTORAL

Michael Flitner

Noise has a physical, technically measurable side. Its negative health effects are directly related to the exposure to certain sound pressure levels.[1] Yet, the disturbing and annoying properties of noise are not just a matter of physics. Noise comes with meaning. It spreads into a meaningful world, it makes sense as it occurs, and the noise events are then further infused with secondary associations and interpretations. Thus, a woman from a village in the south of Germany recalls the beginnings of her political engagement against aircraft noise in the following words:

> I think I was just weeding then, and I thought: my god, this is gorgeous here—the birds, the church bells, and the wind in the leaves. And then, when it clearly started, when I abruptly realized it … waves, always like waves, around noon or in the afternoon around four o'clock…. That's when they had opened up [the region].[2]

A new flight corridor has been established; waves of airplanes roll over the sky and disrupt or replace the cherished sounds that were audible before. This is a fairly common account of people affected by aircraft noise, and two facets of it merit a closer look. Firstly, the woman makes reference to a specific soundscape of a good, relaxed, and somewhat traditional life. Secondly, she links her decisive experience to changes in flight paths and to a condensation of the noise experience in waves that are being formed in certain times and places. I will look into these two specifications of the spatiotemporal noise situation and reflect on their implications in an urban setting.

The first aspect reminds us of a classical literary motif. In his insightful book *The Machine in the Garden* (1964), historian Leo Marx has shown how North American writers of the nineteenth century constructed what he calls a "pastoral ideal" to contrast with the emerging industrial world. Remarkably, these writers have quite often used the *acoustic* dimension of the modern age in their construction, which they opposed to the sounds of a pre-industrial, rural world. In the nineteenth century, it was in particular the whistle of locomotives that stood for the aggressive irruption of the industrial world into the rural idyll.[3] A beautiful example of this literary trope was delivered by Nathaniel Hawthorne (1844) in his *American Notebooks*. He begins with a description of the old, harmonious soundscape that clearly resembles the quote above:

> *A bird is chirping overhead … Now we hear the striking of a village-clock, … a sound that does not disturb the repose of the scene; … we hear at a distance mowers whetting their scythes; but these sounds of labor, when at a proper remoteness, do but increase the quiet of one who lies at his ease, all in a mist of his own musings. There is the tinkling of a cow-bell, a noise how peevishly dissonant if close at hand, but even musical now.*

The clock, the bell, the whetting are not natural sounds like the chirping of birds or the wind in the leaves. If they are not too close, however, they even increase the quiet peacefulness of the rural setting.

> *But, hark! There is a whistle of the locomotive—the long shriek, harsh, above all other harshness, for the space of a mile cannot mollify it into harmony. It tells a story of busy men, citizens, from the hot street, who have come to spend a day in a country village; men of business; in short of all unquietness; and no wonder that it gives such a startling shriek, since it brings the noisy world into the midst of our slumbrous peace.*[4]

Hawthorne is not just defending the rural economy here. Rather, as Leo Marx put it, this literary trope highlights the alleged "moral, aesthetic, and in a sense metaphysical superiority of the pastoral world,"[5] which is threatened by the urban, commercial forces. This old literary argument has not lost its appeal up to the present day. We can find many similar arguments today, in particular when interviewing people living in suburban areas around airports. In articulating their annoyance brought about by aircraft noise, people often refer to sounds that are described as better and more natural in qualitative terms, and they bring in their ideals about nature and the city, about living with nature, and the good life in their gardens. We can conceptualize this process as the construction of specific interpretive frames that structure and fuel environmental conflicts.[6]

Hawthorne's "noisy world" is urban, of course. The city is noise. With Michel Serres, therefore, the city mouse is immune to noise. In an urban context then, it is less obvious to con-

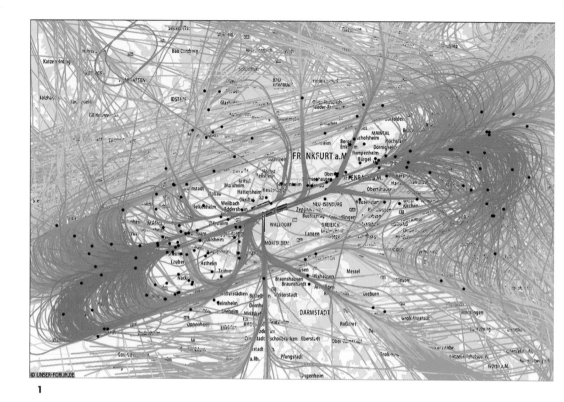

1

sider noise or din too negatively, since they seem to belong to the urban realm, in a certain measure. Nevertheless, disturbing and annoying noise also exists here—generated by cars, neighbours, factories, trains, and leaf-blowers. It is Manhattan, of all places, where the main character in the movie *Noise* (played by Tim Robbins) turns mad because of the blaring car alarms. Yet, if we look a bit closer into the arguments of those concerned by aircraft noise, we find little mention of the intense, lively, and noisy city as a whole. The city as a spatial unit even plays a remarkably small role in the empirical, largely qualitative materials I am aware of dealing with aircraft noise. Instead, we can identify a range of recurring micro-settings that seem characteristic for disturbing noise situations.

Very frequently, the spatial references in interviews relate to smaller units of everyday lived spaces; in particular, they include balconies, terraces, and gardens:

> *I have a balcony with a table down there. I used to make my corrections there and enjoyed it, but you can't do that anymore, you can't concentrate anymore. And then I come in, I close the doors and windows, and naturally, in summer this is very, very annoying.*

The place at the table on the balcony, an open window, a chat over the fence: quite often such examples are also linked to certain times during the day or the week, and to the seasons.

1 Flight paths around Frankfurt airport. Source: Deutscher Fluglärmdienst E.V. (DFLD).

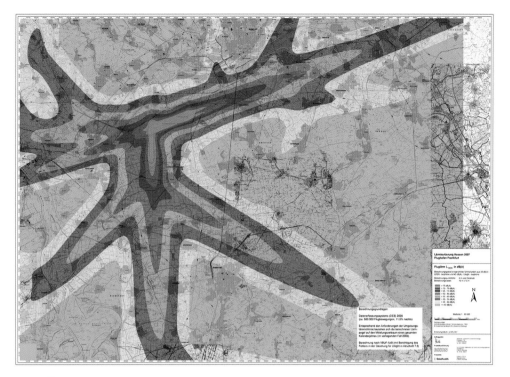

2

The balcony on a summer evening, the terrace on a weekend morning: it is these small, time-space constellations that seem particularly critical for the annoyance caused by aircraft noise. The sensitive microsettings are hooked into the larger, techno-political regimes of flight paths. These regimes are influenced by the hardware on the ground—in particular, the direction of the runways, and the larger-scale flight corridors and rules as determined by the respective national and supranational authorities. The neat images of fixed trajectories displayed by airports and air traffic authorities around the world suggest a well-defined situation, with corresponding acoustic effects. Yet, this suggestion is misleading in several respects. Not only does the meteorological situation modulate the sound substantially, more importantly, most airplanes do not fly exactly along the foreseen trajectory but deviate from it dozens or hundreds of metres to the left or right, and also in terms of height. This disorderly, unforeseeable situation is often described as disquieting, and from an individual, situated point of view, it clearly adds to the disturbance and annoyance with regard to the noise. Radar images of the real flight paths give a rough impression of this situation.

The perception of flight corridors as rather chaotic and arbitrary is common among the people exposed to aircraft noise. It can be exacerbated by security concerns regarding dangerous facilities, such as chemical plants close to flight paths near airports like Frankfurt or Miami. As technical, legal, and equity concerns mix in complex ways with administrative

2 Noise contours at Frankfurt airport. Source: Hessisches Landesamt für Umwelt und Geologie (HLUG).

Base map provided by Hessische Verwaltung für Bodenmanagement und Geoinformation, license number 2014-3-33.

procedures, the determination of flight paths is not transparent to most people concerned. It seems prone to influence from vested interests and largely beyond democratic control. The "techno-organizational management" of the related conflicts usually sidesteps larger political questions such as siting decisions, mobility patterns, or the different public subsidies to air traffic.[7]

The technocratic handling of noise issues certainly contributes to the fact that noise levels can explain only about a third of the variation in annoyance in the population around airports in quantitative surveys. One factor, which has so far received little attention beyond the notorious night-time disturbance, is the role of the specific timing of noise events or, more precisely, their socio-temporal setting. Both interview quotes above have already highlighted the importance of certain moments in time: the structuration of the year through the seasons, the working day with its work time, the afternoon when people come home from work, or the weekend where many are outdoors for at least a few hours. Thus, noise is very time-sensitive, even more, it is entirely context- and time-dependent in its occurrence and perception: this is not just the neighbour's TV during the night-time, but also the charter flights on Saturday mornings or the "men of business" flying back to their home base every workday's late afternoon.

Again, looking into the interview materials regarding aircraft noise, we find a lot of statements where the sensitive times are conceptualised as very specific *social* times, times of being with the family, and more importantly still, times of being together with peers and friends. It is in these moments where people seem to feel and dislike aircraft noise most. Noise is a communicative disruption and a bodily experience that cannot be rejected or denied. One is being overwhelmed by the noise, overwhelmed at least for a short moment, overwhelmed in the presence of friends who inevitably notice the situation. The peers or friends witness the interruption of communication in the house or in the garden, they experience the interruption of a normal communication:

> *Sunday I had visitors and we sat outside ... when a flight comes you can't talk anymore and then the people ask: "Is it like that all day? That's impossible!"*

Friends or colleagues may make remarks about it—or the resident anticipates that they might make remarks or have thoughts about the situation. In particular, for suburban homeowners who have moved to a region where aircraft noise prevails, or built houses there, the noise seems to operate as a concrete, corporeal denial of the good life, a sudden proof of the non-achievement of an entirely successful life.[8]

Thus in several cases, my interview partners seemed to feel ashamed in front of others. They wouldn't mind the noise so much when they were alone or in the family, where everybody knows and shares the situation on a daily basis. Again, this was said mainly in the suburban parts of town, where noise levels encounter the gradients of real estate prices. The pastoral

FÜR DIE ZUKUNFT BASELS
Ja
13./14. JUNI
FLUGPLATZ-VORLAGE

3

ideal, we could conclude, is more endangered in the green zones of the outer city than in the inner, truly urban parts.

The absence of such shame may facilitate, on the other hand, processes where noise annoyance can develop into a productive social and political force. Thus, Guillaume Faburel writes about his research in the environs of the large Parisian airport at Orly, where aircraft noise contributes to territorial structuration by "strengthening community ties and the logic of local identity through the mechanisms of resistance that it induces and the mobilisation of exclusive resources."[9] In other cases, declining housing costs due to airport noise have simply led to strong social or ethnic segregation, with some groups forming "airport-related communities" like the South Asian community in the borough of Hounslow near London's Heathrow airport.

3 Poster in favour of the enlargement of Basel airport (1953).

Graphics by Max Alphons Petitjean.

The establishment and stabilization of flight paths above these communities brings us back to a last, decisive element in the time politics of airport noise. This is the system of noise measurement and calculation, and more specifically, the averages and mean values that are constructed to represent noise around airports. The complex procedures were aptly illustrated by one interview partner on the French side of Basel airport:

> *Just imagine that on Monday morning you hit your thumb with a hammer and you average that to the whole week—[that] doesn't hurt anymore, does it?*

Although the complex noise indicators have been finally harmonized on a European level in recent years, they remain largely inadequate for representing aircraft noise disturbance or annoyance. In situations around most airports, noise does not come like an even, steady, relatively uniform sound stream—neither over the day or night, nor over hours or minutes. Rather, it is marked by a rush of sounds: distinct noise events with a wave-like pattern.[10] Accordingly, the typical noise contour maps of airport locations have little to do with the socio-temporal noise experience of people living around them.

Downtown in the big cities, far enough from most airports, the sight of airplanes on their flight paths may add to the feeling of a big, exciting, and connected world, and their humming is just part of the urban symphony. Aircraft noise annoyance grows as this symphony fades, moving towards the suburbs, where the elated dimensions of city life wear off and flight paths come closer to the ground.

Endnotes

1 For other studies about the health effects of aircraft noise see L. Jarup et al., "Hypertension and Exposure to Noise Near Airports: The HYENA Study," *Environmental Health Perspectives* 116 (3) (2008): 329–333; A. Huss et al., "Aircraft Noise, Air Pollution, and Mortality From Myocardial Infarction," *Epidemiology* 21(6) (2010): 829–836; and the recent debates in the *British Medical Journal* Vol. 347 (2013).

2 Quotes are from my interviews translated from the German and French originals, documented with more detail in M. Flitner, *Lärm an der Grenze: Fluglärm und Umweltgerechtigkeit am Beispiel des binationalen Flughafens Basel-Mulhouse* (Stuttgart: Steiner Verlag, 2007); and M. Flitner, "'Nous sommes une poubelle...': Echelles de reconnaissance et engagement de la société civile," *Annales de Géographie*, 668 (Juillet/Août): 397–413.

3 cf. K. Bijsterveld, "The Diabolical Symphony of the Mechanical Age: Technology and Symbolism of Sound in European and North American Noise Abatement Campaigns, 1900–40," *Social Studies of Science*, 31 (1) (2001): 37–70; for an overview of the sounds of trains and airplanes in musical works, see Hans-Joachim Braun, "'Movin' on': Trains and Planes as a Theme in Music, in ed. Hans-Joachim Braun *"I Sing the Body Electric": Music and Technology in the 20th Century* (Hofheim: Wolke, 2000) pp. 106–120.

4 Nathaniel Hawthorne, *The American Notebooks. The Centenary Edition of the Works of Nathaniel Hawthorne*, VIII (Columbus: Ohio State University Press, 1972 [1844]) here pp. 246–249.

5 Leo Marx, *The Machine in the Garden: Technology and the Pastoral Ideal in America*. (New York: Oxford University Press, 1964) p. 99.

6 See G. Towers, "Applying the Political Geography of Scale: Grassroots Strategies and Environmental Justice," *Professional Geographer* 52 (1) (2000): 23–36; and H. E. Kurtz, "Scale Frames and Counter-scale Frames: Constructing the Problem of Environmental Injustice," *Political Geography* 22 (8) (2003): 887–916.

7 Building on Chantal Mouffe's emphatic notion of "the (post-)political," Oosterlynck and Swyngedouw have termed such an approach to environmental issues "postpolitical governance"; see S. Oosterlynck and E. Swyngedouw, "Noise Reduction: The Postpolitical Quandary of Night Flights at Brussels Airport," *Environment and Planning A*, (42) (2010): 1577–1594.

8 For a more detailed reconstruction of social noise situations, see Flitner, *Lärm an der Grenze* pp. 89–103.

9 G. Faburel, "Le bruit des avions, facteur de révélation et de construction de territoires," *L'Espace géographique* 3 (2003): 205–223. My translation. In the French original, Faburel uses the expression "ciment communitaire."

10 R. Murray Schafer already stated in 1969 that "the whole world is an airport"—but he later erred in his assumption that future developments would make aircraft noise a "continuous" sound that is "not localized." R. Murray Schafer, *The New Soundscape: A Handbook for the Modern Music Teacher* (Toronto: Berandol Music, 1969) p. 61; R. Murray Schafer: *The Tuning of the World* (Toronto: McCelland and Stewart, 1977) p. 86.

BAD VIBRATIONS: INFRASOUND, SONIC HAUNTINGS, AND IMPERCEPTIBLE POLITICS

Kelly Ladd

You wake up in the middle of the night. It's dark. You might hear something, but it is difficult to tell. You know it's there, you can feel it in your belly, a nauseous, nervous tightening in your stomach. If only you could hear it clearly! If only you could record it! The other members of your household are sleeping soundly; they are not "sensitive." A few of your neighbours are. You meet periodically to discuss these strange symptoms, these not-quite noises. Most believe that it is the nearby steel plant or the newly-built wind farm, although there are those that claim that the vibrations in their bellies are caused by covert government military installations, still others blame UFOs. How is a sound making you sick? You sigh, roll over, close your eyes, but sleep does not come.

When we consider toxicity, or more specifically, the ontology of toxins, we immediately think of synthetic chemicals such DDT in the 1950s, which Rachel Carson famously brought to the world's attention or, more recently, endocrine disrupting BPAs in plastics. Perhaps we have read stories about the vast amount of heavy metals in our city's soil, such as lead, which was recently correlated to high levels of crime.[1] Understood in this way, while toxins may radically differ from one another in molecular structure and effect, they

1

nonetheless share, as Stacy Alaimo argues, a form of "materiality," [2] no matter how micro-
scopic or difficult to detect. When they are discovered in the body, unexplained symptoms
are given a causality, threshold levels can be set, and environmentalists can be mobilized
regardless of how politically fraught, contingent, and often futile. But how can causalities
be made, thresholds set, and environmentalists mobilized for something that that leaves no
visible trace in the body? This is the question inherent in the opening vignette, an imagined
scene drawn from a collection of first-hand accounts of sensitivity to infrasound, a usually
inaudible sound wave that occurs at less than 20 Hz.[3] It is important to note that in my
ethnographic fieldwork, where I interview infrasonic "sensitives," the word "sensitivity" is
controversial. Many feel that it implies that their bodies are somehow different, or that their
bodies have a kind of supra-sensible agency. One sufferer I spoke to says she prefers the word
"injury," in order to locate the locus of harm outside of her body, but that there is no term
to describe this relationship. For the purposes of this text and for lack of a better descriptor,

1 Zug Island 3: Image from
the cover of the Gregory F.
Fournier's novel *Zug Island: A
Detroit Riot Novel* (2011), about
1960s race relations in Detroit.
Source: photograph by Bill
Deneau.

I will retain the language of "sensitivity" because of its pervasiveness in the literature about these kinds of environmentally caused illnesses—the World Health Organization defines a similar phenomenon not as an illness but as a sensory "ability"[4]—but I maintain, that with sufferers/infrasonic sensitives it is inherently problematic.

The focus of this essay is one site of rumoured infrasonic pollution, Windsor, Ontario, Canada, which lies directly across the Detroit River from Detroit and the United States border. The hypothesis is that the chemical and steel plants on Zug Island (figures 1 and 2)—owned by United States Steel—are responsible for producing a wide array of low-frequency noises, from inaudible vibrations felt in the body to a constant low drone. The phenomenon is most commonly referred to as the Windsor Hum, placing it in a broader history of mysterious noises and vibrations. The Hum[5] is a catchall phrase that has been used to describe a multitude of unexplained acoustic phenomena: for example, the well-known 1990s Hum in Taos, New Mexico, which was often described as a humming, rumbling, or droning noise not audible to everyone. The New Mexico Hum has been attributed to a vast array of different causes, including secret underground nuclear tests, low-frequency radio waves, and naval antenna arrays. The mystery around the Taos Hum reached such a fever pitch that it inspired both an episode of iconic 1990s television shows *Unsolved Mysteries* and *The X-Files*. In the fictional version of the Hum, Mulder eventually deduces that a series of violent and fatal eardrum explosions in New Mexico were caused by a US Navy antenna array that was emitting low-level electromagnetic frequencies. In Windsor, researchers are currently attempting to record these low-frequency sound waves using microphones designed to record the infrasonic resonances of meteors.[6]

When it comes to infrasound poisoning, researchers more or less agree that extreme infrasound exposure causes a whole host of different symptoms that range from joint pain and bowel collapse to feelings of awe, revulsion, and nervousness.[7] "Soundless Noise," a 2003 collaborative experiment between sound artists and psychological researchers, showed that people who attended a symphony with an inaudible infrasonic note playing, were far more likely to report feeling moved by the music.[8] Similarly, psychological researchers have speculated that infrasound might be responsible for reported experiences of hauntings.[9] There is even some speculation that evangelical churches covertly use background infrasonic resonances to increase churchgoers' feeling of devotion.[10] As such, while the more serious symptoms of infrasound poisoning remain controversial, there is nonetheless a general agreement that infrasound moves bodies to *feel*: it is an *affective* toxin. What researchers cannot agree on is *how much* exposure to infrasound is toxic or how to even begin to measure the effect of its affect.

Infrasound, in its affective relation to the body, does not carry with it the more intelligible markers of toxic harm. Thus, the ontology of this kind of imperceptible toxicity is elusive and slippery, emerging only in the moments when it becomes perceptible to sensitive bodies. In her book *Sick Building Syndrome*, Michelle Murphy argues that the ability and inability to register environmental illnesses as concrete objects depends on "domains of imperceptibility," which are the various structures that render chemical exposures "measurable, quantifiable, assessable and knowable in some ways and not others."[11] In the case of the Windsor Hum, understanding the various domains of imperceptibility that make it perceptible as an object amounts to tracking how causality is marshalled, deployed, and sedimented by sensitives and scientists as they attempt to draw links between acoustic frequencies and somatic symptoms. In doing so, ways in which infrasound toxicity and Hums are made and unmade in this landscape become perceptible.

Making multiple, entangled causalities perceptible is akin to what Anne-Marie Mol has called an "ontological politics."[12] Mol describes how multiple realities are made and enacted through various practices and how there is usually a political reason for one reality becoming entrenched as dominant. In the case of the Windsor Hum, the dominant reality is predicated on the assumption that causality can be distilled to a singular relationship and this cause-effect relationship can be easily represented: there can only be one cause and one Hum. By conceiving of multiple Hums, the emphasis is drawn away from establishing causal links between somatic symptoms and the environment, towards understanding the conditions of possibility for these symptoms. This, in effect, amounts to an *imperceptible politics*, which allows for a flexible and open conception of environmental illness as opposed

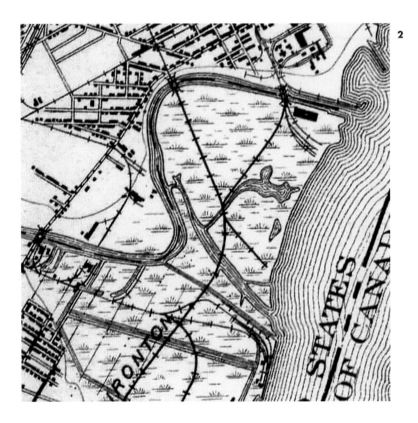

2 Zug Island, map showing its proximity to the Canadian border (undated).

to one that is predicated on a singular cause and effect relationship; traditional modes of knowing that seem to break down when brought to bear on an immeasurable and immaterial toxin. Following feminist science studies scholar Karen Barad's work on "intra-action," which reworks "traditional notions of causality,"[13] insofar as the boundaries of an object can only ever be created through intra-actions between human and non-human agents, this phenomenon can only be understood in terms of how causality is *made* and *enacted* instead of focusing on whether or not claims of somatic distress are true.

Already, as attention is shifted to the conditions of possibility for perception, multiple causalities begin to emerge, as claims of illness come up against failing manufacturing, limited job prospects, and cross-border politics, in an already heavily polluted part of the country. The Windsor Hum and its rumoured source, Zug Island, are a particularly complicated environmental entanglement to chart. Before it was a European settlement, the marshy swampland at the mouth of the Rouge River was a vast Native American burial ground. After it was annexed, it lay fallow until the nineteenth-century furniture baron Samuel Zug decided to buy the land and build a dream home for his wife. Despite the lavish attempt to impress her, the marshy dampness proved too much for Mrs Zug and the couple abandoned their home ten years after construction. Zug eventually sold it as a dump for local industry in what was one of the biggest land deals in Detroit history. Bought by Detroit Iron Works at the turn of the century, it is now owned by United States Steel and is one of the only active coke producers in the US, and is one of a few working steel plants left in the Detroit area, making it an invaluable resource in an economically devastated area. In its current iteration, Zug has become a heavily regulated space; the public is not allowed to set foot on or take photos of the island. Because very few Windsor residents have ever been to Zug, it has become a site for local myth making and its inaccessibility makes it loom large on the horizon as a mysterious, ominous, and foreign space.

As rumours swirl around the smokestacks of Zug Island, another difficulty faced by those claiming to be sensitive to infrasonic frequencies is that, while there is a general agreement that infrasound has deleterious effects on the body, infrasound is shot through with resonances of suspicion and conspiracy theories. Importantly, the term conspiracy is not necessarily negative in relation to a theory or an individual but instead, denotes a marginal figure or concept. Conspiracy theories evince a "desire to map an unmappable system,"[14] and it is this desire that undergirds many of the causal claims sensitives make about their bodies and their environments. This desire functions as a productive force that moves sensitives and scientists to distil and make perceptible causal connections between bodies and environments. A figure that looms large in this landscape of rumour, conspiracy, and suspicion is Vladimir Gavreau, the Cold War-era cyberneticist, who worked at the Electroacoustic and Automation Laboratories of the Centre de la Recherche Scientifique in Paris in the 1960s, where he was developing mobile robots for use in battlefields.[15] According to low-frequency sound lore, Gavreau inadvertently stumbled onto the potential of harnessing infrasound as a weapon when his lab workers began reporting daily instances of nausea. He discovered that a badly installed ventilator fan was emitting a low-frequency vibration. Gavreau believed it was the inaudible low-frequency noise that was making all of the lab workers sick. He immediately shifted his attentions from cybernetics to acoustics, and spent the remainder of his career attempting to weaponize infrasound in the form of an infrasonic whistle (figure 3). It is also rumoured that he had to create an infrasonic shield to protect soldiers from harming themselves while using it. Despite its many failures, weaponized infrasound nonetheless captured the Cold War imagination: rumours circulated that the French were developing a deadly acoustic weapon that could kill within a five-mile radius. There was something about a lethal, inaudible acoustic weapon that many, including Beat author William S. Burroughs and glam-rock icon David Bowie, found to be a captivating metaphor for state violence.[16]

In the end, weaponized infrasound never really took hold and Gavreau's dream of a silent, long-range, murderous vibration dissipated. However, fears about infrasound still linger at the edges of our cultural imagination. We are reminded of the many inherent suspicions[17] accompanying any kind of sensitivity to an environmental trigger that is difficult or impossible to measure. Many sensitives are deemed to be mentally ill by the medical community.[18] However, the perceived misattribution of causality for a sensitive's somatic symptoms is not necessarily considered a psychosomatic illness. Instead, sensitives are often diagnosed with a general somatoform disorder, a catchall category to describe somatic symptoms that seem to have no cause. These are "objectively real" symptoms that are abnormally "present[ed] and interpret[ed]" by sufferers.[19] Articulated differently, a sensitive's sleepless nights might be considered a "real" symptom, but her claim that they are caused by the nearby steel plant is "abnormal." Sensitives are considered mentally ill unless they follow sanctioned avenues of causality. When a sensitive draws conclusions from her lived experience, an overabundance of these rogue suspicions becomes a symptom of mental illness. Conversely, staying attuned to an imperceptible politics shifts the focus away from veracity toward potentiality, and thus works to circumvent this rigid distinction between rationality and irrationality, sense and non-sense, or between truth and conspiracy, which marks environmental illness. Instead of focusing on objects of knowledge that are severed from their conditions of possibility, the focus remains on objects-in-the-making and on the *doing* of causality, which shifts the focus onto how certain causalities become "abnormal," and also the inverse, how causality is done "normally." In the end, sensitives have the double-duty of being both healthy and sick: the sensitive must appear (mentally) healthy before she can officially become (physically) sick. Hence, those who claim to be able to sense infrasound are caught in a Batesonian double bind between two meanings of *non*-sense: as non-rational or non-scientific, and conversely, as beyond the perceptible.[20]

Because of these movements from illness into conspiracy, those who are sensitive to infrasound are becoming increasingly paranoid about being portrayed as paranoid, and are extremely suspicious of outsiders. For example, Adam Makarenko, a Toronto filmmaker

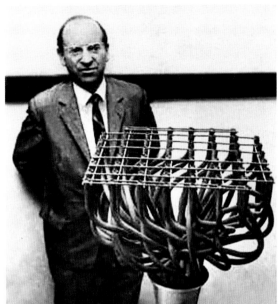

3

making a documentary about infrasound in Windsor, had to promise that he would not mention any connection to conspiracies before sensitives would speak to him. They were worried he would undermine their attempts to be taken seriously by the medical community. The filmmakers described the sensitives in Windsor as keenly aware of the need to separate themselves from other Hum groups, whom they consider environmental conspiracy theorists. The Windsor-Essex Hum Facebook Group, an online space for those sensitive to infrasound in Windsor, moderates its comments closely and any comments linking infrasound to popular conspiracy theories such as UFOs or the most common explanation, the High Frequency Active Auroral Research Program funded in part by the Defense Advanced Research Projects Agency (DARPA), are quickly deleted.[21] Nonetheless, the filmmaker himself has developed a complicated cosmology involving secret military bases to describe the phenomenon.

Also, like infrasonic sensitivity, suspicion is an affective state: one feels suspicious, often without being able to pinpoint an actual object of suspicion. And, again like imperceptible toxicity, suspicions do not need to be rational or have concrete causes; they are often shadowy and unclear. Suspicions are unsettled, potential causalities. Sensitives are thus constantly "working" to transform this multidirectional, suspicious tangle into intelligible, linear, easily representable, settled causalities.[22] In the process, certain bodies, places, and things become suspicious. To avoid becoming a suspicious, marginalized figure—the conspiracy theorist, the mentally ill—sensitives need to firmly attach suspicion to objects in the environment, while avoiding having free-floating suspicions rub off on them. In mapping

3 Vladimir Gavreau and his infrasonic whistle. While this image has been widely circulated in recent literature focusing on Gavreau's work, its provenance can not be verified. The uncertainty surrounding this image mirrors the mystery and conspiracy that surrounds his work.

an unmappable system, sensitives mime the causal practices of scientists, while also working to become recognized as sick by the biomedical establishment.

Thus, in a suspicious spirit, this imperceptible narrative does not offer any kind of resolution or attempt to debunk or uncover a hidden truth, or to prove a causal relation between Zug Island's steel plants and Windsor's Hum phenomenon. Instead, it is concerned with teasing out the various causal threads that animate the scientific controversy surrounding an imperceptible environmental illness. Moreover, by moving from a causal towards an imperceptible politics, the emphasis shifts away from the veracity of illness claims to their conditions of possibility and impossibility, while simultaneously tracing how "suspicion" and "causality" are deployed. In doing so, multiple relations between bodies and the environment emerge in the form of Hums, Native American burial grounds, sleepless nights, infrasonic whistles, coal and steel production, pollution, and cross-border politics.

Endnotes

1 Kevin Drum, "America's Real Criminal Element: Lead," *Mother Jones* (January/February 2013) http://www.motherjones.com/environment/2013/01/lead-crime-link-gasoline.

2 Stacy Alaimo, *Bodily Natures: Science, Environment and the Material Self* (Bloomington: University of Indiana Press, 2010) p. 3.

3 http://www.thehum.info/

4 Kjell Mild et al., "Proceedings International Workshop on EMF Hypersensitivity" (Prague: World Health Organization).

5 There are have been countless hums that have emerged as distinct phenomena. For example, the Bristol Hum, which has been described as a constant rhythm that is tantamount to torture (James Alexander, "Have You Heard the Hum?" BBC News: http://news.bbc.co.uk/1/hi/uk/8056284.stm).

6 There are many potential sources of infrasound, both natural and man-made. The most common source of atmospheric infrasound is pollution from nuclear tests. In fact, a nuclear explosion causes so much infrasonic pollution that the international nuclear test ban is enforced through atmospheric infrasonic monitoring. Moreover, atmospheric infrasonic recording devices, such as the ones being used in Windsor, have only been usable since the test ban. Previously, the amount of residual infrasonic frequencies in the atmosphere made recording the infrasonic resonance of meteors nearly impossible (see http://www.ctbto.org/verification-regime/monitoring-technologies-how-they-work/infrasound-monitoring/).

7 Seth Horowitz, "Could a Sonic Weapon Make Your Head Explode?" *Popular Science*, 11.20.2011: http://www.popsci.com/technology/article/2012-11/acoustic-weapons-book-excerpt

8 http://www.spacedog.biz/extras/Infrasonic/infrasonicResults.htm.

9 Christopher French et al., "The 'Haunt' Project: An Attempt To Build a 'Haunted' Room by Manipulating Complex Electromagnetic Fields and Infrasound," *Cortex*, 45 (5) (2009): 619–629.

10 Steve Goodman, *Sonic Warfare: Sound, Affect and the Ecology of Fear* (Cambridge: MIT University Press, 2010) p. 16.

11 Michelle Murphy, *Sick Building Syndrome and the Problem of Uncertainty: Environmental Politics, Technoscience and Women Workers.* (Durham: Duke University Press, 2006) p. 9.

12 Annemarie Mol, "Ontological Politics: A Word and Some Questions," *Sociological Review* 46 (1998): 74–89.

13 Karen Barad, "Posthumanist Performativity: Toward an Understanding of How Matter Comes to Matter," *Signs* 28 (3) (2003): 815.

14 Eric Cazdyn, *The Already Dead: The New Times of Politics, Culture and Illness* (Durham: Duke University Press, 2012) p. 64.

15 Daria Vaisman, "The Acoustics of War," *Cabinet* Winter 2001/2002: http://cabinetmagazine.org/issues/5/acousticsofwar.php. See also Goodman, *Sonic Warfare* pp. 18-19.

16 David Bowie described his and Burroughs's obsession with infrasonic weapons, which they called "Black Noise," on a 1974 episode of the Dick Cavett show: "Black-noise is something that Burroughs got very interested in. It's a ... one facet of Black-noise is that ... um ... everything, like a glass if an opera singer hits a particular note, the vibrations of that hit the metabolism of the glass and cracks it, yeah? So a Black-noise is the register within which you can crack a city or people or ... it's a new control bomb."

17 Joseph Dumit, (2005) "'Come on people we *are* the aliens. We seem to be suffering from Host-Planet Rejection Syndrome': Liminal Illness, Structural Damnation and Social Creativity," in *ET Culture: Anthropology in Outerspaces*, ed. Debbora Battaglia (Durham: Duke University Press, 2005) pp. 218–234.

18 Josef Bailer et al., "Evidence for Overlap between Idiopathic Environmental Intolerance and Somatoform Disorders," *Psychosomatic Medicine Journal of Behavioural Medicine* 67 (2005): 921–929.

19 American Psychiatric Association, *Diagnostic and Statistical Manual of Mental Disorder* (Washington: American Psychiatric Association, 2013).

20 Gregory Bateson et al., "Toward a Theory of Schizophrenia," *Behavioural Science* 1(4) (1956): 251–254.

21 HAARP (High Frequency Active Auroral Research Program) is an existing project in the United States funded by DARPA, the Air Force, and the Navy. It is an ionospheric (upper atmosphere) research programme whose goal is developing enhanced radio communications and surveillance. Because HAARP is a high-powered radio frequency transmitter, many believe that HAARP is responsible for most infrasonic and Hum phenomena across North America. Moreover, some conspiracy theorists argue that HAARP is actually an EMF weapons programme and/or a weather control device that has been used to cause recent meteorological disasters.

22 Dumit, "Come on People..." p. 319.

NOISE, LANGUAGE, AND PUBLIC PROTEST: THE *CACEROLAZOS* IN BUENOS AIRES

Leandro Minuchin

The incapacity to name is a good symptom of disturbance.
Roland Barthes[1]

Mayo Avenue had turned into a Babel of political expressions. The threatening and pulsating noise of *cacerolazos* (pot banging) had resurfaced. Seven years after they accompanied the fall of President De la Rua in 2001, they emerged in support of rural opposition to government tax measures. The cacerolazos, have become a consolidated means of civic expression, highlighting two complementary fissures that have since haunted the unfolding of Argentina's representative system: firstly, the inability of oppositional forces and institutional frameworks to canalize and express demands of those who feel unaccounted for or wronged; and secondly, the cacerolazos represent the violation or trespassing of an imaginary limit or border. They mark what is outside the boundaries of consensual politics. An instance when the status quo is no longer tenable. They rarely articulate a clear counterproposal or hoist a political figure or party. The cacerolazos form part of a common repertoire of contention that, although crucial to understand the dynamics of urban civil unrest in Argentina at the turn of the century, has appeared in different historical periods and spread across latitudes. They emerged in Chile, during Allende's presidency to protest against product shortages, and in Spain, to signal a strong opposition to the war in Iraq in 2003. They also served the opposition in Venezuela to stage, in 2010, what they referred to in different social networks, as a global act against Chávez, and more recently in 2013, in Turkey when they confronted the anti-secular urban transformations planned for Istanbul. Regardless of the occasion, the presence of the cacerolazos point to a structural disagreement: an absolute opposition that cannot be contained within political discourse.

The Haussmann-inspired artery, which stood as a physical manifestation of the federal and aristocratic imaginations proliferating in Buenos Aires in the late nineteenth century, was now the terrain where positions regarding the controversial decree that sought to increase the tax levy on soya exports, were being uttered and paraded. In June 2008, the historic Mayo square had become an open theatre, where at night, opposing collectives would assemble seeking to assert their rights and wrongs. While roadblocks and lockouts threatened to disturb the circulation of goods, and the rattle of pots and pans conquered the nocturnal soundscapes of central corners in Buenos Aires, neighbours, party militants, and activists sought to make sense of the fractures and disruptions introduced by the decree.

Disused categories like "oligarchy," "destabilization," "federalism," and "surplus," were debated in open spaces, resurfacing in what Ernesto Laclau and Chantal Mouffe refer to as "discursive nodal points."[2] For those supporting the measure and the government, the categories helped to associate rural production, with vested interests and the conservative political imaginations that governed political discourse in Argentina from the 1930s onwards. For those on the farmers' side, the decree was portrayed as anti-national and a threat to traditional livelihoods. The measure also galvanized dispersed anti-government sentiments on the left, which found value in the decree's attempt to address the issue of extraordinary rent, but refuted the authoritarian and anti-federal tactics they thought were propelling the decision.

The cacophony of noise and voices that populated streets and screens signalled the dissolution and breakage of established categories and institutionalized spatial distributions: farmers were no longer just farmers roaming the pampas plains, the function of streets and squares was subverted, and goods were no longer strictly associated with consumption but with the spread of a nationwide tactic of disturbance that expanded the repertoire for political contention. If the urban chaos in 2001 prompted the demise of the Alianza Government and President De la Rua's administration, the dismantling of a matrix of accumulation,[3] and with it, the instantiation of a new cycle of Peronist political hegemony, the 2008 conflict was governed by struggles of redistribution, a fragmented opposition, and marginal reconfigurations within the Peronist factions.[4] However, despite differences in intensity and scale—and sidelining the analysis of the role played by the Peronist party in each of these crises—the rural struggles marked the consolidation of patterns and rituals of collective action that positioned noise as a constitutive means of political expression.

The rattle of pots and pans in 2001, served as a practice to articulate a wide, unnamed, and ephemeral multitude—through what Ana Dinerstein referred to as a moment of fusion[5]—who temporarily disentangled established dichotomies, or antagonistic social sectors in Argentinean politics: agitated savers, proud of their anti-political positions, found in the

1

protests a shared and common means of expression with the unemployed, non-institution-alized grassroots organizations, and opposing political forces. The cacerolazos framed and delimited a paradoxical moment in political dynamics: at the same time that they fostered a heterogeneous assemblage of voices with enough momentum to disrupt institutional poli-tics, this ensemble of dispersed interests articulated no specific demand other than a call for a complete removal of the political class. The cacophonic sound of the cacerolazos was mirrored by the equally undetermined proclamation, "que se vayan todos!" (Everyone out!). When the cacerolazos resurfaced in 2008, instead of signalling the consolidation of a multi-class, cross-party conglomeration, they were reappropriated by civic and political forces op-posing tax revisions. During the rural crisis, the sound of the cacerolazos were reconfigured as a means of articulating a more discernible, anti-government sentiment, mainly supported by urban and rural middle classes. However, despite being linked to different political pro-cesses and collectives, the cacerolazos developed into a standout instrument within the con-temporary Argentine repertoire for political contention, serving specifically to amplify the claims of dispersed collectives outside established institutional channels, and to expose the limits of party politics when it came to channelling demands.

Echoing the scenes produced during the popular unrest in December 2001, the rural crisis of 2008 triggered a sudden interruption of the stable articulations between language and space. When the tension shifted to Parliament, it was apparent the institutional language of politics no longer contained the voice of multitudes that had taken to the streets to engage

1 Two women bang sauce-pans during a demonstration against Argentine president Cristina Fernandez de Kirchner, and in support of the farmers, on March 25, 2008 in 9 de Julio avenue in Buenos Aires. Photo: Juan Mabromata. Courtesy of Getty Images / AFP.

in an accelerated production of noise, sound bites, and fragmented political declarations not yet crystalized into stable and coherent political narratives. A renewed configuration of urban spaces, the subversion of existing structures, and the assembly of flexible architectures accompanied the rapid formation of political expressions and factions. Streets, squares, and tents staged the transition from an undiscerned cacophony to uncomfortable antagonisms that have since divided Argentinean public opinion.

Political theorists have regularly returned to the apparent mutual codependency of language and space. In *Leviathan*, Thomas Hobbes describes how in the apolitical state of nature, where violence reigns and there is no form of justice, human language and productive spaces are impossible.[6] For Hobbes, the capacity to develop and secure the material and spatial conditions for industry and production relied on the possibility of instituting the legal language of a sovereign power: one that would overcome the dissociated grunts muttered by unprotected individuals and replace them by the codified and rational structure of the law. The passage from the state of nature to a civil state is also a passage from noise to language. For Hobbes, it is only through the consolidation of a political sphere and the legitimacy of a single sovereign figure that the conditions for ensuring the regularities and permanence of speech and space become tenable. In *Leviathan*, where there is noise and no regular or pre-assigned functions to space, there is no possibility for politics. This is also true for Hannah Arendt: in *The Human Condition*, the flow and circulation of words are only possible in a political sphere.[7] The boundaries of the *agora* frame and dictate the possibilities for political action, and the latter relies, exclusively, on the ability to use language as a means of invention and creation. There is no political space for the *barbarians*, who do not speak the civic language. As in Hobbes, noise, disruption, and unsettled spatialities negate the possibilities of politics.

In contrast, more recent propositions have sought to address the instability of language and recuperate the instance of disruption as a fundamental moment of politics. In the work of Jacques Rancière, politics is framed around a double process of interruption: first, politics requires an instance of subversion when the established alignments between words and meanings are broken and a new political vocabulary is invented;[8] second, prompted by this reconquering of a vocabulary by those who were excluded from the political count, politics fosters a renewed distribution and assignation of places and spatialities. For Rancière, the moment of politics relies on the emergence of new names, and these are often instigated by a new spatial configuration: new organizations, new uses for existing spatial structures, or the radical appearance of novel architectural typologies accompany the crafting of new socio-political arrangements. What Rancière does not explore, however, is the process of transition; the mechanisms that foster and create the possibilities for a new distribution of bodies, things, and words in space.

The events in Buenos Aires illuminate the moments and procedures occurring prior to Rancière's political event, and highlight how flexible spatial structures participate in the fluidity and shaping of political discourse. They reveal a set of sequences when noise, discursive fragments, and opposing positions rely on adaptable structures and existing surfaces to experiment and test the suitability of words, associations, actions, and disturbances. In Congress Square, weeks before the crucial vote on the resolution that would eventually prevent the actualization of tax increases for agricultural products, opposing groups set up tents, tables, and inflatable figures to disseminate their views: loyal activists, students, farmers, and grassroots organizations transformed their occupied parcels into adaptable structures where lectures were delivered and petitions were signed. The setting was arranged to promote and instigate discussions. The farmers from Oliva, a small town from the Province of Córdoba, shared their hardships in a tent decorated with letters in support of "rural Argentina," while the militant group La Cámpora, organized seminars in an impromptu classroom, with intellectuals who supported the government's policy. The square was transformed into a singular language machine, assembled to accelerate the circulation of words and statements, creating a sphere where the becoming of future political antagonisms was taking shape. In the square, abstract notions—such as "national capitalism," "individual property," or "fiscal responsibility of the state"—were actualized through personal stories or experiences.[9]

Discarded words, adapted meanings, and the fluidity of imaginaries are formed from a cacophony projected out of transient forms of material support. The tensions between sound and space prompt a political temporality that has often been ignored; a sequence of events that situates, in an uninterrupted line, passages and transitions that allow for noise and cacophony to ignite a political process and obtain the consistency of an alternative political language. By including sources other than consolidated discursive formations, urban studies now have the possibility to develop methodological tools capable of investigating the forms of codependency that entangle language and spatial structures in the articulation of novel political antagonisms. This distinctive socio-spatial dynamic demands a form of ethnography attentive to the way fleeting material supports facilitate the transformation of disaggregated chants and unstable vocabularies, into consolidated fragments of political iterations. By rescuing and exploring the soundscapes that escape the margins of institutional politics, we can illuminate the way noise and materiality serve to frame and facilitate the unfolding of political events.

Endnotes

1 Roland Barthes, *Camera Lucida: Reflections on Photography* (Bungay, Suffolk: Fontana Paperbacks, 1980) p. 51.

2 Ernesto Laclau and Chantal Mouffe, *Hegemony and Socialist Strategy: Towards a Radical Democratic Politics* (London: Verso, 2001).

3 Marcela Cerrutti and Alejandro Grimson, "Buenos Aires, neoliberalismo y después. Cambios socioeconómicos y protestas populares," *Cuadernos IDES* (5) (2004): 1–63.

4 Horacio González, *Kircherismo: una controversia cultural* (Buenos Aires: Ediciones Colihue, 2011).

5 Ana C. Dinerstein, "Que se vayan todos: Popular Insurrection and the *Asembleas Barriales* in Argentina," *Bulletin of Latin American Research*, vol. 22 (2) (2003): 187–200.

6 Thomas Hobbes, *Leviathan* (Oxford: Oxford Classics, 2008 [1651]).

7 Hannah Arendt, *The Human Condition* (Chicago: University of Chicago Press, 1999 [1958]).

8 Jacques Rancière, *The Disagreement: Politics and Philosophy*, trans. Julie Rose (Minneapolis: University of Minnesota Press, 2004).

9 Fieldwork notes: Buenos Aires, June 2008.

ACOUSTIC GENTRIFICATION: THE SILENCE OF WARSAW'S SONIC WARFARE

Joanna Kusiak

… Mangon, with his auditory super-sensitivity, was greatly in demand for his ability to sweep selectively, draining from the walls of the Oratory all extraneous and discordant noises—coughing, crying, the clatter of coins and mumble of prayer—leaving behind the chorales and liturgical chants which enhanced their devotional overtones.
J. G. Ballard, "The Sound-Sweep"[1]

Sound, even as it slips away, remains present. In one of his short stories, J. G. Ballard depicts an alternative urban reality in which a sonic vibration does not vanish after appearing but persists by becoming embedded in the architecture. Not only do walls have ears; they also have memory. Yet as few sonic experiences are worth listening to eternally, Ballard's vision includes a new category of municipal service worker. Equipped with powerful *sonovacs*, these sound-sweeps vacuum clean the urban fabric, in accordance with the norms of what is and is not considered a worthy sound. As with many other urban services, access to the most efficient sound-sweeping is privatized, so only affluent citizens can ensure that their reality is selectively silent, thereby treating themselves to local acoustic delights and avoiding urban clatter.

Alas, there were no sonovacs to clean up the acoustic mess when the conflict over night-time noise—which had been increasing in Warsaw for a decade—escalated into real sonic warfare in the spring of 2013. As in Ballard's tale, the story is one about the privilege of sonorous (de)selection. Yet, the stakes concern the sound-making people and venues themselves, not just the sound vibrations that were to be removed. In Warsaw's gradually gentrifying district of Powiśle, a group of inhabitants from the luxurious gated condos overlooking the

Vistula, took a stand against the noise issuing from the cafés and bars that the municipality of Warsaw had permitted to line the riverbank. Among them was the wife of a renowned architect who commissioned a noise measurement, and then sued the municipality of Warsaw for leasing the riverbank area—situated directly in front of the luxury condos—to a concert venue. This case sheds new light on the class lineaments of the noise struggle. First, it challenges the common perception that the chief actors in the disabling of urban nightlife are "grumbling elderly residents" of relatively low income and education. In fact, Powiśle, prior to its creeping gentrification, was a working-class district, and when it hosted several alternative music clubs in its former barracks during the 1990s and 2000s, the local tenants scarcely made any fuss. Second, the plaintiff's plea for "equal rules and rights" to be applied to "all inhabitants of the district" was dubious at best. Famous for many commercial buildings, her and her husband's architectural office is also infamous for two major investments epitomizing urban inequality in Warsaw: an enormous gated community "Marina Mokotów," for which over twenty hectares of public space was excised relatively close to the city centre; and a luxurious department store called "Vitkac," whose huge, plain black granite wall has, despite long protests, completely blocked access to light for tenants from the neighbouring apartment block.[2] The obviously anti-egalitarian background of the wealthy noise-busters met with virulent responses from the Warsaw cultural scene, including a local newspaper, the *Gazeta Stołeczna*. Siding with the bars, the paper started a belligerent pro-noise campaign with the slogan "Warszawa—tu się hie śpi" (There ain't no sleeping in Warsaw), which has included hiring a group of instrumentalists to play classical music in public venues, pointedly just after official quiet hours. As the conflict escalated, the "culturalists" accused the wealthy tenants of gentrification, of privatizing space, and of thwarting Warsaw from becoming a "normal" modern metropolis with a vibrant nightlife. On the other side, the "new rich" have denied the cultural relevance of what they refer to as "selling beer and vodka," and denounced local café-bars as "out-and-out businesses," and their frequenters as "crowds of drunk, unruly kids."[3]

Although conflicts between night-time economies and tired inhabitants are natural for any big city, in the case of Warsaw something more complex is at stake. In line with Steve Goodman's definition of "sonic warfare," some features of Warsaw's (still ongoing) sound struggle reveal a lot about how sound and silence have been historically used as forces of political class struggle in Poland, simultaneously offering insights into the "economy of attention" in contemporary capitalism.[4]

First, compared with most other European capitals, Warsaw remains a particularly quiet city, such that the level of aggression surrounding the noise struggle has shocked outsiders. Second, few serious attempts have been made even to alleviate the problem through technical measures. Instead, the whole discussion quickly transmogrified into a perversely inverted dispute over the right to the city, in which both groups have been trying to denigrate and symbolically exclude each other from the city centre, with each suggesting that the other move out to the suburbs—either to make noise safely or to enjoy the silence. Last but not least, very little attention had been paid to the fact that the discussion has taken place between two groups that are merely two different types of gentrifiers. In the Warsaw suburb of Powiśle, unlike the typical scenario for a Western city, both gentrification pioneers (students and hipsters) and gentrification followers (the middle-class *nouveau riche*) arrived together, while the majority of its original residents have remained silent.

Of these points, the coexistence of pioneers and followers of the gentrification process is the easiest to explain. Under socialism, Warsaw's development was spread out, included many green spaces, and apartments were allocated according to a principle of social heterogeneity. In the 1990s, residential units were sold to individual tenants rather than to big-scale landlords, making it extremely difficult to fully gentrify any district. Instead, developers went about aggressively gentrifying smaller areas (even single blocks), turning unfilled urban spaces into gated communities. Gentrification in Warsaw has mostly proceeded not according to the principle of the "urban frontier,"[5] taking street after street, but instead (to build on Neil Smith's military metaphor) according to that of artillery shelling, where expensive condos have landed amidst a still very mixed urban structure.[6] An alcoholic, a student, an old lady, a corporate lawyer, and a family may all live within a couple of blocks of each other. Even if the developers have installed gates and cameras to separate the rich, noise has turned out to be magnificently egalitarian, penetrating all fences.

Yet to understand the aggression and doggedness characterizing Warsaw's noise conflict, its class inflection must be further explored, and traced back to Poland's various phases of urbanization. In fact, aversion to noise, and in particular to the sound of people loitering in public space, was already a key element of the revanchist anti-urbanism of the Polish gentry (*szlachta*) at a time when it was beginning to lose power and wealth. Although Polish literature abounds with descriptions of the blaring drinking reveries of feudal lords, the sound of their erstwhile serfs boozing in the city was for this group too literal a reminder of their own demise. Having stitched up feudalism until the nineteenth century, the landed gentry had profited both from free peasant labour and from obliging serfs to buy alcohol from them. When Poland's partitioning led, paradoxically, to the liberation of the peasants and to their increased migration to the cities, it triggered a manorial nostalgia for lost power that still lingers in Polish national culture. In this way, the overtones of anti-urbanism so typical of European Romanticism were further amplified by the gentry's class resentment. In a telling verse entitled "Memory of a Village," Cyprian K. Norwid, one of Poland's national poets, declares that he hates the city with its "yelling, raucous urban gatherings and glare of lights," and compares the metropolis to the "gilded edge of a precipice." The noise that the new urbanites made while enacting their freedoms in the city thus became proof of their barbarism.

In the West, analogical class/noise distinctions were naturally also made, as its upper classes were similarly unwilling to accept the changes that industrialization had made to the social structure and to social norms. As a founder of the Antilärm Verein (Anti-Noise Society), German philosopher Theodor Lessing claimed noise to be a sign of the vulgarization of life in the "raucous hells of the big cities," and that "a refined and educated man will always stand out by his silence and his hostility against a noisy lifestyle lacking discipline."[7] The historian Peter Payer underscores the fact that, despite heavy industrialization, hardly any complaints were registered about the noise of the factories:

> *It was clearly the acoustic expression of the lower classes—their crying and shouting, their uncouth behavior, or even their unsophisticated way they played piano—that especially met with disapproval.*[8]

Although the class background of anti-noise campaigns was initially similar in both Western and Eastern Europe, differences emerged both in the context and the results of this struggle. The nineteenth-century industrialization of Warsaw, limited under Russian rule for political reasons, could not match the tempo and cosmopolitan scope of the industrial revolution experienced by cities such as Paris or Vienna. Thus, where Lessing with his anti-noise campaign was quickly dismissed in the latter city as an "arrogant and hypernervous intellectual," "unable to adapt to modern life,"[9] the multiplication of written and unwritten rules on public conduct in Poland consolidated into what historian Błażej Brzostek calls the public's "solemnity," which placed constraints on popular experiences of urbanity.[10] Indeed, this solemnity continued long after Poland regained independence. In a new master plan for a "functionalist Warsaw," the city was pictured as a modernist metropolis of up to five million inhabitants—a cosmopolitan node right in the centre of Europe. And yet, although streets were widened and buildings erected, a Croatian visitor who spent several years in Warsaw during the 1930s, had good reason to note in his diary:

> *Here you don't sing or whistle on the street, people don't talk on the tram ... no one laughs, no one shouts in this city ... no one is pleased or rejoices, no one smiles; even the hookers walk down the streets as grave as matrons.*[11]

Absent from the streets, it would be wrong to assume that playful, clamorous urbanity completely disappeared from the city. Instead, workers, craftsmen, and Jewish traders lived out their sociability more exuberantly in community enclaves. Daytime bazaars-cum-suburban-dive-bars at night saw the emergence among the lower classes of a noisy, vernacular metropolitanism of interwar Warsaw. Meanwhile, the urban intelligentsia began transgressing the rules of public conduct and jeered at bourgeois sanctimony in cafés, where behaviour considered "crude" on the street gained the status of an artistic provocation.[12] Missing from this (resounding) picture, yet guarding discipline on the streets, was the middle class. In Poland, it emerged much later than the urban bourgeoisie in Western Europe and, in an only semi-industrialized society, its members had to work their way up more arduously while simultaneously enduring the vitriol of the revanchist gentry. Hence, the urban middle class in Poland has been literally born out of the spirit of solemnity. Reproducing the revanchism of the gentry and combining it with the uptightness of an *arriviste*, the core of the emerging urban society in Poland was paradoxically anti-urban in terms of *habitus* and culture. "Horrifying dwellers" (*straszni mieszczanie*) is how Julian Tuwim dubbed them, a poet known for his "loud," onomatopoeic poems reproducing urban hubbub, at the time when the sonic warfare between "café intellectuals" and urban *nouveau riche* was first beginning.

But shortly afterwards another war broke out, from which Warsaw emerged completely destroyed, with its population halved. Migration was essential for the rebuilding of the city, so Warsaw was inundated with thousands of peasant workers. Rising up out of its ruins, the city was loud and often brutal, as lifestyles and survival strategies clashed. Not only the remaining *petit bourgeoisie*, but also the new socialist state responded with moral panic, labelling all forms of raucous and unruly behaviour as "hooliganism." After all, the goal was also to turn peasants into "proper" proletarians, guided by a collective ethics. If, as Boris Groys has claimed, "the Stalin era satisfied the fundamental avant-garde demand that art cease representing life and begin transforming it by means of a total aesthetico-political project,"[13] the crafting of a "total artwork" of everyday life under socialism included redesigning the soundscape through, to use Schafer's terminology, the controlling of keynote sounds.[14] The urban planning of a socialist city included both the timing and the zoning of sound. Privileged sites for loud, collective expression were party rallies, May Day parades, or harvest festivals. The auditory life of an exemplary working-class hero would include neither listening to "imperialist" genres of music, nor engaging in *bourgeois* activities like hanging out in bars, cafés, or restaurants. To protect the sleep of "people of work," several tenant committees fought to have bars situated in residential areas stripped of their liquor licences or closed down altogether.[15] A few remaining and exceptionally lively café-bars served two main categories of client that—especially from the perspective of the state—strongly overlapped: intellectuals and notorious troublemakers.

A soundscape is always political, being "simultaneously a physical environment and a way of perceiving that sonic environment"[16]; not only is it a reality but also a constructed cultural interpretation of that reality. Moreover, it is the newness rather than the loudness of particular sounds that prompts citizens to act.[17] As the numbers of bars and cafés quickly grew in Warsaw after 1989, what for Western visitors is still a rather quiet city, for many locals became a particularly loud one. It is no accident that the sonic warfare escalated in Warsaw just as the first post-socialist generation reached their twenties. Emerging from "party scholarships" (as the EU Erasmus programme is often described), these "drunk, unruly kids" for the first time gave critical mass to the attempt at sonic liberation, in which a newly empowered urban culture tried to emancipate itself from the long anti-urban tradition of public solemnity. This emancipation has been the real agenda of the passionate letters in which local journalists and their readers have pleaded in favour of "city din on the crowded bou-levards."[18] Paradoxically, their opponents from the gated community of Powiśle are indeed not (as they regularly claim) against urban culture as such. They moved to the Powiśle dis-trict *precisely because* it was gentrifying, after two attractive public buildings—The Univer-sity of Warsaw Library and the Copernicus Science Centre—were situated there, attracting a student crowd. However, as the upshot of Poland's economic shock therapy in the 1990s is strong societal polarization (disparities within urban areas are the widest across the metro-regions of the OECD),[19] the wealthy residents of the gated communities felt entitled to in-terrupt any sounds they chose. Indeed, "sound imperialism"[20] has always belonged to the set of privileges enjoyed by the ruling classes in Poland. The arbitrariness of sonic (de)selection was once more confirmed by the Warsaw Municipality during the UEFA Euro 2012 Soccer Championship in Poland. Municipal police had raided bars in Powiśle for months before it started and resumed this practice a few days after it ended, but not once did they do so dur-ing the event itself. After all, the vibrant cafés and bars of this district featured prominently in guides recommending spots for tourists visiting Warsaw for the Championship.

One thing remains unresolved: why has this discussion hitherto transpired only between the gentrifiers themselves, while the solemn majority of Warsaw has kept silent? In Ballard's story, Magnon, the mute sound-sweep with auditory super-sensitivity, performs a trick on the garrulous diva Madame Gioconda: driving with her in a sound truck, he activates the sonovac inside the cabin to full power, sucking up every word she utters, so that reality is suspended for a moment, and she appears just as mute as Magnon himself. But in a world without sonovacs, rendering people mute requires other sorts of tricks—those performed by class structures.

Endnotes

1 J. G. Ballard, "The Sound-Sweep," in *The Complete Short Stories of J.G. Ballard* (London: W.W. Norton and Company, 2010). For another urban interpretation of this story see M. Fowler, "On Listening in a Future City," *Grey Room* 42 (2011): 22–45.

2 Filip Springer, "Śródmieście nie tylko dla bogatych," (2012) http://warszawa.gazeta.pl/warszawa/1,34862,13668712,_Srodmiescie_nie_tylko_dla_bogatych___Spor_o_halas.html. Last accessed 23 December 2013.

3 Dariusz Bartoszewicz, "Mieszkańcy Powiśla: Największy problem to zapach moczu," (2012) http://warszawa.gazeta.pl/warszawa/1,34889,12439323,Mieszkancy_Powisla__Najwiekszy_problem_to_zapach_moczu.html. Last accessed 23 December 2013.

4 Steve Goodman, *Sonic Warfare: Sound, Affect and the Ecology of Fear* (Cambridge, MA: MIT Press, 2010) pp. 5–13.

5 Neil Smith, *The New Urban Frontier: Gentrification and the Revanchist City* (London and New York: Routledge, 1996).

6 Joanna Kusiak, "The Cunning of Chaos and Its Orders: A Taxonomy of Urban Chaos in Post-Socialist Warsaw and Beyond," in *Chasing Warsaw: Socio-Material Dynamics of Urban Change since 1990*, ed. Monika Grubbauer and Joanna Kusiak (Frankfurt/New York: Campus, 2012) p. 301.

7 Quoted in: Peter Payer, "The Age of Noise: Early Reactions in Vienna, 1870–1914," *Journal of Urban History* 33/5 (2007): 781.

8 Ibid. p. 785.

9 Ibid. p. 782.

10 Błażej Brzostek, "Za progiem. Życie codzienne w przestrzeni publicznej Warszawy lat 1955–1970" (Warszawa: Trio, 2007), 122. See also Kacper Pobłocki, "Solemnity and Violence in Eastern European Urban Life," in *Visegrad Insight* 1 (2012): 86–89.

11 Ibid. p. 122.

12 Joanna Kusiak and Wojciech Kacperski, "Kiosks with Vodka and Democracy: Civic Cafés between New Urban Movements and Old Social Divisions," in *Chasing Warsaw: Socio-Material Dynamics of Urban Change since 1990*, ed. Monika Grubbauer and Joanna Kusiak (Frankfurt/New York: Campus, 2012) p. 217.

13 Boris Groys, *The Total Art of Stalinism: Avant-Garde, Aesthetic Dictatorship, and Beyond* (Princeton: Princeton University Press, 1992).

14 Raymond Murray Schafer, *The Soundscape: Our Sonic Environment and the Tuning of the World* (Rochester, NY: Destiny Books, 1993).

15 Błażej Brzostek. "Za progiem…" p. 421.

16 Emily Thompson, *The Soundscape of Modernity: Architectural Acoustics and the Culture of Listening in America, 1900–1933* (Cambridge, MA: MIT Press, 2002) p. 1.

17 Ibid.

18 Wojciech Karpieszuk, "Chcę tłumów i wrzawy na bulwarach", http://warszawa.gazeta.pl/warszawa/1,34862,13607085,Pozew_o_halas_na_Powislu_oddalony__Ale_problem_jest.html. Last accessed 23 December 2013.

19 OECD, *OECD Factbook 2008: Economic, Environmental and Social Statistics* (Paris: OECD Publishing).

20 R. Murray Schafer, *The Soundscape* p. 77.

I WAIL, THEREFORE I AM

Tripta Chandola

Hear this: clanking of utensils; water filling plastic bottles; tender bottoms being slapped; grown-up cheeks struck; raucous laughter in the corners; coins being sorted; technologies of communication, communicating—phones, televisions, and amplifiers—creating, collapsing and distancing words and lives; sellers of wares, necessary, unrequired, and varied, dangling their goods through the prowess of their throats; children otherwise told to "shut up" in the classrooms frolicking about imitating the tongues elders speak—I will fuck your sister, you are a cunt; the elders making claims to the fucking—of mothers, sisters, daughters—with more intent and lost innocence; aazaan on the loudspeaker from the mosque in the corner defining the day for many; the same loudspeaker announcing the find of a young Hindu boy, who if not claimed timely enough will be converted; the precious touch of the hand to the bells in the temples nearby, ting-tong, tong-tong, tinging; the hum of the city passing by; the vehicular conversations, honkingly undertaken; confidences of the most delicate sorts shared across corridors, lanes, and lives; songs of yearning penetrating through; a young girl on the roof remembering the cities she is forbidden to visit; an old man spinning yarn of the lives he has not lived to everyone in general and no one in particular.

This is but a brief listening into of a dying afternoon from a corner of the three slum settlements—camps—often collectively recognized as the slums of Govindpuri, a nearby lower-middle class residential area in South West Delhi. This is a listening of the inside (and its outside) from the inside of Govindpuri by an outsider; however, there are those who remain on its outside refusing to even acknowledge an inside (and thus an outside of the inside). From where they are, what they hear of Govindpuri is all but noise. In this reckoning, sounds in Govindpuri have no intent or imagination; they emerge out of nowhere, conflate and contradict with other sounds sharing the same predicament, to disappear into another nowhere-ness. To these outside ears, the noisiness of Govindpuri has only the singular and absolute purpose to invade and disrupt their deserved silences.

That the heard noisiness of Govindpuri from the outside—namely, the middle-class residents—is not a matter of decibel levels, but a "particular trope of experiencing sounds is significant in defining a 'sense of the self,' which is effectively employed to create social, moral, and political exclusion."[1] In the liberties with listenings I evoke here, the politics of production, performance, and articulation of "noise" as a specific instance of sonic engagement to highlight the broader processes of othering in the city as a sonic premise to further complicate the reckoning of noise—politically and philosophically—in itself. In that, the listening attempted here aims to rehabilitate noise within the sonic triad of "noise-sound-silence," wherein sonicity linearly moves from a state of chaos, through certain validations to an absolute state of calm. I will tease out these negotiations by attempting the biography of a sound—wailing—in the immediate context of Govindpuri, and then extrapolate it onto the broader materiality of the sonic capacities available to Others in the city.

Slums are marginalized spaces in the materiality of a city. And in a city like Delhi, with its hyperbolic transformative agendas to become a "world-class, clean, and green city," these spaces, more than ever, represent the perversity of a past desired to be conveniently lost: poverty, violence, unstructured growth, "over-population," dirt, filth, and noise.[2] Acutely aware of the particular predicament of the sustained, strategic, and everyday violence of marginalization that the slums and its residents encounter, the space, its sociality, and cultural politics have their own modalities to internalize this violence; and in that process deliberately define the boundaries of their own margins and locate their own Others. One section of society in Govindpuri on which this violence of othering and marginalization is inscribed is its women. Gender, however, is not the sole category of othering, and its associative social, cultural, and political disenfranchisements. The considerations of caste, class, communal affiliation, and political loyalties are equally determinant in these processes; however, for the sake of the listenings proposed here, it will be the voices—or lack thereof—of the women in Govindpuri that will form the focus of our attention.

The brief listening of a dying afternoon in Govindpuri is suggestive of the density and intensity of it soundscapes. It is indeed thick. To be heard here—literally, metaphorically, and politically—necessitates employment of effective sonic, technological, and social interventions. Given the space of Govindpuri is highly gendered, the women are denied these techniques of being heard, and thus their entry and assertion into its soundscapes often remain, at best, muted. To then extend masculinity to Govindpuri's soundscape as an overarching characteristic is not an attempt at simplification of its listenings, but an invitation to hear into it from a gender-specific trope. One sound—more accurately an instance of sonic performance by women in Govindpuri—however, has the potential to disrupt the intersecting sonic, spatial, and gendered masculine hierarchies, however temporarily: it is that of a wailing woman.

An emaciated, sickly woman is sought, and quickly found. It is an early, cold, January morning in 2012. The Municipal Corporation of Delhi elections are a few weeks away. I am accompanying, listening to, and interviewing a group of women mobilized from the three camps in support of a local candidate contesting the elections. On the said day, there is a scheduled rally in support of the candidate. The atmosphere in the room where the women congregate is tense, only easing when the required—emaciated, sickly—woman is identified. Preparations are in order—often hasty, tense, and leading to heated exchanges. I am told these are for the rally due in a few hours, but the specifics of the plan are not discussed and there is no room for interrogation of that sort. The emaciated, sickly woman is the hero of the moment; deliberations about her attire, where to get the desired at such a short notice, and assuring, and hushed consultations with her are taking place in a corner. I continue to listen. Eventually we set out.

The stage for this setting is an intersection leading from the camps to the main road. The intent by now is obvious; the group of women intends to block this intersection so that the visit of the opposing candidate into the camps can be stalled. The execution of the intent—the plan, now in motion—is not without its ingenuity and strategic planning. The emaciated, sickly woman, dressed in white, is laid down in the middle of the road on a bamboo plaque usually reserved to carry the dead to the cremation ground. She is covered with a white sheet with her face partially covered. It is evident by now that the role assigned to the emaciated, sickly woman in this planning is to play dead. And she does it quite convincingly. The women congregate around her in semi-circle, completely blocking the intersection. The imminent arrival of the opposing candidate is anticipated, and the women surrounding the un-dead dead woman start wailing in a collective, synchronized, and sincere manner. It is not a cry, it is not a shriek, it is simply a "prolonged high-pitched cry of pain, grief, or anger"; it is indeed an inarticulate "high-pitched sound." And, this sonic intervention has its desired effect. The candidate from the opposing party, and his cohorts, try to circumvent this sonic blockade, so to speak: they try to initiate a conversation with the group of wailing women; they try to placate them; they extend promises of justice delivered—without really knowing what the act of criminality or the grievance being mourned over is. The women, however, refuse to relent, and continue with the wailing. The threat of seeking police intervention to remove this sonic blockade was unimaginable: an assault on a group of wailing women, apparently mourning the death of one of them, would have ruined any moral respectability for the concerned candidate in the community.

Eventually, the opposing candidate leaves without holding the scheduled rally, and the women disperse as effectively as they had claimed the space, sonically. The undead finally awakens, walks alongside the others to the murmurs of applause and admiration, though not without a hint of envy. She—the emaciated, sickly woman—is after all the silent punctum of the incisive and effective sonic intervention: wailing.

If sound in its singular manifestation is to be reckoned as a particular and peculiar intersection of its spatiality and temporality in the site of its origin, then soundscapes are the simultaneity of these intersections. A spatial-temporal matrix can contain more than one sound, thus complicating not only the Cartesian notionalities of space and time, but also of the sonicities it contains. Thus, a sound is not just a moment of insular and individuated instance of utterance, but derives its momentum from the collusions with the multiplicities that abound these matrices: spatial, temporal, sonic, social, cultural, and political. A listener, not unlike a cartographer, traverses through these matrices to "make sense," to hear, to map not by accompanying each sound (or in the case of a cartographer, venturing into every crevice) but by deliberately, unintentionally, and inadvertently leaving most un-listened into. And thus the ears, as appendages which can never be "closed," become the libraries where these listening-intos are archived.[3]

But unlike a library, and an archive, with its robust physicality and Dewey-ian, almost clinical sensibilities, an "ear" remains a highly individuated, and thus an ambiguous site for the production of knowledge. Lending anxiety to this ambiguity and identification of "listening(s)" as a knowledge base is not only the technical matter of ears that cannot be closed, but also sounds that cannot be contained. And thus the individuated hearings are not so much a matter of the ears themselves, but a more insidious and astute question of "but whose ears"? The strategic, systematic, and deliberate privileging of hearings of, and by, certain ears—with political, social, cultural, and moral currencies—then assumes the role of listeners selectively identifying sounds to situate within the sonic triad of "noise-sound-silence." These listening(s) of course do not (and cannot) contain sounds permeating into ears and spaces; instead, they weave sounds together into a logic of those that are contaminated, the ones that are sanctioned, and others that are sanctified thus deliberating, and setting limits, to the permissible spatial-temporal-sonic intersections in a space, moment, and its memory. The ears that dare to hear otherwise, and the spaces where sounds—which disrupt the precariously listened-into spatial-temporal sonicity—abound are either silenced, deliberately un-listened into, or identified as sites of sonic contamination.

It is within this schematic that the outside listening-into of Govindpuri is collapsed into a cacophony of contaminated sounds collectively identified as noise. This reckoning has implications both in the real and rarefied imagination of the slums and its residents—the ears and the space: they exist in a perpetual state of chaos, lacking potential and imagination to move towards a validated, and eventually, a state of calm; the chaotic predicament is not conducive to conversations; thus they deserve un-listening and deliberate silencing; they are deemed unfit to participate into the listenings of and in the city; they are all but noise, a distraction; this chaos emerges not out of structural, social, and political marginalization of these ears and spaces, but from its inherent moral and ethical corruptibility; they are beyond redemption, and thus, not unlike an erring child punished to stand outside the classroom, they are denied recognition as citizens of the state. The slums and its residents therefore perpetually reside in the twilight zone of being un-citizens, loud-uncouth-noisy.

But. However. Nevertheless: the city passes. Listen. The city passes. Lend your ears to the sound that refuses to die, dissolve, and indeed disrupts; let us then revisit the sound which got us here in the first place: the women wailing an undead-dead, an existent non-existent. Wailing is a sound that, in its singular utterances, colonizes the spectrum of the "noise-sound-silence" triad in its entirety, and thus its highly disruptive potentialities.[4] Crying and shouting as distant cousins of this sonic performance are not without this disruptive potential, however, these acts inherently extend an invitation for a negotiation: either a complicity in the act, situation, or moment responded to by crying or shouting; or, a desire to seek redemption and retribution, and often even an acknowledgement of guilt and penance. Wailing is a non-negotiable sonic performance. Seemingly inarticulate in its "prolonged high-pitched cry of pain, grief, or anger" or just as a "high-pitched sound," it is in fact unapologetic, resilient, and assured. In its so-heard incoherence, it carries the currency of being a contaminated sound, noise; in its effectiveness to demand attention of the ears, it is a validation of an emotion intensely felt, a sound; and, in its transcendental potential to silence by demanding complete hearing, it also manifests the calmness of silence. In that wailing comes to haunt the hearings, it disrupts the spatial-temporal-sonic matrices, and in its sonic performance, its potency contains "noise-sound-silence" all at once. Women as systematically muted agents—historically, politically, and sonically—performing the wailing further lends to the anxiety: *if the silenced finally start speaking in tongues that cannot be contained and demand complete reverence, one only wonders at the wrathful gods they will evoke.* The imagery of a group of women in Govindpuri wailing before the body of an undead-dead uncannily evokes the predicament of the slums in the city, here in the city of Delhi. Superimposing the masculine/feminine binary to the cartographic reality and imagination of the spaces in the city, slums most definitely embody the *feminine*, and the sustained, systematic, and everyday violence that it entails. Here, the intent of evoking the binary of masculine/feminine to situate the real, imagined, and desired engagements between the slums and the city is to complicate these reckonings instead of reinforcing them.[5] In their encounters with the "city" in different capacities—for example, as employees, voyeurs, and consumers—the men from the Govindpuri feel emasculated, especially in their interactions with middle-class women as employers and "objects of desire." In these encounters, it is required of them to perform *femininity*, exaggerated by the *silence* they have to maintain. This silencing is instituted by the expectation of non-negotiable subservience in the case of former, and its almost-negligible possibility of actualization in the latter. These displaced (never disrupted though) masculinities, however, are rehabilitated by its exaggerated, perverse hyperbolic performance within Govindpuri's spatiality and sociality where their position, especially vis-à-vis women, is one of dominance. However this performance, with all its violence, does not dissipate uncontested, remaining an exclusive domain of the men. Women, both as individuals, and occasionally as a collective, challenge it, whilst others (who either by the virtue of their social position—mother-in-law, for instance—or by enjoying a certain political legitimacy) not only embrace and internalize its vocabulary but execute its violence on other women and "weaker" men. The identified *feminine*, not necessarily a biological entity contained within gendered qualifications, continues to be a site (both in its pathological situation of a space and a body) where the perverse desire to discipline, destabilize, and destroy can be melodramatically performed. The anticipation lending tension to the punctum moment accruing the *masculine-feminine* dramatics (in either its rendition of space or body) is not a resigned deliberation of the sustenance of the status quo, but the palpable *dread* of a conversation.

The deliberate compulsion to collapse all and every sound of the slums in its hearing by the "dominant" ears—namely, the middle classes—as contaminated and relevant only in its noisy manifestation is merely an attempt to deny the potential of mutable sonicities. And thus to keep the slums suspended in perpetuity as un-heard, silenced, un-dead, and un-existent in the circus that makes the city. However. Nevertheless: *the un-heard do wail; the un-dead do not just cremate themselves into ashes; and the un-existent continue to move across the spatial-temporal-sonic matrices.* In their wailing, they haunt.[6]

Endnotes

I dedicate this essay to my longest listening confidante, Jo Tacchi; and Swaroop Dev, one in the making.

1   I have unpacked the tensions of social and morally determined *listening into* the slums elsewhere. See Tripta Chandola, "Listening into Others: Moralising the Soundscapes in Delhi," *International Development Planning Review* 34 (4) (2012): 391–408; Tripta Chandola, "Listening into Others: In between Noise and Silence" unpublished thesis (Brisbane: Queensland University of Technology, 2010). Here, I establish the manner in which this *listening* not only affects the everyday interactions between the residents of the slums and their middle-class neighbours, but also the manner in which it frames the slum-dwellers as *Others* within the imagination of the city, and its impact on urban policies that strategically exclude the spaces of slums and their residents.

2   In the Indian context, these constructions have a historical, social, and cultural continuity, deeply embedded as they are in the practice of caste discrimination, which are essentially sensorially ordained. However, the evocation of these categories to justify the transformations of the Delhi into a "world-class, global" city attempts to neutralize these negotiations by rendering onto them an ahistorical, modernist agenda. This I identify as "sensorial re-turn in urban planning policies which I argue is, "...continuation of the elitist agenda to contain bodies and conquer spaces. However, the manner in which it is being executed is outside the praxis of caste, class and religion in the name of progress and development, thereby lending it a secular character, which denies it historical continuity and complexity. The sensorial re-turn is acquiring not only a political rhetoric and mainstream support, but also legal sanction." See Chandola, "Listening into Others."

3   Aside: is there a technical, clinical and, even perhaps, a cynical term for storing and sorting listening without reliance on a visual paradigm? Its reliance on a doctrine visually inclined? The insertion of a blind Borges (a storyteller par excellence, but most fundamentally a custodian of knowledge in his avatar as a librarian) is to at once reveal the visual-centric bias in acknowledging and classifying experiences as knowledge cultures and practices and to emphasize that there are indeed other modalities of experiencing—evolving a "sense of self"—arrived at through a mêlée of sensorial explorations. Alberto Manguel (2004), who in his youth read to Borges when he started losing his sight, renders the experience of *experiencing* libraries, stories, and their classification with Borges as "memories of memories," inadvertently displacing the visual bias. See Alberto Manguel, *With Borges* (London: Telegram Books, 2006). The Western, Cartesian, colonial agenda of the visual bias was not without its deliberation to deny of a "sense of self" (by disregarding the knowledge cultures premised on a sensorial reckoning) of the encountered "Others"—the natives. See David Howes (ed.), *The Varieties of Sensory Experience: A Sourcebook in the Anthropolgy of the Senses* (Toronto: University of Toronto Press, 1991), Steven Connor, *Edison's Teeth: Touching Hearing* (2001). Accessible online at http://www.stevenconnor.com/edsteeth/ (accessed 20 March 2014). The "sensorial re-turn is but a particular and peculiar manifestation of this kind of *othering*.

4   Here, the disruptive potential of wailing as a sonic performance by women in Govindpuri is identified as "… a scandal with the sudden intrusion, the unanticipated agency, of a female 'object' who inexplicably returns the glance, reverses the gaze, and contests the place and authority of the masculine position. The radical dependency of the masculine subject on the female 'Other' suddenly exposes his autonomy as illusory." See Judith Butler, *Gender Trouble* (London: Routledge, 1999 [1990]) p. vii. This performance further displaces the male gaze (and hearing) which Žižek identifies as "… endeavors to counter the fundamental hystericity (lie, lack of a firm position of enunciation) of the feminine speech" by laying claims to the very vocabularies which are reckoned to render them incomprehensible, thus divesting the male gaze (and its hearings) of its autonomy. See Slavoj Žižek, *Organs without Bodies: On Deleuze and Consequences* (London: Routledge, 2012 [2004]).

5   The reactions in the Indian media and the middle-class rhetoric to the brutal Delhi Gang Rape case of 2012 are symptomatic of these negotiations. The fact that the perpetrators were residents of a slum settlement in the city distracted attention from the fundamental violence and brutality of the act of rape to the specific case being evoked as a particular pathology of slums. The materiality of this space was identified by most commentators as a breeding ground for rape. It is overpopulated; the people uneducated, and by that stretch uncouth; people here do not experience sex as a "personal, emotional" act, but perform it publicly; men are drunk and women lack morals. And, of course, these spaces are swarm with those alien things: the migrants. The media was replete with such elaborations, with Sheila Dixit, the Chief Minister of Delhi then, even managing to push her decade-long agenda of restricting the entry of migrants in the city in the kitty. See also: http://www.abc.net.au/am/content/2013/s3683181.htm; http://www.theguardian.com/world/2013/sep/07/gang-rape-fear-anger-delhi-slums

6   The potential of wailing—as a particular sonic performance and as a more generic manifestation of the gendered, spatial, and social negotiations—is identified within its capacities to occupy/claim the position of *trickster*, "dispelling the belief that any given social order is absolute and objective," who demands an audience, critical and engaged, instead of silencing this performance, potent with possibilities, by a silent reception. See Mary Douglas, "The Social Control of Cognition: Some Factors in Joke Perception," *Man* (3.3) (1968) p. 365.

CONTRIBUTORS

ANDERS ALBRECHTSLUND is Associate Professor of Information Studies at Aarhus University, Denmark, and his research interests include surveillance, social media, and ethics. He is a member of the editorial board for the peer-reviewed journal *Surveillance & Society*, and has participated in a number of international research projects and networks, including the COST Action *Living in Surveillance Societies* (2009–2013) and *Surveillance in Denmark* (2010–2015).

STEPHEN BARBER is Fellow of the International Research Center, Interweaving Performance Cultures, at Free University Berlin, and Professor in the Faculty of Art, Design, and Architecture at Kingston University, London. His recent books are: *Muybridge: The Eye in Motion* (Chicago University Press, "Solar" series, 2012), *England's Darkness* (Sun Vision Press, 2013) and *Performance Projections: Film and The Body in Action* (Reaktion, 2014). He is currently the holder of a Major Research Scholarship from the Gerda Henkel Foundation.

OLIVIA BLOCK is a Chicago-based composer, who creates original sound compositions for concerts, site-specific multi-speaker installations, live cinema, and performance. Her compositions often include field recordings, chamber instruments, and electronic textures. Additionally, she performs multi-speaker electronic compositions, and compositions for inside piano and objects. Her latest acclaimed LP/download release, *Karren* (Sedimental, 2013), is an electroacoustic and orchestral piece performed by the Chicago Composers Orchestra.
www.oliviablock.net

FÉLIX BLUME is a sound engineer, born in the South of France. He studied sound in Toulouse and at the INSAS film school in Brussels. He mainly works as a sound engineer for independent documentaries, such as *Au-delà de l'Ararat* (2013, dir. Tülin Özdemir), *Killing Time* (2011, dir. Lydie Wisshaupt-Claudel), *Chernobyl 4 Ever* (2010, dir. Alain de Halleux). He also works with video artists, such as Francis Alÿs, Raul Ortega, and Clio Simon. He makes "sound creations," turning his sound recordings into "sonic postcards" produced and broadcasted by ARTE Radio (Fr), Phaune Radio (Fr), Radio Grenouille (Fr), KUNST RADIO (Au), and Idioteca (Sp).
www.felixblume.com

JOERI BRUYNINCKX has a background in Science and Technology Studies. He is a researcher in the department of Technology and Society Studies at Maastricht University, where he received his PhD degree in 2013. His dissertation explores the cultural history of sound recording in field ornithology and is currently being revised for a monograph. His has also contributed to the *Oxford Handbook of Sound Studies* (2012). He is interested in relations between the senses, technology, and scientific knowledge; his current project investigates the organization of listening and other sensory skills in the use of scientific laboratory instruments.

TIM CASPAR BOEHME is a cultural journalist and translator based in Berlin. He regularly writes for *die taz, Spiegel Online, Spex*, and *Groove*, amongst others. His book *Ethik und Genießen. Kant und Lacan* was published in 2005 by Turia + Kant.

TRIPTA CHANDOLA is a Delhi-based ethnographer. She is a research fellow at the Royal Melbourne Institute of Technology (RMIT) and has been a postdoctoral research fellow at the Asia Research Institute at the National University of Singapore. Her essays have appeared in various journals including *Asian Studies Review, International Development Planning Review*, and *International Journal of Cultural Studies*.

STEVEN CONNOR is Grace 2 Professor of English at the University of Cambridge and Fellow of Peterhouse, Cambridge. He is a writer, critic, and broadcaster, who has published books on Dickens, Beckett, Joyce and postmodernism, as well as on topics such as ventriloquism, skin, flies, and air. His most recent books are *Beyond Words: Sobbing, Humming and Other Vocalizations* (Reaktion, 2014) and *Beckett, Modernism and the Material Imagination* (Cambridge University Press, 2014). His website at www.stevenconnor.com includes lectures, broadcasts, unpublished work, and work in progress.

EKKEHARD EHLERS is a composer working in the field of electronic music. In addition to his solo career, he has recorded under the monikers Auch, Betrieb, and Ferdinand Fehlers, and as a member of the duo Autopoesies and his band März. In 2001, he began recording *Plays*, a series of singles to serve as tributes to some of his sources of aesthetic inspiration. He followed this album with the more abstract *Politik Braucht Keinen Feind* (2003), *A Life Without Fear* (2006), and most recently *Adikia* (2012). Since 2000, he has been working on ballet scores for the choreographers William Forsythe and later Christoph Winkler, and theatre music for Ulrich Rasche. As a curator Ehlers has been responsible for the "Lux Aeterna" festival at Berlin's Berghain and "Audio Poverty" at the Haus Der Kulturen Der Welt, Berlin.

MICHAEL FLITNER is Professor of Geography at Bremen University and Chair of the artec Sustainability Research Center since 2010. His publications include *Sammler, Räuber und Gelehrte: Die politischen Interessen an pflanzengenetischen Ressourcen, 1895–1995* (Campus, 1995), *Lärm an der Grenze: Fluglärm und Umweltgerechtigkeit am Beispiel des Flughafens Basel-Mulhouse* (Steiner, 2007), and articles in a range of journals and edited volumes. His current research interest centres on topics of cultural and historical political ecology with ongoing projects in Germany, Indonesia and Ghana.

MATTHEW GANDY is Professor of Geography at University College London and was Director of the UCL Urban Laboratory from 2005 to 2011. His publications include *Concrete and Clay: Reworking Nature in New York City* (The MIT Press, 2002), *Urban Constellations* (jovis, 2011), and *The Fabric of Space: Water, Modernity, and the Urban Imagination* (The MIT Press, 2014), along with articles in *Architectural Design, New Left Review, International Journal of Urban and Regional and Research, Society and Space*, and many other journals. He is currently researching the interface between cultural and scientific aspects to urban nature and urban biodiversity.

ANDREW HARRIS is Lecturer in Geography and Urban Studies at University College London, where he convenes the interdisciplinary Urban Studies MSc. His research develops critical perspectives on the role of art, creativity, and culture in recent processes of urban restructuring, and on the three-dimensional geographies of contemporary cities. He has published articles in various journals including *City, International Journal of Urban and Regional Research, Transactions of the Institute of British Geographers*, and *Urban Studies*. He is currently writing up material from a project exploring the construction of transport infrastructure in Mumbai.

SANDRA JASPER is completing her doctorate on "Cyborg Imaginations: Nature, Technology, and Urban Space in West Berlin" at the UCL Urban Laboratory. From May 2014, she will be working as a post-doctoral researcher on *Rethinking Urban Nature*, a project funded by the European Research Council. She has published essays in Matthew Gandy (ed.) *Urban Constellations* (jovis, 2011) and D. Cascella and P. Inverni (ed.) *What Matters Now (What Can't You Hear?)* (Noch Publishing, 2013). She is the founder of *Stadtkolloquium*, an international research network for postgraduate urban scholars.

KATE E. JONES is Professor of Ecology and Biodiversity jointly at University College London and the Zoological Society of London. In 2008, she was awarded the Philip Leverhulme Award for Outstanding Contributions to Zoology and she is chair of the Bat Conservation Trust. She has published her work in many journals including *Biology Letters, Conservation Biology, Nature*, and *Science*.

JOANNA KUSIAK is a PhD candidate in sociology at the University of Warsaw and Darmstadt University of Technology. Her publications include *Chasing Warsaw: Socio-Material Dynamics of Urban Change after 1990* (with Monika Grubbauer, Campus, 2012) and *Miasto-Zdrój /The Sanative City* (Bęc Zmiana, 2014), along with articles in various journals and edited volumes. Her doctoral thesis examines urban "chaos"—both as an ideological concept, and as a set of empirical phenomena in transforming Warsaw. Her latest project seeks to open a new avenue of comparison between two apparently "deviant" models of urbanism, that of Eastern Europe and the Global South.

KELLY LADD is a PhD candidate in the Science and Technology Studies Program at York University, Toronto, Canada. Her dissertation project charts the toxic relationality of immaterial and imperceptible forms of pollution such as infrasound and low-frequency radiation. She is currently collaborating on a project that examines the larger technological and economic infrastructures that make toxic relations possible. Her publications include a 2011 translation of an interview with Isabelle Stengers for the architecture and political economy journal *Scapegoat*.

GODÉ LOFOMBO is a Congolese musician and bass guitar player. He is known for his collaboration with Pépé Kallé in the 1990s, when he performed with the Empire Bakuba band. He is a co-founder and member of the Delta Force band, which featured rapper and dancer Bileku Mpasi. As a music arranger, he has also done tracks for other Congolese musicians, including Madilu System and Werra Son.

REKOPANTSWE MATE is Lecturer in Sociology at the University of Zimbabwe, Harare, and is completing her doctorate on young people's experiences of coming of age in Zimbabwe at the International Institute of Social Studies at the Erasmus University, Rotterdam. Her research interests are in the broad area of the intersection of social change and social relations in Zimbabwe. Recent publications include an article in the *Journal of Southern African studies* (2012) and a book chapter "From Respectable to Questionable: Women's Narratives of Marital Relations and Sexual Restriction in Widowhood in Harare, Zimbabwe," in Jans Bennett and Charmaine Pereira (ed.) *Jacketed Women: Qualitative Methodologies on Sexualities and Gender in Africa* (University of Cape Town/United Nations University Press, 2013).

LEANDRO MINUCHIN is Lecturer in Architecture and Global Urbanism at the Manchester Architectural Research Centre at the University of Manchester. He has published on themes related to material politics and modern architectural thought in Buenos Aires. His essays have appeared in various journals including *Antipode* and *International Journal of Urban and Regional Research*. He is currently working on a research project focused on constructive practices, techno-popular knowledges, and urban activism in Latin American cities.

TONY MITCHELL is an Honorary Research Associate in Cultural Studies and Popular Music at the University of Technology, Sydney. He is the author of *Dario Fo: People's Court Jester* (Methuen, 1999), *Popular Music and Local Identity: Pop, Rock and Rap in Europe and Oceania* (University of Leicester Press, 1996), and the editor of *Global Noise: Rap and Hip Hop outside the USA* (Wesleyan University Press, 2001). He co-edited *Sounds of Then, Sounds of Now: Popular Music in Australia* (Australian Clearing House for Youth Studies, 2008), and *Home, Land and Sea: Situating Popular Music in Aotearoa New Zealand* (Pearson Education, 2011). He is currently working on an edited volume about Icelandic music.

LOUIS MORENO is completing a PhD at the UCL Urban Laboratory exploring the influence of financialization on the design and restructuring of UK cities. He teaches in the Department of Visual Cultures at Goldsmiths, University of London, and was a researcher at the Commission for Architecture and the Built Environment. His articles have appeared in *City* and *Dialogues in Human Geography*. As a DJ Louis has also produced techno and house music for the labels Counterattack, Footwork, Arcola/Warp and Numbers.

BJ NILSEN is a Swedish composer and recording artist, based in Berlin and London. His work primarily focuses on the sound of nature and its effects on humans. His two latest solo albums—*Eye Of The Microphone* (2013), a personal audio rendition based on the sound of London, and *The Invisible City* (2010), both released by Touch—have explored the urban acoustic realm. He has collaborated with Chris Watson on *Storm* and *Wind*, released by Touch (2006, 2001). His original scores and soundtracks have featured in theatre, dance, and film, including *Microtopia* and *Test Site* (2013, 2010, dir. Jesper Wachtmeister), *Enter the Void* (2010, dir. Gaspar Noé), and, in collaboration with Jóhann Jóhannsson, *I Am Here* (2014, dir. Anders Morgenthaler). www.bjnilsen.com

DAVID NOVAK is Associate Professor of Music at the University of California, Santa Barbara, and co-director of the Center for the Interdisciplinary Study of Music. His work deals with the globalization of popular media, noise, protest culture, urban sound, and social practices of listening. He is the author of recent essays in *Cultural Anthropology*, *Public Culture*, and *The Wire*, as well as the book *Japanoise: Music at the Edge of Circulation* (Duke University Press, 2013).

YUI ONODERA is a composer, sound artist, and architectural acoustics designer, based in Tokyo, Japan. After studying music and architecture, he founded the Critical Path label. He employs materials from various sources ranging from field recordings, electronics, and voices, to various musical instruments, for process-based, restrained electro-acoustic pieces. His solo releases include *Entropy* (Trumn, 2009) and *Suisei* (and/Oar, 2007). He has collaborated with The Beautiful Schizophonic on *Night Blossom* (Whereabouts Records, 2009) and with Celer on *Generic City* (Two Acorns, 2010), and contributed to compilations, such as *Vernacular* (Whereabouts Records, 2013). He has performed live at Tokyo's NTT InterCommunication Center, Iwate Museum of Art, Kawagoe City Museum, and Störung Festival. www.critical-path.info

GASCIA OUZOUNIAN is Lecturer in the School of Creative Arts at Queen's University Belfast. Her research on sound installation art, site-specific sound art, and experimental music has been published in *Computer Music Journal*, *Journal of Visual Culture*, and *Leonardo Music Journal*, as well as the edited collections *Paul DeMarinis: Buried in Noise* (Carsten Seiffarth, Ingrid Beirer, Sabine Himmelsbach, ed., Kehrer, 2010) and *Music, Sound and Space* (Georgina Born, ed., Cambridge University Press, 2013). She is Artistic Director of Optophono, a label for interactive music and sound art. With the architect Sarah Lappin, she co-leads the research group Recomposing the City: Sound Art and Urban Architectures, whose activities are documented at www.recomposingthecity.org.

LEE PATTERSON is an improviser and sound artist who resides in Prestwich, Greater Manchester. Using a number of distinct approaches he has developed a new "voice" for an accumulation of everyday objects and amplified devices, as well as original processes for live sound generation. He has an interest in "overlooked" or hidden sounds with particular reference to landscape and nature. His latest CD album release, a collaboration with Vanessa Rossetto, is titled *Temperament As Waveform* (2013, Another Timbre).

SIMON JAMES PHILLIPS is a Berlin-based pianist from Australia. He trained as a classical pianist in Australia and Sweden, but now works primarily in the field of musical improvisation. He constructs an open sonic atmosphere that provides the audience with time to reflect upon and explore the sound. By controlling the pace of a piece's development, his intention is to affect the perception of time through music. His latest album release is *Chair* (ROOM40, 2014). Outside of his solo work, Phillips spends his time as half of Pedal (with Chris Abrahams), is a member of The Swifter (with Andrea Belfi and BJ Nilsen), and also performs with The Berlin Splitter Orchestra. www.simonjamesphillips.com

NINA POWER is Senior Lecturer in Philosophy at the University of Roehampton and Tutor in Critical Writing in Art & Design at the Royal College of Art, London. She has published widely on European philosophy and politics, particularly protest and feminism.

MERIJN ROYAARDS is an independent sound artist and musician with degrees in fine art, music, and urban design. He is currently enrolled as a research student at UCL's Bartlett School of Architecture, and has performed and exhibited in Europe, China, and the US. Recent publications and speaking engagements include the Sonic Arts Research Centre in Belfast, AHRA's Transgression Conference, and the new journal *Architecture and Culture*. Merijn acts as external affiliate to Recomposing the City at Queen's University Belfast, and is founder of Hybridity, a collective of artists, architects, and musicians who think architecture through time-based media and performance.

ARUN SALDANHA is Associate Professor in the Department of Geography at the University of Minnesota. His publications include *Psychedelic White: Goa Trance and the Viscosity of Race* (University of Minnesota Press, 2007) and as co-editor *Sexual Difference: Between Psychoanalysis and Vitalism* (Routledge, 2013), *Deleuze and Race* (University of Edinburgh Press, 2013), and *Geographies of Race and Food* (Ashgate, 2013).

JOHN SCANLAN is Senior Lecturer in Sociology at Manchester Metropolitan University. He is the author of *On Garbage* (Reaktion, 2004), *Memory: Encounters with the Strange and the Familiar* (Reaktion, 2013), as well as articles in journals such as *Time & Society*, *Space and Culture* and *History of the Human Sciences*. His research focuses on the "ecological" nature of contemporary life, and the human relationship with nature, technology, and place. In his spare time, he edits a series of books on music and place, titled "Reverb," for Reaktion Books, and published *Van Halen: Exuberant California, Zen Rock'n'roll* (2012) in the series.

SCHNEIDER TM is the name for the electric and electronic music projects of Dirk Dresselhaus. His recent releases include *Construction Sounds* (Bureau B, 2012), a blend of field recordings and electronic improvisations inspired by the ongoing construction near his East Berlin apartment, and *Guitar Sounds* (Bureau B, 2013), which featured several pieces originally composed for Carsten Ludwig's film *In der Überzahl* (2013). He has collaborated with former Pan Sonic member Ilpo Väisänen, and worked with Jochen Arbeit, Damo Suzuki, and Japanese dancer Tomoko Nakasato. He also scored films such as *66/67* (2009, dir. Carsten Ludwig) and *Polnische Ostern* (2011, dir. Jakob Ziemnicki), and composed music for theatrical productions and radio plays. www.schneidertm.net

MARIA SURIANO is Senior Lecturer in History at the University of the Witwatersrand, Johannesburg. Her research interests encompass African social and intellectual history, and past and present popular music in urban Tanzania, especially jazz (*dansi*) and Bongo Flava. She has conducted fieldwork in Tanzania since 2000. Her articles include: "'*Mimi ni msanii, kioo cha jamii*'. Urban Youth Culture in Tanzania as Seen through Bongo Flavour and Hip-Hop" in *Swahili Forum*, and "Making the Modern: Contestations over *Muziki wa Dansi* in Tanganyika, ca. 1945–61" in *African Studies*.

VENOZ TKS is a sound recordist working in Los Angeles. Using any recording equipment to hand, he records what is witnessed, using only found sounds. He has contributed to various compilation releases over the years, including *END ID* (Digital Narcis, Japan, 1999). Disregarding sample and bit rates, the quality is not the issue; events occur in a specific time and location and cannot be recreated. They can merely be witnessed. Contact: venoztks@field.nu

CHRIS WATSON is one of the world's leading recorders of wildlife and natural phenomena. For Touch, he edits his field recordings into a filmic narrative, most recently *El Tren Fantasma*, (The Ghost Train, 2011), his 4th solo album. He was a founding member of the influential Sheffield-based experimental music group Cabaret Voltaire. His sound recording career began in 1981 when he joined Tyne Tees Television. Since then, he has developed a particular and passionate interest in recording the wildlife sounds of animals, habitats, and atmospheres from around the world. As a freelance recordist for film, TV, and radio, he specializes in natural history and documentary location sound. His television work includes many programmes in the David Attenborough *Life* series, including *The Life of Birds*, and more recently the BBC's series *Frozen Planet*, which both won a BAFTA Award for "Best Factual Sound" (1996, 2012).
www.chriswatson.net

HEIKE WEBER is Professor of History of Technology at the Bergische Universität, Wuppertal. Her research lies at the intersection of the history of technology, urban history, consumption history, and environmental history. She has published on the history of portable media electronics, including the monograph *Das Versprechen mobiler Freiheit. Zur Kultur- und Technikgeschichte von Kofferradio, Walkman und Handy* (transcript, 2008). She is currently researching the history of municipal waste in Germany and France and co-edited (with Ruth Oldenziel) a special issue on the "Social history of Recycling and Re-use in the 20th Century" for *Contemporary European History* (2013).

BOB W. WHITE is Professor in the Department of Anthropology at the University of Montreal, and Director of the Laboratory of Research on Intercultural Relations (LABRRI). His book *Rumba Rules: The Politics of Dance Music in Mobutu's Zaire* (Duke University Press, 2008) received the Anthony Leeds Prize (2009) and the Joel Gregory Prize (2010). He has also done research on globalization (*Music and Globalization*, Indiana University Press, 2011), theories of reception (*Musique populaire et société à Kinshasa: Une ethnographie de l'écoute*, L'Harmattan, 2010, with Lye M. Yoka), and comparative cultural policy (www.atalaku.net/wsuc). His current research involves an ethnographic study of intercultural dynamics and policies in Montreal, Québec. His next book is entitled *Breakdown and Breakthrough: An Anthropological Theory of Intercultural Knowledge*.

PASCAL WYSE is a journalist, writer, musician, and performer. Along with producing comic strips for the *Guardian* in London, as Berger & Wyse, Pascal has written regularly for the paper and had two weekly columns: "We're Jammin'" and "Wyse Words" (published in book form in 2009 by Chambers). He has written drama scripts, sketches, and produced animation, for Channel 4, the BBC, and Discovery. As a musician and performer, he has worked with the Globe Theatre, Royal Shakespeare Company, and Almeida, amongst others, and is a member of the group London Snorkelling Team. His interests in field recording and film sound can be heard in various films and animations by Berger and Wyse, and the sound design and music for Chiwetel Ejiofor's short film *Columbite Tantalite*.
www.pascalwyse.net

© 2014 by jovis Verlag GmbH
Texts by kind permission of the authors.
Pictures by kind permission of the photographers/
holders of the picture rights.

All rights reserved.

Cover design adapted from the original artwork by
Anna-Lena Kornfeld, entitled 'Sound-to-Silence Ratio'
(2009)

Proofreading: Inez Templeton, Berlin
Design and setting: jovis: Franziska Fritzsche, Berlin
Lithography: Bild1Druck, Berlin
Printing and binding: GRASPO CZ, a.s., Zlín
CD manufacturing: CDA GmbH, Suhl

www.theacousticcity.com

Bibliographic information published by the
Deutsche Nationalbibliothek
The Deutsche Nationalbibliothek lists this publication
in the Deutsche Nationalbibliografie; detailed bibliographic data are available on the Internet at
http://dnb.d-nb.de

jovis Verlag GmbH
Kurfürstenstrasse 15/16
10785 Berlin

www.jovis.de

ISBN 978-3-86859-271-9

CD CONTENT

1
SANDRA JASPER | TUNE IN

Field recording. Berlin, February 2014.
Berliner Philharmonie, G left, row 1, seat 18.

2
BJ NILSEN | HAMPSTEAD HEATH

Field recording and composition. London, July 2012.
Bathing pond in Hampstead Heath.
Published by Touch Music (MCPS).

3
DAVID NOVAK | OSAKA TRAIN SYSTEM

Binaural field recordings. Osaka, June 2007.
Sounds of street-level electric train street crossing, Hankyu limited express platform, and Midosuji subway line ticket platform.

4
YUI ONODERA | ANONYMOUS SOUNDSCAPE

Field recording and composition. Tokyo, Japan, 2013.
Electric guitars, violin, and field recordings.

5
MERIJN ROYAARDS | COMPOSING THE CITY

Percussion and field recordings. London, October 2011.
Sounds recorded in King's Cross, Canary Wharf, Hackney, Blackfriars, and the UCL Bartlett School of Architecture.

6
FÉLIX BLUME | JE VOUS SALUT MARIE CHUCHOTTÉ DANS L›ABBAYE DE LA CAMBRE

Field recording. Brussels, September 2009.
Voices of praying nuns in the Abbey de La Cambre.

7
FÉLIX BLUME | APPEL PRIERE SOIR

Field recording. Istanbul, Turkey, August 2012.
Call to evening prayer from several loudspeakers.

8
KATE E. JONES | BATS

Field recordings. London, June 2010.
Echolocation calls of Noctule bat, *Nyctalus noctula*, Common pipistrelle bat, *Pipistrellus pipistrellus*, and Daubenton's bat, *Myotis daubentoni*.

9
SCHNEIDER TM | ESCALATOR TRANSFORMATOR

Field recordings and composition. Berlin and Lille, 2011–2013.
Partly processed mobile phone recordings of an escalator in Avenue Willy Brandt, Lille, May 2013, and a transformator in Berlin, September 2011. Published by La Chunga Music.

10
BJ NILSEN | HELSINKI, NAPLES, MARRAKECH

Field recordings in Helsinki, Naples, and Marrakech. February 2014.
Published by Touch Music (MCPS).

11
LEE PATTERSON | DIPTYCH FOR SINT-KATELIJNESPLEIN

Field recordings and composition. Brussels, September 2012.
Recorded with hydrophones.
While walking through Place Sainte-Catherine, I spotted hundreds of aquatic insects in a shallow pool and fountain. I knew that these water boatmen could be quite vociferous, being mostly Micronecta with some coroxids also. Upon placing hydrophones into the water, I was surprised to hear not only the Micronecta calling to one another (the coroxids were strangely silent) but also the metro trains arriving at the station below. Both were accompanied by the footsteps and wheeled cases of passers-by on the cobblestones above—vibrations transmitted through the solid substrate into the water. I returned two days later to make further recordings but the fountain pool had been drained of all water along with the insects that inhabited it. Lee Patterson

12
SIMON JAMES PHILLIPS | #2
(EXCERPT)

Piano. Berlin, August 2008.
Recorded by Peter Lenaerts in Podewil, Berlin.
Instant compositions scored in real-time in one uninterrupted movement through different rooms and spaces. A piano player improvises in an empty room. Over time the recordist travels around and away from the piano and explores first the space, and then the adjacent rooms and floors of the building. While the pianist plays with the acoustics and reverberation of the room, the sound is further shaped and transformed by how the recordist uses the different rooms and their features. The architecture becomes an editing device that continuously changes the texture and quality of the recordings. Simon James Phillips

13
OLIVIA BLOCK | UNTITLED FOR PIANO, BELLS, CASSETTES

Composition. Chicago, February 2014.

14
BJ NILSEN | ABNEY PARK CEMETERY

Field recording. London, April 2012.
Sounds of various birds including Blackbird, *Terdus merula*, Robin, *Erithacus rubecula*, Dunnock, *Prunella modularis*, Blue Tit, *Cyanistes caeruleus*, Great Tit, *Parus major*, Wren, *Troglodytes troglodytes*, and Magpie, *Pica pica*. Published by Touch Music (MCPS).

15
MATTHEW GANDY | ABNEY PARK WOODPECKERS

Field recording. London, January 2011.
Great Spotted Woodpecker, *Dendrocopus major*, with Magpie, *Pica pica*, and other birds in the background.

16
MATTHEW GANDY | CACEROLAZOS

Field recording during demonstration. Buenos Aires, June 2008.

17
PASCAL WYSE | HONKY

Field recording. Lyon, October 2007.
Recorded from hotel window on Place Bellecour during a taxi strike.

18
GODÉ LOFOMBO | BAMBINGA FARDC

Music. Kinshasa, Democratic Republic of the Congo, 2009.
Intro/Outro BJ Nilsen Reinickendorf, near Tegel Airport.
Field recording. Berlin, Germany, February 2014.

19
MATTHEW GANDY & BJ NILSEN | CHAMISSOPLATZ

Guitar improvisations and sound collage.
Berlin, March 2014.

20
CHRIS WATSON | STREET MARKET

Field recording. Ramnagar, Uttarakhand, Northern India, January 2011.
Published by Touch Music (MCPS).

21
VENOZ TKS | STRAWBERRY SELLERS

Field recording. Marrakesh, Morocco, February 2014.
Published by Field Music (MCPS).

22
EKKEHARD EHLERS | MARIA & MARTHA

Composition. Berlin, Germany, 2006.
Originally released on the album A Life Without Fear (2006).
Published by Freibank.

The Acoustic City CD was curated and compiled by BJ Nilsen and Matthew Gandy.
All publishing rights belong to the artists except where stated.
We would like to thank all the artists and contributors featured on this CD for their kind support.
Thanks also to Mark Pearson for assistance with the identification of bird songs and to
Rudolf Thome for permission to use dialogue taken from his film Berlin *Chamissoplatz* (1980).